P9-DTO-500

NO LONGER PROPERTY OF
SEATTLE PUBLIC LIBRARY
JUL 19 2017

Praise for *Song of the Plains*

"Linda Joy Myers has written a remarkable, heartbreaking, and hopeful story. *Song of the Plains* is a memoir of fierce longing and a quest to understand the fragile bonds of family. Myers stitches together her past, finding solace in the landscape of the Great Plains and weaving in elements of story like a poet, detective, artist, therapist, mother, daughter, and historian. The fascinating and fractured women in this memoir will continue to whisper their songs for generations to come."

—MELISSA CISTARO, author of *Pieces of My Mother*

"Linda Joy Myers, already an established thought leader in the memoir genre, solidifies her legacy with this meditation on ancestry, place, generational pain, healing, and redemption. The author's consistently braided themes of memoir as art, craft, and psychological process are enhanced by her longstanding career as a marriage and family therapist. The writing is cohesive and evocative, the research impeccable, and the ultimate triumph over both nature and nurture compelling."

—KATHLEEN ADAMS LPC, Director, Center for Journal Therapy, Inc., author of *Journal to the Self*, and editor of *Expressive Writing: Foundations of Practice*

"*Song of the Plains* is a poetic work of art that deftly weaves an intergenerational tapestry of the author's ultimate healing and self-redemption. Threads of a child longing for love and the need for a maternal bridge that children need to thrive are woven throughout. Linda Joy Myers' elegantly crafted memoir gives hope to readers yearning to break the legacy of childhood trauma and it inspires us to undertake necessary work to accept ourselves, own our worthiness, and take our rightful place in the world."

—DONNA STONEHAM, PhD, author of *The Thriver's Edge: Seven Keys to Transform the Way You Live, Love, and Lead*

"Linda Joy Myers is a warrior—a solider with a pen who fights her way through a painful family history to an unexpected place of profound understanding and gratitude. This beautiful memoir is for anyone who wants to cull deep meaning from their past and find peace and healing on the other side."

—Rev. Susan Sparks, author of *Laugh Your Way to Grace: Reclaiming the Spiritual Power of Humor*

"Linda Joy Myers's search for continuity in her family history brings to mind E. M. Forster's quote, 'Only connect the prose and the passion, and both will be exalted." Her search for connection deeply resonates in a time when social media makes connections that are broad but shallow. Rooted in place and personal stories, *Song of the Plains* is an antidote to the superficial and the faux. Myers's writing plumbs the depths of real experience. This important narrative is crafted to last."

—Sue William Silverman, author of *The Pat Boone Fan Club: My Life as a White Anglo-Saxon Jew*

"Intelligent, heartfelt, and tenderly observed, *Song of the Plains* is a memoir about identity, storytelling, and the healing power of telling the truth. Raised in a family haunted by secrets, Linda Joy Myers set out on a journey to discover what the women in her clan were hiding—and *why*—as a way to untangle the legacy of inherited-but-hidden trauma. As Myers writes, 'If we hide or don't tell our stories, part of who we are goes missing.' If you've ever puzzled over your own missing pieces or questioned who you might be without your own secrets, this beautiful book will help light your way."

—Mark Matousek, author of *Sex Death Enlightenment* and *The Boy He Left Behind*

"*Song of the Plains* is an emotional and captivating read. From the very first page, Linda Myers leads the reader on a journey into the inner landscape of a complex family dynamic that invites curiosity and empathy. Myers is a brilliant storyteller, weaving together well-researched details with answers to plaguing life questions that reveal the reality of 'home'—turning a preconceived definition on its head. This story touches readers in a way that stirs compassion for the complexity of people and their role in a larger framework known as 'family.' It makes one wonder about their own sense of home and what they've come to believe about it."

—TINA M. GAMES, author of *Journaling by the Moonlight: A Mother's Path to Self Discovery*

"The descriptions in *Song of the Plains* are downright elegiac. I felt I was standing on the red earth in Oklahoma, feeling the wind in my face. This next volume of Myers's quest for understanding and forgiveness of her foremothers and family will inspire anyone seeking to understand their roots."

—SHARON LIPPINCOTT, author of *The Heart and Craft of Lifestory Writing*

"We all have stories that change our lives. Sometimes we remain silent, but the silence only gives the story more power. In *Song of the Plains*, memoir expert Linda Joy Myers goes deeply into her own life story and reveals how she transformed it into a new one that helped her move forward with hope and love. Another moving healing journey related to family relationships from Myers, this book is a must-read for anyone who wants to explore—and heal—the past."

—NINA AMIR, best-selling author of *Creative Visualization for Writers*, *The Author Training Manual*, and *How to Blog a Book*

"For years, as I considered the mystery of my childhood, I wondered, 'Who were these people who molded me?' *Song of the Plains* asks that question and explores the decades-long saga of the author's search for answers. Like an ancestral detective, Myers peers into the evidence and follows historical bread crumbs, attempting to make sense of her family's earlier lives."

—JERRY WAXLER, author of *The Memoir Revolution*

"Beautiful and lyrical, this memoir is achingly honest. We see the narrator, a strong woman who not only survived her early life—abandonment, rageful attacks, and betrayals—offering us the story of her struggle and ultimate redemption. Through writing her story she shows us a way to find our own, modeling the kind of bravery and grit it takes for us to embark on our own journey."

—JUDY REEVES, author of *Wild Women, Wild Voices* and *A Writer's Book of Days*

"Myers, a skillful and poetic storyteller, recalls scenes from a childhood spent in the long shadows of her mother and grandmother. We follow her shero's journey as she attempts to disentangle her spirit from the legacies of the past and finds the lost stories that are the key to freedom."

—HOLLYE DEXTER, author of *The Fire Season*

song of
the plains

a family memoir

LINDA JOY MYERS

SHE WRITES PRESS

Copyright © 2017 by Linda Joy Myers

All rights reserved. No part of this publication may be
reproduced, distributed, or transmitted in any form or by any
means, including photocopying, recording, digital scanning,
or other electronic or mechanical methods, without the prior
written permission of the publisher, except in the case of brief
quotations embodied in critical reviews and certain other
noncommercial uses permitted by copyright law. For permission
requests, please address She Writes Press.

Published 2017
Printed in the United States of America
Print ISBN: 978-1-63152-216-1
E-ISBN: 978-1-63152-217-8
Library of Congress Control Number: 2017933977

For information, address:
She Writes Press
1563 Solano Ave #546
Berkeley, CA 94707

Cover design © Julie Metz, Ltd./metzdesign.com
Interior design by Tabitha Lahr

She Writes Press is a division of SparkPoint Studio, LLC.

Names and identifying characteristics have been changed to
protect the privacy of certain individuals.

For my children and grandchildren;
may you know the power of your own history.

Contents

The Great Plains is a wonder of contrasts.

The deep-indigo night sky is splashed by a wash of stars scattered across the dome above your small self.

In the white brilliance of daylight, it echoes with lonely notes from meadowlarks and red-winged blackbirds resting on stark tree branches and fence posts, dangerous barbed wire trembling in the wind.

The sounds of the birds and the sense of space, so large you can't grasp them with your two-dimensional mind, etch the edges of your loneliness, giving it form, making your heart reach out for the simplicity of light and wind, red dirt and birdcall.

In this moment you are at one with All That Is.

You are free.

Introduction

"Home" is a world full of emotion—it's a place, a house, a land, a landscape, a vision, a refuge. It's imagination and long-ing. For some, home is a safe place; for others, standing under the wide-open sky during a storm is safer than the four walls of any house.

As I grew up, the landscape of northern Oklahoma, bisected by the old Chisholm Trail, was home to me. It was a land of emp-tiness, space everywhere as far as the eye could see, the grasses flattened by the incessant wind. Our version of skyscrapers were the wheat elevators, white towers that rose up at the end of the road, but when you got closer, the elevators were by the railroad tracks, the cars ready to gather up the harvest and ship it east. Long ago, the cattle drives moved north on the Chisholm Trail to the markets in Dodge City.

The history of a place leaves a permanent imprint, though you may not know it. It whispers its secret stories and offers up mysteri-ous landmarks—a deserted cabin, ruts from westward trails, graves marked and unmarked. For as long as I can remember, I tuned in to these whispers—more like vibrations, or a vision caught in the corner of my eye. From a young age, I knew that my family was repeating history, locked into some kind of pattern that separated us. It interrupted the course of love, leaving distance and pain. All my life I've tried to understand the heritage I was born into, especially my maternal line—I knew almost nothing of my father's family. As a child, I picked up on clues about who we were and where we came from as I listened to the adults whisper or laugh at stories around the kitchen table. My great-grandmother Blanche opened up this box of secret tales and set me on my course to search for the truth, and to sense the truths that were covered by lies.

To know things that are not provable by objective means puts you in a category of mystic or crazy or obsessed. I prefer to call it intuitive. All artist types, psychics, healers, and mystics tap into other realms, but many suffer for it. I always felt that if I discovered enough of the stories and dug into the past for information, I'd find out why my grandmother and mother left their daughters when they were little girls, why they shouted and threw things. I wanted to understand why I couldn't shake the sense of darkness and loss that put its arms around me all my life, as it did them.

When you dig into the past to discover the truth, the world will tell you that you should "get over it"—the past is the past. The world will judge you and ask, "Are you *still* thinking about all that stuff?" People will look at you as if you're nuts.

But William Faulkner had it right: "The past is not dead. It's not even past."

I've been pleased to discover studies about epigenetic DNA research in the field of neuroscience, which prove what psychologists and contemplatives have known: that we are a story-making species. We need to make sense of what has happened to us and what our heritage is so we can become our best selves. The recent epigenetic research affirms that the answers to all our questions are buried deep inside our bodies. It also reveals how trauma may be inherited through DNA and various cell transformations. We carry the DNA of grandparents and great-grandparents. The traumas they suffered mark our genetic patterns and are passed down to us. This research affirms what my body has always told me: I'm a part of everything that's happened; the darkness that I sensed was not just about me. I wasn't crazy to follow the thread or to embark upon this quest. In this book, I've stepped into the shoes and inhabited the hearts and minds of my mother and my grandmother, and in doing so I've come to see them through new eyes—the eyes of compassion and love.

Over the last four decades, my work as an artist, therapist, and memoirist has helped my own healing. Through my teaching, I've helped others find the words and images that lead them to a new perspective about themselves, home, and family. In this new memoir, I'm trying to understand the historical, psychological, and genealogical roots of my own family. I realized, as I assembled all the parts of our story, that I've been doing this research all my life.

Song of the Plains traces my path from curious child inspired by the power of my great-grandmother's stories through the forty years of research about my family I felt compelled to do. Through the years, people would look at me askance—the usual raised eyebrow in response to my telling them that I'd yet again gone back to the library microfilms in the village where my mother was born, that I'd roamed through cemeteries and courthouses trying to discover our genealogy long before Ancestry. com existed.

Members of my extended family in Iowa looked at me with some suspicion—perhaps afraid that certain things they wanted to keep hidden would be revealed. I followed the clues, spending long stints on Ancestry.com once I discovered it, trying to find information about my family: dates, addresses, names, ages, even journeys to foreign climes. If we hide or don't tell our stories, part of who we are goes missing. I knew that if I could weave new fabric into the tapestry of my family, fill in what was missing, I could find redemption in a story that had so much heartache.

The truth can be a difficult muse to court. We will not like everything we find. Some information may be shameful and embarrassing, but ultimately the truth frees us from our mistaken assumptions about who we are—and who we are not. We're always becoming. We can transform our lives from darkness into light.

part one

Time present and time past
Are both perhaps present in time future
And time future contained in time past.

—T. S. Eliot, *Four Quartets*

CHAPTER 1

Beauty

It's more than eyes and hair, the curve of a cheek, the shape of a lip, a smile, a happy temperament. We inherit many things in our genes, but here's a question: How much is nature, how much is nurture? Science tells us that our cells are marked by what has happened in the past long before we became embodied, and that we carry fragments of our history from ancestors whose names we don't know. Yet we come into the world with our own story set in the stars, our own fingerprints and personality, our own magic and shine.

As we make our way through life on this planet, we question who we are and where we came from. Hints whisper to us in the darkness—ghosts of our history, the sense of what's hidden, secrets. I have always wondered, if we search for the secrets and hidden history, can we recover lost years and lost people? Can we repair the lost connections and create new relationships? Is it crazy to try? How do we weave together what was broken?

I suppose you could say I'm obsessed with trying to fit together all the pieces of my fragmented family. I always wanted to know more about them, about the history that kept entering my childhood like a wave that kept rolling toward us. I could feel its unstoppable force.

I was lucky—my curiosity about history was seeded by the stories my great-grandmother Blanche told me as we lay together in her featherbed in Iowa when I was eight years old. As I listened to her tell me about my grandmother as a little girl and my mother as a baby, I'd close my eyes and imagine them small, like I was.

What I learned as I gathered up the threads of our stories is that everyone has a point of view, a particular lens through which they see the world. My grandmother had her version, and Blanche had another. I always yearned for my mother to tell me her story, but instead she acted it out—sometimes screamed it out—and in the end, I was left with fragments about her life. There was so much more I didn't know. I had to find out what happened to my mother when she was a little girl who had been left behind by her mother, just like I was. What were the stories she couldn't remember or tell?

Our story is about my search to understand what happened to my mother and her mother, and the legacy of the generations that came before us. I wanted to understand the ways in which we were all marked by loss, the way the wind in the Great Plains bends the trees and lifts the earth in shapes that change the landscape forever.

Until the recent advent of Ancestry.com and other online resources, you had to learn your history through "direct research." Your fingers rifle through gritty index cards filed in the dusty archive boxes lining spider-webbed shelves in the backs of libraries and courthouses. You lift up huge leather-bound books from the shelves and flip through hundreds of pages of births and deaths and marriage records, translating calligraphic handwriting in black ink, each name shaped like a poem, each name someone who lived and died and was memorialized in these records.

The books I found in the courthouses in Iowa were stacked to the ceiling, draped with inches of dust, the thick books holding clues to people long forgotten. I wondered if anyone alive had ever heard of the names I saw in them.

Another place to find your kin is in a cemetery. The aroma of fresh grass greets your nostrils, and birds sing on nearby trees. In this bucolic setting, you tramp between the rows of headstones. You see names carved in old stones that are almost unreadable, names lost to the ravages of weather and time. Angels lean inexorably toward the earth, where the ancient loam will absorb the stones.

Looking for people with whom you share DNA is a physical experience of sweat and dust and frustration. But when you find them and brush the powdered leaves off the dimly chiseled names, you notice the severe framing of the person's life: date of birth to date of death. You can't help but wonder about your own future stone, how the austere dates of your beginning and ending will one day be marked under your name, and how in, say, one hundred years, no one will remember you. No one will know who you were—unless you leave a story behind. And even then, the trails of your existence will gradually disappear into mist.

Perhaps the current DNA testing, genealogical research, and family stories and memoirs are a popular way to link ourselves to what may seem to be invisible threads to the long arc of time. For as long as I can remember, I have been obsessed with learning about people I've never met, especially direct links to my mother's kin. I had a living father whom I hardly saw, and I lived in a world of women. The family that I could claim and that, for a time, claimed me was my mother's side. It is their tale I seek.

I have now found what I can through my genealogical research, which leaves me with even more questions, but I'm content with having many dates and facts from our family story. I want to share these with my daughter, but when we gather during the holidays, we are in the Present. In moments of quiet, during our celebrating and opening stockings and presents, I find myself thinking about the long-ago stories I've uncovered, the heritage that is ours. As I look around the room, our DNA legacy is evident in the faces of my daughter and grandchildren—the impressions of five generations, that harks back over 120 years. Such moments reveal the most obvious gifts from the past, in bone and blood and flesh.

Several times a year, I visit my daughter, Amanda, her husband, Frank, and their two children, Miles and Zoe, in San Diego. It is in them that I notice the hints of what Louis, my grandmother's father, left us. He died at twenty-one in 1894, two months after his wedding to Blanche, my great-grandmother, most likely unaware he had fathered a daughter. I think of him as the boy who offered us his beauty before he died. He gifted my grandmother her good looks, looks passed on to my mother and me, mixed with other DNA. Again, I see him in the curve of cheeks, the lips and eyes, of my daughter and her children.

My daughter gave my granddaughter, Zoe Joy, my middle name. She's lanky as a colt, with long blond hair and a no-nonsense approach to life I wish I'd had when I was her age. And I love how she loves to read—I like to think it's a passion that runs through the generations. My grandson Miles takes after his father, with his Italian looks and bent for art and creativity. My daughter's dark eyes and face remind me of my mother in a heart-tugging way that honors the heritage of genetics. My daughter grasps my hand and puts it by hers, saying how much they look alike.

Her hands remind me of my mother's and grandmother's: slim hands that are strong, hands that work and soothe, hands that echo the women she never knew but who are deeply embedded in my psyche and our history. As I hold her hand, I'm reminded of how much I loved my mother's hands, too. It's been twenty years since she died and that part of our story ended. It was a rocky ending to a struggle to be loved, to try to understand her. We were both abandoned daughters, both partially raised by her mother, my grandmother, which left many holes in our family story. By now the stings of the past have smoothed into "that's what happened then; that's only part of my story." I'm aware how much the past has formed and shaped me. There were so many pieces that were missing, too many unanswered questions about why and when the fractures in our family happened. But my search has offered new ground to stand on, a deeper understanding than I had when I was young.

Aware of my fragmented past, my daughter understands the importance of family for me. By now, we've worked out some of the rough periods our relationship endured. When she was a teen, there were times of disconnect and discord, but when she entered her twenties, we experienced a gradual walking toward each other. A deeper healing came when she married Frank; this was a time when past issues with my ex-husband, her father, were put to rest.

What a difference it makes to forgive and let go. You're free to enjoy life and even laugh at your old self, tenderly and with compassion. I wish the family I grew up with had been able to find that kind of resolution. Amanda and I sit together, watching her children play. They are innocent of the darker history my daughter and I know about. We know that we've created a new pattern for her children. We're the first mother-and-daughter friends in four generations, passing on the gift of love and a new story for those who will come after us.

CHAPTER 2

Etched

When I was a child, I watched and looked for clues to the drama unfolding between my mother and grandmother. They were beautiful women, soft of cheek, with dark hair and eyes that promised glamour and dreams. From my beginnings, I was cast in a drama that had started before my birth. My mother, Josephine, was left behind by her mother as a young child, and my grandmother grew up most of her life with her grandmother. Gram's mother, Blanche, was a tough farm woman who worked hard and knew too well the pains and sorrows of life. The sharp winds of fate—ancient, deep patterns of heartache and struggle and love—were etched on our bodies and souls, all of us, as surely as we were carved from the blood and bones of our ancestors. Genetic patterns are carried from generation to generation in ways that are unconscious, yet they whisper to us the hints that can save us.

The landscape of the Midwest shaped our family, the everlasting sky and prairies of the Great Plains, where my body clicks awake with a cellular awareness that I've returned to the land of my origins. A place where the winds stir dirt and bone and memory. Where the clouds reach to the heavens.

This—the landscape of home—would lure me back with its winds and desperate clouds and endless expanse even when there was no house to return to and everyone had died. All family stories are made of fragments, moments in time, and these linger in our minds as long as we are alive. Each fragment is a piece of the family puzzle, and woven into each fragment is a nugget of wisdom. Each is composed of dark and light reflections of our journey through time, through the arc of our lives on Earth.

My story and the stories I've discovered about the generations on my mother's side of the family have taken place over 160 years—not a long span of time in history. But the United States is a young country, only 240 years old, so, as you can see, my family story is embedded within most of the history of America. Not that there are heroes to write about, or heroines, or famous figures. But what moves me is trying to discover the truth in the lives of my mother and grandmother, women I loved. Their story, dramatic as it was, ultimately shaped me into a writer, a therapist, and a historian. I wanted to know the forces that shaped them, all the things they never told me—because we spent years apart. I yearned to understand the mysterious world of the adults, people who cried and shouted, who took fast trains, who smoked and churned out letters in cursive and, in the end, became lost in their own dramas. I wanted to understand where things went wrong for them, what path they might have taken to achieve different outcomes. Maybe there could have been fewer tears and fewer fights. "What if . . ." became my watchwords, as I tried to imagine alternative outcomes. In the end of my searching for answers, I would find out that your imagination can go only so far, but it can also save you.

‡⁂—⁂

I was four years old when our family history began to etch my life and psyche in ways that I remember. Clouds of smoke billowed into the air around the heads of my mother and grandmother as their voices ratcheted to a crescendo in the small house in Wichita where Gram had invited us to live a few weeks earlier. My mother paced back and forth across wooden floors, heels click-clicking. "I'm going back to Chicago," she announced with conviction in her voice, alerting me to danger.

Not long before, we had lived, she and I, in an apartment in Chicago—my parents had split up before I was a year old. My mother sang to me as she fed me applesauce in my toddler chair; she helped me get dressed in my seersucker sunsuit to go to the park. I wore a babushka, she called it, to keep my fine blond hair from blowing in my eyes, a frequent hazard in that windy city. Then a train ride across big spaces of fields, the blur of trees as they went by. As the train rushed us through the Great Plains, she told me the names of things I'd never seen before. "Horses, cows, barns, birds, weeping willow trees."

Then we met my grandmother in Wichita, where she'd made a cozy apartment for us in the basement of her house, with pretty blond furniture and a colorful rug. As soon as we arrived, my mother and Gram began arguing, their voices tense, bodies stiff, gritting their teeth, pacing, smoking. But when Gram smiled at me, her dark eyes were warm, her smile just like my mother's.

Then, too soon, came my mother's announcement that she was leaving. My stomach felt empty; my heart pounded with dread. *No, she can't go. She can't.* I'm not sure when she left, exactly; it's a blank in my memory. The train took her away. She told me not to cry.

I was living happily with Gram when the Visitors came: a tall, toothy woman with beady eyes, and her sharp-nosed husband, trailed by four lanky kids—three boys and a girl. Gram said the man was her cousin. The boys, a tall one about twelve and his two younger brothers, picked up my dolls and looked under their skirts, waving the dolls, whom I considered my friends, back and forth wildly with bucktoothed glee. They circled me like raptors while their sister whined. I kept glancing into the living room to see what the adults were doing. They seemed to be laughing like old friends, Gram talking in her funny accent, her cigarette in a cigarette holder. Finally, the Visitors left.

Afterward, I tried to comfort my dolls. I had gotten several new dolls and a new buggy for my fifth birthday, after my mother left. I loved my dolls, but when they were bad, I spanked them with a spoon. I'd feel remorseful, hold them and cry, "Sorry. I'm sorry I spanked you so hard." I was not sure how many apologies would make things okay again or who was really bad—they or I.

I played with the neighborhood kids and once asked to sleep overnight at the house next door. That night, a terrible panic welled up in me in the dark. I began to cry and couldn't stop. I felt alone in the universe, adrift without anyone, though Gram was next door. I was afraid the adults would get mad, but I finally woke up the mother and asked her to call Gram. When I saw her kind face, relief poured over me. She wrapped me in her arms and told me everything was fine. She settled me under the covers of my bed. I felt safe, but shaken by what had happened, by the power of feelings I didn't understand.

Later, though I don't know how long—perhaps a few months, or it might have been weeks—Gram came into my room, looking upset. She'd just gotten off the phone with my mother. Tears streaked her makeup, and her eyes drooped with sorrow, "I'm sorry, Sugar Pie, but your parents want you to live with those people." I knew she was talking about the Visitors. I could see she didn't want to tell me this.

I felt hollow again, as a wind was blowing through our house, through me. I begged, "Please don't send me away. I'll be good. I'll eat all my prunes. I'll . . ."

She cried so hard, I had to quit begging. "Your parents have custody of you, and they want you to live with people who have children."

For the next week, I followed her around, telling her I didn't want to go. She cried and washed my clothes, carefully placing them in a small suitcase. I couldn't understand why she had to do this when she didn't want to. It seemed to me that adults did whatever they wanted. I kept hoping something would change, but the people came one afternoon and swept me away, and after that, nothing would be the same again. I wonder now, was it just my own fears that were squeezing me breathless, or was I also feeling what had happened to my mother when she was young?

The first evening, the mother called me to the front porch. She told me I had to brush my teeth every day and I had to mind her. I nodded. She narrowed her eyes at me. "Now that you live here, I am your mother. Call me Mother."

I stared at her as she rocked in a chair, smiling with all those white teeth. I couldn't believe what she had asked of me.

"You have to mind me. Say it now."

I stiffened my knees. I could find no way to utter the words. The standoff continued as early evening moved into darkness. Cicadas. Crickets. Porch lights snapped on. Trains spoke with their lonely whistles. I saw my own mother's face, her lovely face, with soft cheeks and perfect lipsticked lips and dark eyes. I could still feel the softness of her fingers on my face. I knew who my mother was. My knees were shaking after standing for so long.

"We can stay here as long as you want." The woman grinned again. "But you won't go to bed until you say it."

After darkness fell around us, my knees wobbled and my stomach rumbled. I could see I was in trouble there and I was on my own. I would have to obey her. I thought an apology toward my mother and said the word, hating the woman as much as a five-year-old can. Scared for what would happen in that strange house.

A year later, after spankings for trying to find extra food, for being "late" walking home from kindergarten, for lying about messing up the mother's piecrust when her daughter did it but lied; after the boys teased me mercilessly, pointing and making fun of me for what, who knows; after a sixteen-year-old male friend of theirs molested me in the basement; after being blamed for things the other kids did; after listening to the boys being beaten with a belt; after giving up hope I'd ever leave that place; after noticing that my inner light was fading, I found myself dumped at Gram's so they could have a vacation without a sick child.

I had seen Gram only once, for half a day, since the Visitors had spirited me away. Feverish and confused, I heard the mother, Vera, say they didn't want me on their vacation. I had been sick a lot that year and punished for it. "You have to stay in your room while we go play in the snow," she'd say, as if I had planned to be sick, as if I did it to her just to be irritating. Sometimes she spanked me for being sick, and she always shamed me for it.

That day, a day that would change everything, as they left Gram's house, I lay on the bed, a fuzzy light around me, everything blurry and out of focus. Gram appeared like an angel as she tucked me in, whispering that everything would be all right. I tried to smile when she brought me soup and knelt at my side, murmuring comfort. But I had nothing to say.

As the days passed, Gram appeared worried; parallel lines made grooves between her eyes. She coaxed me to talk to her and brought me applesauce, which used to be a favorite, but I had become a silent child, one who disappeared deep inside. As if observing through mist, I watched her talk to me, using her charm on me, but all I did was rock in the rocking chair that was once my mother's and hold a doll. Trembling, I waited for the scary people to come back.

One morning, I broke through my silence. I couldn't bear to eat the egg Gram had fixed for me. It was runny and disgusting, but I was too scared to tell her what was wrong. What if she got mad? What if she punished me? The boys had made fun of me for not eating eggs and thumped my head with their fists while their mother laughed. I sat in front of the messy egg in a bowl and tried not to throw up.

"Please, Sugar Pie, tell me what happened there." Her eyes were dark with worry, moist with her tears, and soft with love.

She knelt on the floor and begged me to tell her what was wrong. My silence began to break somewhere inside. Perhaps I *could* trust her; perhaps I began to talk because I just couldn't hold it all anymore. Between sobs, sentence by sentence, I told her everything except about the boy in the basement—I didn't have words for that, and besides, I thought it would embarrass her to hear what he had done with that pink thing, how he had tried to put it on my bare body.

She patted me and cried and kept whispering, "Oh, Sugar Pie."

After we both stopped crying, her eyes flashed with anger. She rushed to the phone to call my parents. She yelled into the black receiver connected to the wall phone in the kitchen. As she talked and paced in jagged circles, telling the tale of my last year with "those people," its long cord twisted along the doorway. What kind of trouble was I causing everyone now?

First, she confronted my mother in the tense, singsong voice I remembered from before. "They did terrible things. You have custody of her; what are you going to do about this?" A pause, her eyes narrowing, and then an explosion: "Of course she's telling the truth! You should see her, all skin and bones. She isn't the same child!"

It was strange to hear her talk about me as if I weren't there. In my disconnected state, I was secretly glad she was defending me. Usually people did not believe children, which was why you didn't tell anyone anything, but Gram listened and she seemed to believe me. Skin and bones? All I knew was that when my stomach hurt, I couldn't eat. I felt wispy, as if I weren't there at all.

It went on, that long afternoon when Gram fought for me. She called my father and yelled hard words at him, too. I watched from a distance, the words penetrating the mist off and on. The previous year, during a weekend visit, I had seen that my father, accompanied by his smiling new wife, wouldn't take me away with him if I told him the truth about my life in that house, so I stayed silent. If I told him and he didn't take me away that day, Vera would beat me. A photograph taken of me that day shows fearful eyes and no smile.

As Gram continued to pace back and forth, fierce and angry, twisting the curly black phone cord, she shouted, "That's enough! She will stay with me from now on."

I wondered if she meant it. I was nothing but trouble for everyone, an unwanted burden. I spent the next few days nervous, asking her over and over again if the family would take me even if Gram wouldn't let them, or if Gram would change her mind. She kept reassuring me, her soft voice and kind eyes inviting me to trust her, but fear had been my companion for too long.

Finally, the family came back, cheerful and smiling. I hid in the bathroom and listened to Gram tell them I would stay with her, that she had custody now. No one yelled or screamed. I was shaking when I emerged but plastered a smile on my face, trying to pretend I wasn't terrified. The woman flashed her teeth in her version of a smile, and they all left without me. I stood for a moment in the quiet, trying to test whether this was all real. Gram bustled around, clearing up the coffee cups. I went into my room and sat on the bed. I held my dolls, glad to be reunited with them. Gram came in and gave me a comforting smile. "It's okay, Sugar Pie. They're gone, and you will live with me now."

I was happy that she was assuring me that everything was fine, but I had no belief that what she said, what any adult said, was true. At any time, adults made decisions you couldn't do anything about.

For the rest of my childhood, I had nightmares that they would come to steal me away, about the basement where the boy molested me, and about the spankings, which spun out in dream after dream. I'd wake up shouting and then remember that Gram was in the next room. All the years I lived with her, I was grateful that she had saved me, and at the same time I was prepared for a possible rejection. For years, even into adulthood, I would have dreams—nightmares, really—of how to survive on my own if I had to, mentally adding up what to pack: sturdy shoes, warm sweaters, spoons, a can opener, bread, paper and pencil, some good books, coins stolen from Gram's purse. I would be alone, with no hope of rescue.

Gram moved us to Enid, Oklahoma, when I was six. I would find out later it was to live near her best friend, Helen, whom she'd met during World War II. All around us, the past made itself known. We lived in the Land of the Red Man, as the name Oklahoma was translated, and as a child, I could feel the history there. Oklahoma glorified the pioneer past: the land rush of 1889, the conquest of the "Indians." We lived near the Chisholm Trail, renamed Highway 81. Movie theaters, cafés, streets, and towns had Indian names: Cherokee, Osage, Apache, Comanche, Arapahoe, Waukomis. As the cicadas throbbed in hypnotic, sultry rhythms in the summer, I'd peer through my eyelashes across the street from our house, where I saw/imagined Indians riding their horses in the dusty field. Everything was dusty and burnished brown and gold: the shape of the men, the horses whirling gracefully by the gully and under the big old cottonwood tree that feathered our neighborhood with its cotton floss in the spring. It had a thick skin and its branches rose to the sky.

Over time, I learned what happened to the Indians. I felt a squeezing in my body, a sense of loss that we killed them off, wondering at my own silent guilt, even though it happened before I was born. I believed that the land, the dirt, the trees, the sky, and the rocks had witnessed the history of what happened there. The land recorded it; the history of everything that occurred was embedded in every rock and every grain of red dirt. History marked us with invisible particles upon our skin. Later, I would learn that this is true: we inhale the dirt and dust, it becomes part of our bodies—earth to earth, dust to dust—and that history lives in our very cells.

There was always the wind. It whirled and swirled, kicking up dust and revealing, if we cared to look for it, secrets just under the surface, particles of bone and earth that shimmered from the great inland sea that covered mid-America thousands of years ago. The land spreading before me horizon to horizon was wise and eternal, carrying the imprints of the past. I would lean into this wind, eager to learn about the land and absorb its whispering lessons. If I could learn about what came before our time here, perhaps I could understand everything better; maybe I could make sense of my family, too.

The small house we moved to on Park Street was filled to the brim with things that Gram had brought from her life in Chicago: an oversize satin brocade couch and chair that took up nearly half of the small living room, a huge mahogany desk with inlaid wood edges. Wine-colored Oriental rugs adorned hardwood floors. Gram wanted to create an artistic, European look and supervised decorating the house with "French" wallpaper in a flowery green-

and-maroon pattern. Over the couch hung a "copy of a Rembrandt," she liked to brag, a dark, brooding presence painted in brown and black, filling the house with the history of art and a hint of Europe. Her furnishings proved that Gram was different from everyone else—no one else in that middle-class town had heavy dark furniture or busy French wallpaper. They didn't use real silver or china, although when we used it, we ate on TV tables. Lace curtains on the windows and bedroom furniture—substantial mahogany twin bed sets—demonstrated that she was different and better, and a higher class than everyone else. That's what I figured out about her as the years went on.

She'd talk about the importance of fine furniture, clothes, travel, and education, and how the "hoi polloi" lived useless, ugly, and artless lives. I felt embarrassed that she insisted both of us represented a higher status. I wanted to be "normal." I didn't want to stand out, but, as I would come to understand, she had something to prove. She appointed me her representative in her desire for status—an uncomfortable fit for me.

In a photograph of my grandmother taken in the early 1950s, just after she took me in, she is wearing a silk shirtdress, her hair coiffed, her hip jutting out. She looks glamorous standing by her new Nash Rambler. She was an attractive, vibrant woman who seemed full of vim and vigor, as they say. I loved watching her sit at her dressing table, carefully applying her makeup, powder, and rouge. Her lips were rich with colors of red and wine, and she always, always dressed up before going out, wearing dresses and suits made of silk, wool, or soft cotton that draped luxuriously around her slim frame. She wore hose, the seam running up the back of her leg and fastened with a garter belt, and expensive shoes. As most little girls do, I loved watching her dress. In those days, her slightly graying hair was tinted blue—all the rage then.

Soon after we moved to Enid, she found a piano teacher and I began weekly piano lessons. "You need to become someone

Gram 1950—with her Nash Rambler

other people can respect and admire," she told me. I enjoyed picking out the notes on the white and black keys, though practicing was not fun when the other kids were outside playing. I didn't know yet that by playing music, I gave her the opportunity to live a life she had never had but secretly desired. Through me, she would have her piano, she would have the recitals and concerts she missed growing up in a poor family in Iowa, and she'd be admired for what she had created—a young self that she never had but that I now embodied. Of course, I knew nothing of this then.

Some afternoons, she'd put on the long-playing records by Tchaikovsky, Beethoven, or Brahms. She'd dance and hum to the music, her face lighting up; she loved classical music and the lifestyle she associated with culture and grace. Gram would let me paw through her closet and caress her silk dresses, evening gowns, and feather boas. I loved touching her gowns and slipping leather shoes, in pale blue and forest green, from the bottom of her closet. Sometimes Gram told the stories connected with the clothes: a voyage by ship that took her to England. A hefty black trunk was perched in the back of the closet; her face lit up as she pulled it out. Eagerly, I unlatched the brass fasteners and opened it, delighted by the miniature hangers and little drawers with leather pulls. The inside was wallpapered with a pink-and-cream pattern, and the outside was stamped with colorful stickers, faraway destinations. As I opened and closed the drawers, I tried to imagine the ships and what it must have been like to cross the huge Atlantic Ocean. When she talked to me about where she had gone, her eyes flickered toward the past, toward another era in her life.

Her hair pouffed around her happy face as she told me about her trip—or was it trips?—to England. "I even got to dine at the captain's table," she breathed, her eyes glittering with the honor of it as she savored the memory. I gathered that not everyone was invited. She showed me a photograph of her on the deck of a ship, looking slinky like a movie star as she leaned against a bench behind the captain. She wore the latest-style suit, bearing a fur collar, and a jaunty hat on her head, and she held a cigarette in its ivory holder at a daring angle, looking like an older Lauren Bacall and movie stars from the 1930s.

I can remember the tone of her voice as she breathed, "Oh, England—it's so beautiful, with its cathedrals and ancient cemeteries. And the castles . . . You could imagine how it was in the sixteenth century." She grew quiet, then said, "One time, as I stood in one of the castles, I saw myself living there in another time. I've always felt I was born in the wrong time."

There she was, my grandmother with a big imagination, a world traveler. Who she was to me changed in that moment. She was not just my grandmother; she was someone else, a romantic figure of dreams. I could see her then, the young woman who used her middle name, no longer Lulu. It was Frances who traveled across the Atlantic Ocean with her trunk and her silk dresses, far away from her crude Iowa farm origins. Later, I learned that you can leave your origins, you can change your name and your clothes and your hair, but everything you have ever been is a part of you, and you can't escape that. She tried to get away from her origins, those rough farm people, barefoot, poor, and uneducated. I would find out her whole life was about this escape. And it didn't quite work.

When you are away from someone a long time, they become mist and dream. You make them up; they become characters in a fiction story. You begin to wonder what the truth is, but then there's the advantage in your dream world—you make things happen the way you want them to be. You can dream of good endings, of your mother rushing back from the train, changing her mind, her arms open, her face crumpled with missing you so much she tells you that she can't live without you. Maybe she'll say she's come back to take you with her. In reality, that might not be a great idea. But if you measure that act on the "love scales," which you keep track of in your body and heart, it would mean everything if she would say it or want it. It would mean you finally matter, that you are the most important thing in her life for a change.

It was a great dream every time, every year, as I counted down the days until my mother's next visit. It's not necessary to say here that this dream never happened in real life—she didn't come back to get me and change her mind about leaving. The reality is another dimension, one that's made of the color gray and wet tears and socked-in-the-stomach disappointment. There's a sorrow that seems to flow through the bloodstream, but you learn not to notice it—that's not the feeling you want to have. I was an eternal optimist. Each time my mother arrived, I had the same dream-illusion—the yearning, waiting for her to descend from the train and look at me. Then the reality.

Now, I wonder if it might have been like that for my mother, too, that yearning, that dreaming, as she replayed her own mother's visits when she was a little girl and her mother had left her behind. As my mother emerged from the steam billowing around the silver train that rushed toward the station in Perry, Oklahoma. My heart beat heart beat a little faster when I saw her slim form, dressed in a lovely suit, her red hair gleaming in the sun. At that moment, the dream was better than reality. She would smile; she might let me get close to her for a moment, for a cool hug. Then her body would stiffen and her eyes would rise toward her mother for "the glance." Gram would stand with her hand on one hip, not quite glaring, looking vaguely impatient. And they would begin the silent contest, the one that came before the word battle that would follow in a few hours. I'd lose my mother at that moment to whatever it was between her and her mother, their history, the story they'd already lived and fought about. I didn't know what those struggles were about yet; I knew only of the breath-holding tension, the lack of enough oxygen to breathe. I remember wanting them just to love each other. Wanting them not to fight. Every. Time.

You can't stop storms in the Great Plains. They are inevitable as they roll down from the Rocky Mountains, sweeping as they do in their great curtains of black, jabs of lightning, mountains of clouds rising in ever-growing layers to disappear into the heavens above. You must bow to the great power of the wind. All you can do is step outside and lift your face to the smell of rain, to the heavens. These are forces that you learn to surrender to; you learn to wait for them, to expect them, even to welcome them, their power greater than that of any human.

There were other kinds of storms, too—the smoke, sharp voices, and cadences of shrieking, followed by a concrete silence that weighed heavily on my body. My stomach ached for the dream that seemed so real before my mother arrived. This time, they would love each other, if only my "real" mother, the one I'd dreamed of, the mother I'd waited for whose caress soothed me, would not disappear in the middle of a fight. They were always about money, about all the things she did wrong: lose jobs, beg money from Gram, be lost in a fantasy about one boyfriend or another. Worse, they would even fight about me: who could best take care of me; whether I should be allowed more freedom; how much my father should visit; and, later, if I should be allowed to wear "teen" lipstick or what kind of clothes. While Gram was very careful and controlling of what I did, Mother thought I should be allowed to go skating or ride a bike, which Gram wouldn't allow. I secretly agreed with my mother but could say nothing. Mother encouraged me to have fun and not just practice and read and study all the time. Later, when Gram brought me a bra, which was a big stepping-stone for a skinny girl like me, and I was grateful to her, Mother thought I was too young for it, though I was fourteen. She seemed to want me to stay a little girl. Perhaps because she realized she'd missed my childhood.

As they fought, I closed my eyes and held my breath for a softer tone, hoping they would remember something nice about each other, that they would connect somehow, wishing they weren't upset. In those first years, my excitement would build each day during the months I waited for my mother to visit. I imagined the delicious thrill of seeing her, falling into her beauty and the soft tenderness I remembered. I never learned to approach her visits differently until I was much older, and even then I'd stick with my happy fantasies. The truth is, I liked to tilt reality in a positive direction. If I expected slightly less but left room for something more or better—maybe the best would happen: my dreams *would* come true. I would use that illusion method until one day it would become clear that it wasn't such a good idea—I couldn't make people into something they were not.

Later in my life, I'd use the Illusion method to dream up relationships that were better in my imagination than they were in reality. Boyfriends and husbands might be too controlling, or not present, or abandoning, but through my rose-colored glasses, they were perfect. They would disappoint or leave me, but I never gave up. But that's who I was, who I am. I'd rather hold out hope, even now, to leave room for the possibility that love, or the desire to sustain a thin thread of connection or forgiveness, will finally become Real. One day, things will come right.

I wonder now what it was like for my mother when she came and went from that humble train station stuck in the middle of the Great Plains. Over the years, I learned how parallel our paths were. Her arrivals and departures were almost identical to what her own mother had done. Through trying to understand what happened, I came to understand that she, too, was abandoned by her mother—by both parents, really; she had a search for identity, like I did; and she was confused about men and love. We were intrinsically different, but the parallels couldn't be missed. I was not glamorous like Gram and Mother, instead practical, cautious, and shy. Until my forties, I wished I could be more like them, I wanted to be as lovely as they were. By my forties, I'd been in therapy for a few years and began to realize their beauty was fragile, based on the physical. They were beautiful, but they were both trapped by anger, judgment, and grudges. But when I was young, my breath caught at their beauty.

CHAPTER 3

Walking Storybook

Wafting somewhat loosely in the wind, assailed by stomachaches and afraid of losing the only person who wanted me, I adjusted to being with Gram. When the nightmares came, she soothed me with gentle strokes of her hands, whispering that I was all right. She enticed me to eat and bought steaks to make sure I had iron. She was trying to make up for my malnutrition at Vera's, where I got rickets. As the years passed, school, with books and reading, was a thrilling discovery. The stories took me away as the pages unfolded their magic. A new kind of comfort wrapped its arms around me: worlds that existed in my mind, worlds that offered escape from anything unpleasant.

Summer hits the Great Plains hard, the ever-present wind grabbing leaves and tossing them about in a whirl of sound. Heavy rain and dark clouds promised a cocoon where I could dive even deeper into books on those days that crackled with electricity. We could see the storms heading toward us from the west, great walls of black clouds, a sense of urgency in the air, an inevitability. We had to surrender to it.

In June that year, I was eight, between the storms, intense heat infused our house, which had no air conditioner, only a small black metal fan that swung back and forth. One day, Gram put a kerchief over her hair and scurried around, doing the dishes, scrubbing the sink, and taking out the garbage, looking determined but happy. She took suitcases from the garage and told me to put in everything I would need for the summer.

"Where are we going?" I asked, packing dolls, doll clothes, shorts, socks, sandals, and my nightie. I had a separate stack of books.

"To Iowa, where my mama lives. I miss her so much." Gram blew the smoke from her cigarette and paused in her scurrying, a tender look on her face.

I was surprised to hear that she had a mother, but of course everyone had to have a mother. I felt silly that I'd never thought about it before. Missing mothers was something I was used to. In my room, as I was packing, I opened the chest of drawers, where a rabbit-fur muff my mother gave me when we were in Chicago was folded in tissue paper. I held the soft fur against my face, caressing it as if it were her. It held the scent of my mother, and for a few moments, she was with me. I wrapped it back up so it would be safe, so I could come back and get it out when I wanted to be with her.

The next day, sweat poured down my body as we tucked into the backseat of the Nash Rambler a thick satin comforter to cushion my fall in case of an accident—this was before seat belts. Off we went, a warm wind blowing across the car, slightly cooler coming in from the window. Gram relaxed into smiles and pranced perkily around the car when we stopped for gas. She played the radio and smoked and talked about Blanche, her mother. "Mama—I miss her so much. She's getting old, so I need to see her more often. You be polite to her. She's very old and must be treated with respect."

For three days, she drove us across the flat plains of southern Kansas, which gradually led to hilly uprisings through Missouri and into Iowa, the amazing wide spaces of land rolling out before us. Gram loved driving and became more alive as we went, chatting with waitresses when we stopped, smiling flirtatiously at the young men who pumped gas and washed the car windows. That trip was my first taste of the vastness of the Great Plains. The skies went on forever and the open spaces were lonely, but there was something I loved about the enormity of the land and sky and the wind, the way that wind bent trees on their sides and plastered my dresses to my body. I would turn my face and body into it as it blew so hard I had to gasp to take a breath.

On the last day, Gram excitedly pointed out towns she knew the names of as we approached the land where she was born. Then we arrived at the Martin Mink Farm, near Muscatine, which belonged to Edith, Gram's half sister, and her husband, Willard. All of them, including their twenty-six-year-old son, Billy, rushed out from the house to greet us, along with an old woman who I figured must be Blanche, Gram's mother. Finally, I got to meet her. Her skin was wrinkled, and her back was hunched over. Tears came from her eyes as everyone offered quick hugs. Blanche looked like a wise old woman, her dark eyes clear as she took in everything. She patted me on the head and wiped her eyes. We all made our way to the house while Gram chatted about the trip. Everyone kept patting me and smiling at me, as if they knew me. As if I belonged with them. For the first time, I began to see what "family" meant.

You feel everything on your skin when you are young—the breeze makes the hair on your arms stand up. In this new place, the aromas in the wind offered me a mix of mud and animal shit and gravy and pie, green growing things and the musty smell of the past. The famous Mississippi, with its scent and movement and mysteries of time, was only a mile away. I watched my grandmother change from her formal self into someone who seemed younger and more vulnerable. She hovered around her mother with a different kind of look on her face than I'd ever seen, as if wanting approval. Blanche seemed a bit formidable, with stern glances, sharp elbows, hard lines in her face, and heels that stomped across the floor—not a person to be hugging. But she intrigued me. I had never seen anyone so old or wrinkled.

The day moved quickly as Aunt Edith, a smiling, kind woman of soft speech, served homemade apple pie, vanilla ice cream, and coffee. A couple of hours after that, she stirred up a huge feast of fried chicken, mashed potatoes, and gravy. Uncle Willard puffed a pipe after dinner and chuckled deep in his throat. He wore plaid shirts and overalls, and his fingers and square teeth were stained with tobacco. Billy kept smiling at me and asking me questions about school and books. He asked if I wanted to go with him and his father later, if Gram allowed it, to feed the mink in the pens. The men interested me: they had their chores; they looked and acted so different from women. Without a father, I wanted to know the world of men, and I liked the way they smiled at me.

I was a little terrified of Blanche—she seemed so fierce, with her beetled dark brows, clunky shoes, and somber face—but she was nice, too. She asked me about school and showed me her embroidery work, tiny stitches that made flowers, and asked me if I wanted to learn. I poked my fingers a few times, but I felt proud when I learned to make flowers and leaves with pretty colored threads. That night it was an honor to be assigned to sleep with her in the featherbed upstairs. After she put her teeth in a jar by the bed and told me to turn out the light, she began lisping her stories to me. The crevices of her face were softened by moonlight as it fell upon us. She told me about her life as a mother raising seven children on a farm. She churned butter and baked bread in a wood cookstove, even in sweltering summers. She cooked meat, gravy, mashed potatoes, corn on the cob, pie, cake, and coffee for twenty harvesters and her family. I learned about hard work, horses and wagons, instead of cars, and chores that had to be done every day. The women helped deliver each other's babies, and some of the babies died.

She was silent for a few minutes, breathing in and out. I didn't know if she was asleep. I felt on high alert—there was so much to learn from her. She'd opened my eyes in just a few minutes to her life in the nineteenth century, a landscape of wonder and stories.

She took a breath and whispered, "You never know how things will turn out. Lulu's father . . . we were married in 1894, January first, New Year's Day. The snow was high, and it was a sunny day." She paused. "His name was Louis, and two months later he was dead. The pneumonia."

Startled, I stared at her, barely able to make out her face as she lay on the bed in the moonlight. I must have gasped or sighed or something as I tried to understand that time long ago when he died, and to grasp that he was Gram's father. "You can't know when you're young the things that will happen."

I took a breath and asked, "So Gram's daddy died?"

Her curls rasped on the pillow as she nodded. I lay there silent, not knowing what I could say to her. At eight years old, I could hardly imagine death. *Gram's daddy died* repeated itself in my mind over and over again. What did he look like? Did Gram miss him like I missed my father? How did not having a father make her feel? I knew what it was like to miss someone. Was she lonely like I was?

The next morning, I gazed at my grandmother, smoke scribing lazy gray circles around her head, wondering if she was lonely as a little girl without her father. It occurred to me that she had been a little girl once, that she had been born from Blanche. That she had a history; she had come from somewhere and lived a long time before she'd become my grandmother. Until then, I had never thought of her as a regular person—she was just Gram.

She would sit at Edith and Willard's kitchen table, the morning light pouring in from the window as she smoked a cigarette, laughing and telling tales about a trip to Europe. The looks on the faces of Edith, Willard, and Blanche made it seem like they had heard it all before, or maybe they thought she was exaggerating. Was I sensing another story beneath the one she was telling?

The next afternoon, I couldn't stop thinking about all the things that Blanche had told me. I wanted to be near her and see if there were more stories, so I followed her out to the garden. The earth smelled fresh, and bugs were flying everywhere. She gestured to the plants, and as she named each one—tomatoes, strawberries, onions, and beans—the garden began to be a world I could understand. It had its own language, and gardening was another thing she was an expert at doing. She grumbled about the weeds and stooped over low, her dress riding up in back, exposing rolled-up cotton hose and the backs of her knees. As if continuing with a story already begun, she talked about my mother, Jo'tine, and my grandmother—Lulu. I was still getting used to the idea that to these people, Gram had an entirely different name—Lulu, instead of Frances.

"Those two, they should be ashamed." She shook her head and made a *tsk-tsk* sound. It interested me that she was talking about her own daughter that way. "All these years, the way they talk to each other . . ." She shook her head again.

I knew what she meant: their tense bodies lined up like warriors across the room, their pretty faces distorted with anger. Mother had just visited a few weeks before, and all I wanted was for them to get along. I missed Mommy so much, but after the first gentle hello, her perfume wafting over me, her eyes settled on her mother. For a few minutes, maybe it was longer, they talked about Mother's work as a secretary, the weather, but then somehow they were arguing, their voices rising higher and higher, cigarette smoke circling both of them as they spat out angry words.

"That Lulu, she left Jo'tine behind when she was a baby." Blanche dug the spade in to take out a clump of weeds.

I tried to understand what she had just said. Gram left my mother? Then my mother would have been alone, like I was, without her mother. Until then, it hadn't occurred to me that Blanche knew everyone—she was the mother of the mother of my mother. Thinking aloud, I said, "You knew Mommy when she was a little girl?"

Blanche pulled out a dandelion and threw it down. She chuckled. "Sure I did. Little Jo'tine came to live with my mother—her name was Josephine, too. She was a sweet little thing, not like she is now. But things never was right between them after that."

Now I was learning about Blanche's mother—another Josephine—and I wanted to know why she called Gram Lulu.

"That's her name: Lulu Frances. 'Course, when she went off like that, she wanted us to call her Frances." I could tell she thought that name meant Gram had been fancying herself up too much.

"Went off? Where did she go?"

"Off gallivanting."

Gallivanting—I wasn't sure of its definition, exactly, but I guessed it meant that Gram didn't stay home where she belonged, and left my mother behind with Blanche's mother. Each question led to more mystery—all the adults had to know this story. Just as I had realized the previous night, grown-ups remember the past; they carry it around with them. They see the world through memories of what happened. You can sometimes see it clearly on their faces.

Blanche attacked the weeds ferociously, clicking her false teeth. I could see that she didn't approve of what had happened between her daughter and my mother. "Those two, they fight like cats and dogs. It's a terrible shame." More teeth clicking.

Suddenly, I was tired. I pulled a few weeds with Blanche, the aroma of the rich soil filling me with a yearning I didn't understand. She knew everything—what had happened between

Mother and Gram years ago—and she'd lived through all those things she'd told me about the night before. I decided that she was someone to stick close to. The stories from the past might have some of the answers I needed about why things were so complicated and why I'd get that knot in my stomach when I thought about my mother.

I let Blanche tramp ahead of me toward the house while I thought about the shocking news that Gram had left my mother when she was little. It was sad, but it made sense that they fought. I thought about what had happened just before we'd left for our trip to Iowa. My mother, her beauty always making me melt a little, stood opposite Gram in the living room of the house on Park Street back in Enid, but she didn't look so beautiful right then. The lights were on, the air in the room mustard yellow. They looked like soldiers, hands on hips, smoke swirling around their heads, as the air crackled with voices shouting blame: "It's your fault." "No, it's yours." Both of them tried to prove how wrong the other one was for so long, it made my head hurt. I was invisible to them in the heat of the battle. Every muscle of my body was pulled tight. I loved them both. Did I have to choose? Why couldn't they just love each other?

My heart pounding at my boldness, and unable to stand the tension any longer, I pushed myself between them and begged them to stop. As if shocked, they hesitated for a moment, a startling silence falling into a room cloudy with smoke and hints of the past, but then they moved into another battle position and started in again, the volume only slightly lower. They were swaying back and forth, as if taking invisible blows. My stomach ached and my neck was stiff. Finally, my mother stomped across the wooden floors toward my room. She threw bottles of her makeup into her suitcase, the sweet scents wafting up toward me, an aroma that existed only when she arrived.

I followed her in and said, "Mommy, don't be mad. Please don't leave. Can I go with you?"

A frown appeared between her eyes, her voice hoarse and deep. "I have to go."

Her body seemed to close in on itself; her face turned from me as she folded her sweaters in tissue paper. The rustling was too loud, like leaves crackling at the start of a storm. I knew she would go to Gram's best friend, Aunt Helen's, house first, before she would leave for good, but the whirlwind of the fight—Gram in the living room, crying; Mother still seething with anger, eyes troubled and hands shaking—the whole mess of it paralyzed my mind as I tried to figure out what to do. Couldn't I help them make peace? It seemed to me that was all they needed to do—say they were sorry. Try to talk softly.

I went to Gram, who was huddled miserably on the couch. I wanted to make her feel better, but she barely managed a weak smile when I knelt before her, and then Mother was in the dining room, dialing the phone to call a cab. Gram slammed down her coffee cup, and Mother stomped to the door, flinging out sharp sentences of blame and finality. The door closed behind her, and the night swallowed her up. When would I see her again? Would she ever come back? In the living room, the battlefield was quiet, too quiet and dark, and everything felt like needles on my skin. I didn't know how to help them love each other, but if they didn't, what would become of us?

In Iowa that first summer, after Blanche gave me those clues to the past, I had to know everything about the Iowa family. Windows into the past opened up at the kitchen table at Edith's house after supper. A reminiscent quality began to emerge in the stories around the table, the old stories, the "remember when" stories. I could feel the past tiptoeing up to us in the cadence of their voices, deep, throaty tones hinting that they were remembering special moments. I could see in their eyes that they were traveling back in time. There was a lot of history behind them—Blanche and Gram were born in the last century, Edith and Willard early in the new century. Their son, Billy, was in his twenties, and he loved it when the family stories started up. He'd help Edith dig the shoebox of photos out of the hall closet.

A wistful mood came over everyone as they gathered around the boxes and photos in the middle of the Formica table. Willard's antique clocks ticked and tocked, and as the hours passed, they chimed out the time.

This exploration of time and memory began when I was young, and every year after that, we celebrated the old stories. In a reverent, almost spiritual celebration of those who were gone, they nibbled on memories as if they were a treasured dessert. When the photo box was opened, everyone pawed excitedly through layers of black-and-white photos, talking about the branches of the family, the houses where they'd all lived. Most of the photographs were small squares with crimped edges. Image by image, time fell open as we gazed upon the faces of people who were captured in a single lived moment long ago. "There's So-and-So, and, oh, I forgot that Uncle What's-His-Name always had a pipe"—their memories seemed to gather in a rush of remembering. I saw ill-fitting suits, grouchy-looking faces, stiff poses, all kinds of horses and carriages, dogs and cats, and vintage cars. Very few of those serious German people smiled. There was a photo of Blanche taken when she was young, her unsmiling face different from now only in that it wasn't wrinkled. She had the same high cheekbones, pointed nose, and severe mouth.

They all laughed as they looked at photos of Edith's half-brothers and -sisters, my great-aunts and uncles. In one photo, they were barefoot, their clothes ragged, as they posed under a tree on a farm, chickens wandering in a blur through the background. Blanche talked about how hard those days were, doing the wash each Monday in the yard, having barely enough money for food and clothes, though nearly everything was created by hand on the farm.

Then a hush fell over the group when a sepia-toned photo of a young man slipped onto the table.

"Oh, there he is," Blanche said.

"Who?" I asked, peering at the photo. The man had large brown eyes, a serious but sensitive-looking face, and a short haircut.

"Louis," whispered Blanche. "Lulu's father."

I glanced at my grandmother, who was quiet—or was she sorrowful?—as her eyes lingered on the image. There he was, the man Blanche had told me had died a few weeks after marrying her. He was a very young man, almost a boy, in the photo, while Blanche's face and body all these years later registered the passing of time. His face was innocent and open, and I noticed he had none of the hard edges of the other people in the family pictures. We all watched Gram as she looked at her father.

"It's the only photo we have of him, the only one," Blanche said softly.

She laid the photo to the side, away from the pile on the table, where we could keep looking at him. I saw hints of Gram and my mother in his lips, his large, soulful eyes, and the shape of his face. I looked at Blanche and Gram. Even though I was very young then, I could see it was Louis who echoed through my grandmother, offering his gift of genes to us.

Louis Garrett, age 20

The moment was broken by someone talking about the "hard times" back then, the Depression. They talked about other pictures, friends they had known and where they had lived and who was related to whom. I noticed that Gram was quiet, but I didn't know what to say to her. It seemed harsh to say nothing, but I didn't want to say the wrong thing and make her sad. She had never told me about her father. There were so many photos of people Gram didn't know. She asked about who certain people were and what certain events were, so I knew she must have been gone and not have been part of those stories.

As we continued to sift through the collection, dozens of sharp-faced ancestors showed up: Blanche's mother, Josephine; her brothers and sisters—the Stinemans. Finally, I heard the names of the aunts and great-aunts and great-great-aunts and uncles and cousins: Hidelbaugh, McGill, Dickerson, and Letts. After a while, a silence descended as the clocks ticked and chimed. It became clear that sometime in the past Gram had slipped away from the tight weaving of family into the "gallivanting" Blanche had told me about. I knew there were more stories and secrets that lurked behind these stories. What I didn't know was that it would be a project that would last a lifetime.

It seemed to me that everyone at the table wanted to step through the windows of the photographs and return to a moment in their past. Less than a mile away, the Mississippi River flowed heavy and full between its wide banks. A levee kept the river from flooding as it used to, but it was still a powerful force. It was a mythic river, sacred to those who first set down their moccasins on its banks in a time before regular time, when we started measuring history. It had its own stories. Mark Twain had lived in Muscatine and wrote about the river. Before the lands were "settled," the Sac and Fox hunted and fished and trapped along the river. There may have been a tribe called the Mouscatin—how Muscatine got its name.

The Great River watched my family plant their fields, ride their horses, raise their children. Herons roosted on tree branches; fish swam downstream. The footprints have long been washed away, a time when the land was open forests, when the tall and short grasses of the prairies flowed like waves across the land—a wild, magical place.

CHAPTER 4

God Love Ya, Darlin'

$\mathcal{S}$ ometimes new family members get adopted in, especially if there is a need, a hole in the heart. Though they may be "new" friends, they seem to fit in with us naturally, as if we have always known them. They may become closer than blood family; they rest near to our hearts and cheer us on. It's not uncommon for children to call their parents' friends "aunt" or "uncle," making the family adoption official.

We called my grandmother's best friend Aunt Helen. She was woven into my life more closely than my parents were. Her husband was called Uncle Maj, so named from his stint as a major in the army during World War II, when my grandmother met them in Texas. Gram would "winter in the South," in San Antonio, and, according to Aunt Helen, the narrator of the story about their meeting, my grandmother fascinated them. They all met at a San Antonio hotel near where Uncle Maj was stationed.

Aunt Helen laughing

I could imagine Gram sweeping in, wearing a sophisticated outfit, her makeup and hair perfect. As she spun stories about her travels to Europe, she must have seemed extraordinary to these Midwestern, conservative people, one of the most interesting women they'd ever met. At that time, my grandmother was used to being on her own. She had made her way across the ocean and traveled in foreign countries by herself at a time when it was not acceptable or usual for women to have such adventures.

Uncle Maj, who always stood erect and proud like a soldier, his white hair combed neatly, his brilliant blue eyes never missing a thing, was a certified public accountant in Enid. He had lived there with his first wife and daughters before his wife had died, a few years earlier. Helen and Maj were in their late fifties by the time I knew them. He became the closest thing to a father I'd have—not in embraces or sitting on laps, but in showing me how he treated everyone with respect, how he loved Aunt Helen, glanced at her with a twinkle in his eye. How he believed in peace, even when he refereed wars between Gram and Mother. The way he winked at me in amusement.

Aunt Helen, with her Southern accent and cooking, wrapped everyone in her warmth. She had a talent for making everyone feel wanted and loved and special, from our family to ladies at the church to the children and grandchildren of Uncle Maj. She had no children of her own but seemed to adopt everybody. Over the years, Aunt Helen acted as a buffer between my grandmother and me—she always thought Gram was too strict. She and Maj. were the only witnesses to what I believed was my grandmother's true nature—sophisticated and smart—despite the times when she fell into her darkness. I still grieve Aunt Helen, but I'm blessed with dozens of letters that bring her back to life.

In the early years when I lived with Gram, every weekend we'd pack up some clothes, my dolls, books, Gram's cigarettes and makeup to trek to Aunt Helen's house on the other side of town. We traveled in our Nash Rambler down bumpy Market Street, a road rutted with the copper-stained dirt that blew continuously on the wind. This was considered the southernmost street in town because no one (white) cared to acknowledge that there was an entire black community on the other side of Market, where the roads weren't paved. It was considered off-limits, as was socializing with any people of color, unless you wanted to hire one as a maid.

I don't believe that Aunt Helen followed all those societal rules. I seem to remember that she took food to families in that community, though she wouldn't have bragged about it. I observed that Aunt Helen's philosophy of life and choices contrasted with Gram's. Aunt Helen took being a Christian seriously—she went to church and believed in putting into action her efforts to heal and help people; she spent time taking care of older people who had no one. She cooked for them, did errands, and took them to church or shopping. I met quite a few of these gentle, white-haired, fragile ladies, whose eyes were full of memories. They would look at Aunt Helen with speech-less, teary thanks.

Helen's mother, Miss Daisy, who was in her eighties, lived with Helen until she died. Miss Daisy was from Virginia and gave off the air of a classic Southern woman, with her rose-scented bath powder and good manners. Her wrinkled fingers could speed across the baby-grand piano in the living room, inspiring Gram to tell me to practice more so I could play like Miss Daisy. We spent every weekend at their house, Gram and I sleeping together in the double bed, the sheets a soft cotton that smelled of the sun, the bedspread fluffy white chenille. I loved running my fingers across the little bumps. Her room smelled of perfume and powder and sun and fresh air. I loved to inhale the aroma of all the delightful things on her wooden dressing table—its round mirror catching the reflection of everything in the room. When she saw me opening the bottles, I held my breath, but she just smiled and let out a belly laugh. "God love ya, darlin'—you go right ahead. Which scent would you like me to put on your wrist?"

Every week, Aunt Helen baked loaves of bread. Gram and I would arrive to a home filled with the aroma of yeast and love. Gram and Helen's friends, Bob and Willi Jean would gather on Friday and Saturday nights to play bridge. Bob was bald, his wife tall, with strong features, and they both loved to laugh. They'd all make jokes and stay up late, playing cards and telling stories. I'd listen from the bedroom to their voices as they wove comfort and a routine I could count on.

Helen's delicious Southern recipes for Sunday dinner gave us something to look forward to and balanced out Gram's inabil-ity to cook anything. Aunt Helen's house became my true home. A good sport, and seeing my need for a pet, she would defy my grandmother's rules against my petting her cat: "They'll give you a disease. They'll bite you!" Aunt Helen would whisper for me to follow her to the back porch, where we'd kneel down so I could stroke her fluffy kitty. I'd sink my fingers gratefully into the soft fur, its purring a comforting vibration in my body.

Aunt Helen's welcoming personality was the opposite of Gram's formality and edgy critique of everything low-class or without style. They were an oddly matched pair. Aunt Helen was round and soft, approachable and a good listener, nodding and smiling when you talked, peppering her responses with "You don't say; I do declare!" Unless she was going out, she wore cotton housedresses and an apron. Her big belly laughs and body-crushing hugs, which she delivered frequently, surrounded me in warmth.

As the years passed she became a witness and mediator of the dramas that unfolded in my family—my mother's dramatic visits, Gram's sorrowful lamentations about her daughter. Gram and Mother would fight for hours within the first few moments they were together, but it was understood that my mother could leave Gram's house if the fight got out of hand and rush over to Helen's. A day or two later, after they had both cooled off, Gram and I would visit Mother there. In the meantime, Helen would have heard all about the fight from both of them. She would counsel them to let it go or to try to forgive. She'd nurture my mother the way she nurtured me, with hot chocolate, good cooking, and a calm household. Helen and Maj's house was like Switzerland, a neutral zone.

Over the years, Aunt Helen became the unhappy witness to the war between my father and my grandmother. Aunt Helen would eventually intervene, to disastrous consequences. Anyone who didn't completely agree with my grandmother was unforgivably disloyal. When I was fifteen, when Gram believed Aunt Helen had betrayed her, she stopped speaking to her. Gram lived in an either/or world—either you were all the way on her side, or you were the enemy. Finally, Gram finally relented and spoke to Aunt Helen again, but by then we hardly ever spent time at her home. For the rest of my life, I would long for those days of my childhood when they laughed and told stories.

Later, as the darkness descended upon her, Gram was not kind to Aunt Helen, but she simply would not give up being Gram's friend. Speaking of loyalty—Aunt Helen demonstrated it in many ways. She would show up at my piano and cello recitals, orchestra concerts, and award ceremonies, even after Gram stopped going. She was a peacemaker at heart, always wanting the best for everyone. She gave with her whole heart, and she loved my grandmother until the day she died, despite how poorly Gram treated her. Aunt Helen was always ready to forgive and forget. I watched these lessons carefully and decided that she modeled what I wanted to create in my life.

Every Sunday, Aunt Helen would arrive, wearing her church dress, carrying a casserole or baked chicken for Gram's dinner. She'd sit in the maroon velvet chair opposite Gram and listen while Gram ranted about my mother, father, and me—anyone who stirred her anger. Aunt Helen would nod and say, "Uh-huh, you don't say, uh-huh, I declare" for about forty-five minutes. Then she'd laugh and add something encouraging, like, "You have to get up off that couch, Frances. Get some new duds; do something with yourself."

Gram would growl back, but Aunt Helen would keep smiling. Finally, she'd take her leave, saying, "Now, you just get up off that couch and put on your makeup. You'll feel a lot better."

Gram would grouchily reply or make a face, but Aunt Helen would cheerily say, "Good-bye, Frances," put on her coat, and drive away until the next week.

I'd watch this in silence, hiding in the hallway, wondering how Aunt Helen could still be kind to my grandmother after being treated so badly. I resolved not to follow my grandmother's path of darkness. Aunt Helen showed me, and everyone she met, unconditional love. I carry that love with me, that ache of sorrow for her. She held the light for us; she loved us with her whole heart.

CHAPTER 5

Secrets and Ghosts

During my first summers in Iowa, I learned that I had a grandfather. Gram sat me down in front of her on a chair in Edith's living room, her face soft, her eyes warm and concerned, as if there was something delicate about what she had to tell me. "Your grandfather Blaine is your mother's father, and we were married a long time ago. He lives in Wapello, a few miles away, and I want you to meet him."

I had a grandfather? I kept learning new things about Gram when we were in Iowa. I had known her as someone who was alone, not young or married. She had always been my grandmother, without a past. I smiled at her and leaned in to hear more. Her eyes were so dark they seemed black, glittered as she said, "Your grandfather and his wife, Bernie, want to get to know you. We'll pack a bag and I'll drive you there. They want you to stay for a few days."

My mother's father—another new relative I didn't know about! And why was Gram acting so strange? That morning, she got herself "gussied up," as they called it, rouged and powdered and coiffed, and applied crimson lipstick. She put on a silk shirtwaist dress that flowed around her slim body and kept looking at herself in the mirror. I could hear hushed comments from Edith and Blanche as we got ready. There seemed to be stories that dropped into a well of silence between Gram's questions: "Got your suitcase?" "Do you want to take your favorite doll?" The way Edith and Willard looked at Gram—*Are you sure you should take her to him?*—made me wonder what was going on. *Whisper, whisper.* I didn't know what everyone was up to, but there was something about my grandfather and Gram that flamed the air.

The pink Nash Rambler, the deluxe model Gram was proud of, sped down the highway, a gray ribbon that wound itself between rolling hills of cornfields sporting golden silk top hats. Puffy white clouds scudded across the blue sky. We came upon two-story white farmhouses with red barns and silos and smelly pigpens on each side of the road. Other farms dotted the distance, highlighted by silver silos that glittered in the sun. They towered above each farm, giving the feeling of endless corn and farms and rolling hills, an image from a Heartland postcard.

Gram told me about Grandpa. "We were married when we were very young, and we lived in Wapello, where your mother was born. His father owned the newspaper, and he worked there, too. Later, we got divorced and he married a new wife—that's your grandma Bernie—and they had a daughter, Jean."

Another new relative? My mother had a half-sister? I found it hard to imagine Mother as anything but a lone child. As we were about to pass over a bridge marked Iowa River, Gram put on her turn signal and pulled to the side of the road. She smiled into the rearview mirror, applied more lipstick, and fluffed up her hair. I fidgeted, staring down at green water flecked by sunlight.

Dragonflies zipped by, sparkling, iridescent, and quick above the ripples of the stream.

Finally, she drove on, her knuckles white as she gripped the wheel. "I don't like bridges," she muttered, then glanced a couple of times into the mirror. We passed the cement plant and the Dairy Queen—the town was about three blocks long—and turned right in front of a small house with peeling paint and a garage surrounded by hollyhocks blooming vivaciously in red, pink, white, and yellow.

Gram pulled into the driveway and tooted the horn. Her hands shook as she lit another cigarette. A moment later, a silver-haired woman and a man with gray hair combed back from a large forehead came out. They smiled as they welcomed me and greeted Gram with a slightly cool, "Hello, Frances." Oh, she was Frances to them.

Gram acted stilted, holding her body in glamorous poses I'd never seen before. She spoke with the English accent I'd seen her use when putting on airs in other social situations.

Behind the masks of smiles, the weight of the past seemed to rise up like a thick white curtain of fog. I kept looking at them, wondering at what was not being said, as Gram got out of the car. Grandpa knelt down to talk with me. I smiled back at him, noticing his blue eyes and kind face, and tried to make sense of what I was feeling, wishing I could understand what was behind the big curtain of things unspoken.

The fog of history hovered around them near the colorful hollyhocks, plants that were nearly as tall as Grandpa, where the bees were buzzing. He and Gram stayed by the hollyhocks, talking alone, while I helped Grandma Bernie fix lemonade and put some cookies on a tray. She kept looking out the window. When she carried out the pitcher of lemonade and glasses, there was a stiffness in her smile and something about her extreme politeness when she offered the lemonade. It seemed to me like they'd all had a difficult conversation a few weeks earlier and were now picking up where they'd left off, all of it in code.

The smiles seemed real, but their eyes suggested bitterness or sorrow, planting more seeds of curiosity about them. I couldn't have imagined then that I would spend several decades later on trying to understand the mysteries conveyed in those few minutes.

Finally, it was time for Gram to leave. She hugged me and told me to be good and to call her at Edith's if I got homesick. Bernie and Grandpa waved good-bye, clearly relieved that she was leaving.

It was a memorable week with Grandpa and Grandma Bernie. They fed me delicious fried chicken, mashed potatoes, and green beans from their garden, and, of course, lovely, ripe red tomatoes. Grandpa would pray over it until the food was cold and slimy—he carried a Bible and believed in being a good Christian. They were gentle with me, used kind voices and smiles, and encouraged me to have fun.

Blaine and Bernie's daughter, Jean, had two children. I was interested in meeting my aunt, a tall, dark-haired woman who warmly introduced me to my cousins Joanie, six, and Kenny, ten. Joanie and I played dress-up from Bernie's dress-up box, tying on large scarves as skirts, draping ourselves in jewelry, and putting funny hats on our heads. One hot day, we were playing in a huge tin tub when Grandpa sprayed us with cold water from the hose. We grabbed each other, lost in fits of giggling. There, I was allowed to be a little girl with nothing to do but play, instead of always reading and practicing music. In the mornings, the sun shone in through the gauzy white curtains, waking me up to another day of adventure, chatter, fun, and good food. Every night I felt cocooned in safety and tenderness.

One afternoon, I heard Grandpa cry out. I looked out the window to see him kneeling in the driveway, Bernie bending near him. I could hear her murmuring that he was trying, that everything would be okay, God would help him. Later, I asked

Linda Joy and cousin Joanie, 1953

her what was wrong. "Don't worry about him, honey—he's fine now. He used to drink too much. He made some mistakes, and he . . . well, he needs to forgive himself. He's found Jesus now, and he's okay, but sometimes he . . ." Her voice trailed off, and I wasn't sure what she meant. Maybe that was part of the past I had sensed when Gram was with them.

Over the years, Gram and I went back to Iowa in the summers. A couple of times, she braved the Iowa winter weather and drove us up for Christmas. She had chains put on at a gas station some-where in Missouri, and when we arrived, her brothers laughed and patted her on the back for bravely driving through snow and ice on her own. Christmas was held at the home of my Aunt Grace, one of Gram's sisters, and was a huge family affair, with Blanche, the matriarch, in the seat of honor, surrounded by children, grandchildren, and great-grandchildren. Nearly thirty people gathered by the twelve-foot Christmas tree, decorated lavishly and piled high with presents. Gram didn't bother with trees and decorations at our house, so such elaborate rituals entranced me. Blanche opened all her presents first. It was fun to see Gram laughing and chatting with her family, losing her fake English accent. I watched her with fascination as she turned back into Lulu, the young woman who had grown up there. I wondered what my mother and father were doing for their holiday.

Gram's brothers were big and loud and plaid-shirted, hardworking men with thick hands and deep voices. They all worked hard and were clearly "in charge," the bosses of their families. The women wore aprons and laughed with the children, chatting together as they served food all day. The aromas of ham, fried chicken, roast turkey, and pork chops filled the air, followed by cookies and cakes and pies—a table of plenty.

Every summer when we arrived for the Iowa visit, Gram and I followed a routine. We'd stay for a week with Edith. She took me under her wing and taught me how to cook. I helped her make fried chicken, gravy, and mashed potatoes; pot roast and vegetables; pies and cakes and cookies. Cooking and baking became our ritual for as long as she was alive. She taught me how to iron and how to hang clothes on the clothesline. The sun-kissed sheets would slap me gently in the face. I'd breathe in the aroma of sun and fresh air and home, taking in the traditions handed down to the women in the family.

After our time at Edith's, we'd head into town to Blanche's house, with its single-seat privy out back and a wood cookstove in the kitchen that she used in the summer and winter. From her home base, we'd take Blanche around to the farms and houses where her children lived—"visitin'." The landscape of Iowa—its lush green grass and trees, buzzing cicadas and flies—became my own. At night, lightning bugs magically illuminated the soft landscape, freshened by summer rains. I could sense the river from wherever I was, like a compass.

One of my uncles owned a dairy farm and raised horses. He taught his daughter, who was my age, how to ride and compete in horse shows. I loved getting to know their farm world, the barn and stink and mud and flies and cows. I would beg Gram to let me go outside with my cousin and uncle into that mucky world. His wife said, "Oh, she's safe; let her have fun and go out to see the cows."

"But she might get hurt." Gram frowned and Blanche chuckled.

My uncle laughed. "You kiddin'? Cows don't hurt nobody."

I ran outside before anyone else could object, following my cousin out to the barn behind her father, who was calling the cows in. The odor of manure mixed with the pleasant smells of milk and hay. He showed me how he milked the cow, then put my hand on her soft udder. "See, just gently pull on the teats, like this." He yanked, and milk sprayed delightfully into the bucket. Cats of all sizes lined up to catch a spray gone wild, purring and rubbing against his legs, but he kicked them away. I cried out and looked at him in horror.

He laughed. "Aw, hell, you can't hurt none of them. They're just cats."

I rushed over to make sure the kitties weren't hurt, but I couldn't catch them. I stared at my uncle, trying to understand why he would kick a cat. Was that how everyone on farms acted? He was Blanche's youngest son, and one of three brothers. They all seemed rough, but were they cruel, too?

Besides horses, cows, and pigs, he raised tomatoes, which were harvested in July and August. I noticed the people with dark skin and hair in his tomato fields. At lunch, all of us were at the table: Blanche, Gram, my uncle, and his wife and daughter. I asked him about those people out in the fields.

"Oh, them's just the Mexicans. They're here to pick the tomatoes." He looked disgusted.

"What are those small buildings in the fields?" They were made of wood and were not much bigger than Blanche's privy.

"Aw, they live there like animals." He shook his head. Everyone else at the table went on eating their iceberg lettuce salad.

"What about the children out there in the sun?"

"Jesus Christ, they're just dirty Mexicans."

"Don't they have another house?" I couldn't believe all those people were living in one tiny wooden house in the middle of the field.

"Hell no—that's good enough for 'em. We hire 'em up for the harvest, and then they go back. I *hope* they go back. We don't want 'em here—that's for damn sure." He shook his head again, as if to rid them from his thoughts.

I wanted to like my uncle—his cows and horses and farm and pigs and chickens were wonderful—but I couldn't get my mind around what he was saying. My uncle's wife seemed to notice that I was disturbed. She said, "This is how they earn money, and they move from farm to farm."

He went on, "None of them is worth a plugged nickel. They're lazy and deserve what they get. I have to go now and mow the back forty." He got up and slammed the door on the way out.

Blanche shook her head, and Gram took a long drag of her cigarette. Talking about people that way seemed to mean nothing to her. I found out that everyone in the family talked that way about Mexicans and black people—they looked down on them. My relatives believed in divisions of class and color, and worried that "those people" would get too uppity and threaten what they'd worked hard to earn. It would be a while before I learned that this kind of thinking was called "racist," but even without knowing that word, I felt it was all wrong. Even Gram didn't seem bothered by what her brother had said. No one cared about the little children wandering in the fields in the hot sun. They looked hungry and sad, and I wanted to help them. In a way, they reminded me of how I felt at Vera's—lost and rejected. They might have even been hungry. I felt ashamed, but at the same time I was grateful that this family welcomed me at all.

All these things crowded my mind that day after lunch. I went out by myself to think for a while. Acres of rolling cornfields spread out as far as the eye could see. The farm was on a hill and down a narrow gravel road. From there I could see other farms, the houses looking like Monopoly pieces in the distance. I sat down on a rock, the sound of flies and buzzing bugs murmuring hypnotically. The scent of earth, the soft wind rustling the trees, wove me into the heart of the land, but my body rebelled against relaxing into it. I wanted to go out to the fields and apologize to the families for my uncle. He didn't care that their children were dirty and wore rags. But he was part of my family. In Blanche's stories I had learned about farm life, but seeing it for real was different—how long my uncles worked every day, the way they treated animals, a kick, a shove, the bloody killing. I'd witnessed Blanche kill a chicken, its headless body spurting blood and running around. I tried to understand the harsh streak I was seeing. I'd hidden in my heart other things about the Iowa family that I didn't like. There was so much to figure out.

After a few minutes, the warm breeze and the view of golden fields of corn topped with the blue sky, everything in slight motion from the wind, comforted me. The land and its gifts, the natural way the trees leafed out, the sounds of the animals, connected me to beauty. I listened to the sound of the insects and enjoyed the way the sun warmed the muscles of my body, pushing aside what bothered me. I didn't know that's how we create two worlds in ourselves—the world we see and accept and the world we cover up. For many years, this would be how I managed the dark and light parts of my family: what I was willing to see, and what I tried to box up and put away. One day I would see it all as a whole vision, and it would break my heart, its beauty and its sorrows.

The past does not disappear. As we grow older, we're still tethered to it and it clings to us like that fog I saw around my grandmother and Blaine. Everything exists at once; there's no separation. There's no escape, no way out of the truth—good or bad. When we accept this, we can find freedom.

Time and history knit us into a dream, the dream of life unfolding, and the dreams of everyone whose blood beats in our veins become our own.

Not until I was eleven and in Iowa again for the summer did the puzzle piece about my grandfather Blaine and my grandmother slip into place. By then, Gram had begun her slow slide into a harsh and negative figure, but there were still times when she was warm and delightful. She seemed to become smaller and more vulnerable around her mother, Blanche, but she was also the travel guide who would drive Blanche to interesting sites in the Nash Rambler and conduct tours of the area for Blanche and her sister Aunt Dell, who was a few years younger than Blanche and lived in a nursing home. All the years we visited the nursing home or picked up Dell for one of our jaunts—to Herbert Hoover's birthplace or to the Amana Colony—Blanche would get shaky and bite her lips, saying, "Ya got to promise me you'll never put me in one a them homes."

Blanche lived to be ninety-two and died in her own bed at home. But that summer morning when I was eleven, that was ahead of us. The day started with Blanche filling her cookstove with wood; the crackle of the fire, the smell of smoke, and the aroma of coffee boiling in a saucepan filled the kitchen. Gram finally came in, sleepy and wearing a flowered robe that made her look as if she had just stepped out of an impressionist painting. Blanche was deeply engrossed in reading the morning paper.

"Hmm, Lula, you'd be interested in this. Betsy [So-and-So—I don't remember the name] has come home to visit her family. Remember her?"

Gram shook her head and frowned into her coffee cup. Blanche went on, "I'd think you'd remember her. You borrowed a dress from her when you ran off to get married."

Gram's face grew red, and she slammed her coffee cup on the table. "I did no such thing!" She pushed her chair back and ran out of the room. I watched in fascination as they began to argue—I'd never seen anything like this before with them. She tried to hush Blanche, who stubbornly went on: "We couldn't look people in the eye. We were so ashamed."

I knew I should get out of their way, so I went to the bedroom, where I could listen in. I came to understand that Gram and Blaine were underage when they ran off to get married. No wonder there was such a sense of unspoken history when I first saw them together.

The fight between Gram and Blanche continued, both of them shouting at each other. They were discussing an event that had been buried for years—Gram was in her sixties when this fight erupted, and Blanche in her eighties. We were supposed to pick up Dell that day and go on one of our drives, and we were already late. Finally, they began to speak more softly. I peeked out from the bedroom to see Gram crying, her arms around her mother. That was out of the ordinary, too—any affection like that.

I would never see my grandmother through the same eyes again. Even though I didn't know the details and couldn't ask, the story about the secrets and their fight lingered in my mind.

One day, that story would help to explain why my grandmother wouldn't allow me to date boys.

The stories that have the most juice are those no one will tell you. For forty years, I tried to find out more about their elopement when I began to do family research. I looked for wedding announcements in the newspaper archives and records at the local courthouse but found nothing. Dell's daughter, whom I had not seen for years, learned through relatives that I was doing genealogy research and that I was trying to learn more about my grandmother. She mailed me this news article shortly after my mother died, when I was fifty years old.

April 6, 1911
High School Girl in an Elopement
Miss Lulu Garrett Weds Blaine Hawkins at
Des Moines?
At opening of spring vacation she leaves city
supposedly for Sterling but goes to Des Moines.

An elopement which displays a wealth of romance was that which it would seem was brought to light yesterday when Mrs. J. P. Stineman of 1021 Iowa Avenue received a communication in which information was given to the effect that Miss Lulu Garrett, who resides at the Stineman home, had been united in Marriage to Blaine Hawkins at Des Moines, IA, on April 4. The letter which conveyed the announcement of the nuptial event was from Miss Garrett. Mrs. Hawkins, who is less than eighteen years of age and has been a student of the Muscatine high school, left this city at the opening of the spring vacation and declared at that time that she was going to Sterling, Ill., to visit with the La Grille family, formerly of Muscatine. It appears, however, that the girl proceeded to Des Moines, where she met Mr. Hawkins and the matrimonial event took place that had been previously planned.

The groom is the son of R. G. Hawkins, editor of the Wapello Republican, and is well known at Wapello. He left there a short time ago for Des Moines and had been employed as a printer in the Capital City. He is under 20 years of age.

The many Muscatine friends of Mrs. Hawkins will be surprised to hear of her marriage, as not the slightest intimation had been given out as to the romantic turn which affairs were given.

Doubts the Story

R. G. Hawkins of Wapello, the father of the youthful benedict, declared this morning that he was uninformed as to the marriage of his son and expressed some doubt as to whether the marriage had taken place. He stated that his son is employed as a linotype operator at the Chronicle at Toledo, Ia. Young Hawkins admitted the truth of the report when communicated with over the long distance phone today, but declared that he wanted to keep the marriage a secret.

You know how it feels when there's completion—a new equilibrium, the sense of a puzzle piece being slipped into place. When I was eleven, thanks to overhearing that fight between Gram and Blanche, I began to see how long people can keep secrets. When I learned that Gram had lied and created a persona that was for public consumption, I became aware that she was human and fallible. That idea had never occurred to me before—she'd seemed all-powerful and always right about everything. It was the beginning of the end of my innocence. Learning these secrets made me more determined to find out more, especially the stuff no one wanted you to know. I had to develop sleuthing skills akin to those of Nancy Drew, my heroine. I didn't know the term "unreliable narrator" then, but I sensed that I'd need to bring my own curiosity and intelligence to the mysterious entity that was my family to find the real truth, whatever that might be. I was set on the path of uncovering mysteries.

CHAPTER 6

The Mystery of Men

As I grew up with my grandmother, men were a mystery to me, and I was never sure what "father" meant. Our house was completely female—no men's shaving equipment, no raised toilet seats. When a man, like my father or one of my music teachers, came to visit, Gram would stiffen, not happy to have them in our feminine space. I, on the other hand, thought men were captivating. They were like mythical beings, distant and hard-to-understand creatures who appeared suddenly in my life when my father visited or when we went to Iowa.

Men became my research project; I made a study of them. Their scratchy beards were fascinating. I'd rub my hand across Uncle Willard's face, or my dad's when he was around. I'd watch girlfriends with their fathers; they had an intimacy I wanted with my own father—a safe intimacy: doing homework or going out for ice cream or helping in the yard.

Uncle Willard, a father figure until the day he died, was plaid-shirted, with a ready sense of humor, thick fingers that tamped the tobacco in his pipe, hands that made boats and fixed cars and built mink cages. Working hands. When he relaxed after lunch at the kitchen table, he'd clamp his pipe between his yellowed teeth, tamp in the tobacco, light his match—and if I was lucky, he'd let me blow it out and make a wish.

Uncle Willard and Billy ran the mink farm. Twice a day, they mixed up special food and fed the hundreds of mink, in heat and cold, rain and snow. They mated the mink and supervised the birth of kits. In the winter, when the adult mink were ready and their fur was thick and silky, they killed them, gutted them, and stretched their skins on long racks in the basement, to be shipped off and made into mink coats and stoles, popular back then. I wondered if the ladies who wore them had any idea of the hard work of raising the mink as they draped those garments around their shoulders.

Willard had another son, K., the "bad seed" son. I heard he was a wild man who drank too much and hit his wives. There were hush-hush whispers when he got in trouble, and Edith's face took on a pained look, but generally the attitude about his shenanigans seemed to be "boys will be boys."

The men in the Iowa family worked hard: they built houses and fixed cars; they raised cattle and horses, hay and corn, sugar beets and soybeans. One uncle was a butcher, another a carpenter. All the things they could do made them seem larger than life, but they all had their troubles: alcohol, hints of affairs, cruelty. Secrets were rife, bubbling under the surface. Blanche confessed to me in tears one day, "You can't never predict what your kids will do. They'll break your heart." I didn't understand, but I was happy that she'd confided in me.

I turned up the volume on my sleuthing—wondering how I could find what was going on beneath what I could see. Later, I'd learn there were words for that: "text" (what is said) and "subtext" (what is not said but suggested).

Despite their conflicts, my father and grandmother were not so different. He came from a farm, too, and considered himself lucky to have escaped it. By the time I knew him, he worked in white-collar offices and looked like Fred Astaire, long and lanky, wearing polished wingtip shoes, fedora hats, and finely tailored suits. His Old Spice entranced me, and his masculinity fascinated and repelled me. My father was a force of energy, always buzzing from the moment he got off the train, but I didn't have an everyday life with him, as other girls did with their dads—no ordinary days of casual conversation or kid activities. His visits were high-intensity and full of complications.

Uncle Maj was an everyday part of our lives and shone his respectful and kind light upon us. He was Gram's age, so I didn't think of him as a "father." Perhaps I took him for granted because he was a part of my life as soon as we moved to Enid. He was simply Uncle Maj, with his military posture, his wise blue eyes, his funny jokes, and his abiding interest in what was in the newspaper. On every visit there was the crackle of pages and a running, belted-out commentary about the news, accompanied by a chuckle. He and Helen had separate bedrooms—Uncle Maj snored like an elephant—and his room was full of faded hardback books, his suits all hung up neatly in his closet, his shoes polished and lined up as if he were still in the military.

Years later, he would look out at me from an eight-by-ten, formal black-and-white photograph. He'd been tucked away in a folder, but as I compiled research from my genealogy folders for this book, I found him and put him on my bookcase. He might be in his early fifties in the picture. His strong, direct gaze makes it seem as if he's staring right at you. He's wearing his major uniform and an official-looking cap with an insignia. I don't know where this photograph came from—if it was Gram's or if Aunt

Helen sent it to me—but I'm grateful for it. I look into his face, touching the contour of his firm jaw; he's not smiling, but he's looking pleasantly out of the frame, as if to say, *I'm still here.*

Uncle Maj

He wasn't one for intense, dramatic emotions, though he seemed to tolerate them in Gram and Mother. Back then, I didn't realize how handsome he was. He was about six feet tall, even in his seventies. He smoked a pipe and had a way of clearing his throat loudly. We spent nearly every weekend at his house, and I grew used to his ways. In the mornings, he'd be fully dressed but wearing his leather bedroom slippers. They would slap militarily on the wooden floors as he padded about. The best part of his personality was his turns of phrase: he called Aunt Helen the Little Round Woman, said with such affection you knew he adored her, and she always laughed. His other phrase was an exclamation: "great balls of sheet iron." Aunt Helen laughed heartily at all his jokes and phrases, ever an appreciative audience.

She was indeed round and soft and motherly, nurturing us always with her Southern cooking. She'd fix something called "glop," frozen vegetables and okra and hamburger all bubbled in a delicious tomato sauce. Uncle Maj was grateful to her; he relished every Southern meal she prepared. He'd sit down in his spot at the table with some formality. He'd slide his white cloth napkin out of his silver napkin holder, monogrammed with "RCM," which stood for "Russel Claire Marshall," and place it in his lap. There would be a quick prayer of thanks, then "pass the beans," with a wink, because there were no beans. For every meal in the spring and summer, he'd place a single rose, often a deep-crimson beauty, in a silver vase in the middle of the table.

On soft summer evenings, he would take me around to all his beloved rosebushes, cradling flower buds in his large hand, presenting them to me in a formal introduction, naming the roses so I was properly introduced. Their seductive aroma bathed us in an ecstasy that can be received only in a garden of one hundred rosebushes, or perhaps in heaven. Uncle Maj and Aunt Helen's property had two backyards, one that opened out from the back porch, and the other extending all the way to the alley several hundred feet beyond the house. The garden was edged with pink, white, yellow, and red roses, and more were planted diagonally through the middle. He'd show me how to prune them, and the right way to clip a rose to grace the vases in every room. We had to watch out for thorns, but he was undaunted by them, considering blood wounds a necessary sacrifice for beauty. He was a military man with strict standards and ethics about right and wrong, and he always stood tall and stately, but his heart was soft with roses and the worlds of little girls. He carried a sturdy love for Helen and my grandmother, a quiet love, understated.

I, too, plant rosebushes, inspired by Uncle Maj—twenty bushes, not one hundred. I'm not an inveterate gardener like he was, but my rosebushes have been kind to me, producing blooms in profusion, offering me their delicious scents. I clip them, Uncle Maj's voice in my ear: *Isn't she a beauty?*

Beauty. He offered me that, and, coming from a man, it

has a different flavor than it would from a woman. And he gave me the feeling that, around him, things could be managed, life's messes could be straightened up. He'd intervene in the middle of fights that broke out between Gram and Mother, raising his voice slightly, his deep, firm tones cutting through their argument. "Now, look here—that's enough!"

A blessed silence would cut through the din, and, to my surprise, they'd stop fighting. He was the only person who could stop them. Ever the referee, Uncle Maj would get them to take a break and sit on opposite corners like prizefighters. Each would take out a cigarette; then a red flicker and the snap of tobacco. Aunt Helen would look gratefully at Uncle Maj and chatter in her Southern way about time for coffee and homemade cake, and how about some whipped cream with that. They offered compassion and love to my grandmother and mother, as if they were out-of-control children who needed strong parents. Aunt Helen and Uncle Maj were at the heart of our family until the story was over.

At the end of Gram's life, when I was twenty-six, they were at my side, helping me pick out her casket and clothes, driving me two hours to the Perry train station as we followed the hearse winding through the brown winter landscape of the Oklahoma plains. As a CPA, he took care of Gram's finances, and after the funeral, he organized her papers and her will. He found $2,000 tucked into books in her house and noted all the money in her accounts.

There's a letter Aunt Helen wrote the year before Uncle Maj died—I was in my thirties then. He was sick, she was not sure what was wrong yet, and she was worried. She wrote: "Uncle Maj says he loves you and thank you for the birthday wishes. He will write when he feels better." A few months later, her letter announcing his death arrived. It was unbearable to think of having no more evenings in Uncle Maj's garden with his roses. I didn't know then that I'd see Aunt Helen only one more time in my life, or that I'd have to live for decades when they were alive only in my memory. How I wanted to drive up to their house and hear Uncle Maj mutter, "Great balls of sheet iron" and have Aunt Helen enfold me in her soft embrace.

I bring Aunt Helen alive when I make homemade bread, though it can never be as good as hers. I walk in my garden, imagining Uncle Maj, cupping the flowers in my hand like he did, lifting the face of the rose to my ten-year-old grandson so he can treasure it, passing to him my love of roses, planting the seeds of memories in his heart.

The war between my father and grandmother started when I was ten. She began her rage campaign against my father, triggered by what, I don't know, but she focused on money: he was stingy, he was selfish, he was . . . I don't remember, but she would take the war with him all the way to their deaths, decades later. I'd be trapped in a chair next to my grandmother as she dictated her verbal attacks. She called him a bastard, accused him of being stupid and uneducated and selfish, calling him out on every mistake she thought he'd made. I'd have to sign my name to this document, my stomach in a guilty knot. He'd write back angry retorts, addressed to me. I was bad, I was disloyal, how dare I write such lies. On and on it went, every few weeks. I knew that Aunt Helen and Uncle Maj didn't approve of Gram's hateful attitude—they tried to help her see some of his good qualities and reminded her that he was my father, after all—but nothing they said, even mildly and respectfully, changed her mind.

My father fulfilled his financial responsibilities—he sent a check for $100 every month, equivalent to about $500 today, though she criticized him for sending "just" that amount. All these years later, I wonder if Gram was angry about things that had happened when he was married to my mother. I also wonder now, in light of my therapy work with families, if she sensed that he had wandering hands. She never knew that he "taught" me to kiss on his visits, or that one night, when she allowed me to spend the night in his hotel room when I was eight, he put me on top of him in the hotel bed and pretended he was a horse and I was riding him. I thought it was a fun cowboy game at first—I was into cowboys and cowgirls and horses—but I soon realized something wasn't right about it. I didn't know much about men and boys and their "private parts," but I sensed that something was wrong with my riding him that way. I knew that *he* knew it was wrong when he said, "Don't tell Gram about this. She wouldn't understand." From then on, we had our uncomfortable secrets.

Why did these men choose me? I would think about the molestation at Vera's house, and that Aunt Edith's son, Billy, had touched me in ways he shouldn't have. Sometimes when we were alone, as I padded about, following him and Willard while they did chores, he'd slide his hand over my body. I would deftly move to another part of the room or go outside, careful not to make him mad, worried that I'd be blamed if anyone found out or if he got angry. I had the feeling that no one would believe me, or that I'd be blamed if I told. I didn't want to destroy my bubble of happiness at Edith's, a happy place except for Billy's occasional touches. I stuffed down the shame that stayed with me about Billy, telling myself he was like a brother—I'd learned from Blanche that they'd had a baby daughter who died at birth, and I was like a replacement. I thought maybe this is what brothers did.

I knew I couldn't say anything against him. Everyone adored Billy—he was so helpful; he was the loyal son. He was part of my "adopted" family. Plus, I needed things to stay carefree in Iowa. It was where Gram relaxed; she didn't yell at me as much and allowed me to do things with family members without her constant supervision. She, too, liked Billy—he had attended college, and, unlike the rest of the Iowa clan, he valued books, took art classes, and had a darkroom. Everyone was impressed with his special talents. He and Gram had long, philosophical conversations in the living room about books. When I was an adult, he joined me in researching our family history. I'd always try to avoid being alone with him, but he'd sidle up to me and make a suggestive comment. Every time, I'd say, "Billy, you're like a brother to me." He'd make a face and retreat, but on the next visit, he'd pull the same moves again. I figured it was just the way the men were in the family.

The list of dangerous men included Uncle Ray, Gram's eldest half brother. All his other siblings looked up to him, including Gram—he held a place of honor as the oldest son. The first winter we drove up to Iowa in the snow, he offered to help Gram get the car unstuck, and I was to ride with him in his old pickup to his house. The truck smelled of gasoline and old leather. He turned on the truck engine and it idled for a few minutes in the cold to warm up. Suddenly, he lurched toward me and planted his squishy lips on mine. Why did these men want to kiss me? What was wrong with me?

Shaking from cold and surprise, I slid away from him, careful not to make him mad, confused because I thought he was some kind of god, as everyone had conveyed to me, and to children, gods are perfect. I wanted to erase what he had done. He became one more male relative to watch out for.

As the years went by, when the family went visiting, I'd see his eyes scrape over my body, and though I maneuvered myself not to be close to him, he'd find a way to zoom in and plant his hand on my ass when no one was looking. I'd shift away, embarrassed and angry that I hadn't escaped him. How was it that no one else noticed his loose hands? He had a wife, a daughter, and two grandchildren, one of whom would kill himself in his twenties. I had to wonder how Ray treated his wife and daughter and my cousins. Or did he just pick on me? What was I doing wrong? Years later, I'd put these memories together and realize how much abuse was rampant in the Iowa family.

Gram's legacy regarding men was twofold: she taught me to hate and mistrust them, but she also saw them as useful. They fixed things—they mowed the lawn; they understood the physical world—and they were supposed to protect you. On our trips to Iowa, she put a man's hat in the back window to suggest we had a "protector."

Her attitude about men and sex was clear, though. When I was nine years old, she said, "Men want only one thing. Are you going to give it to them?"

"Don't give them what they want; they'll just leave you if you do."

"Girls who give in are sluts, and they will amount to nothing."

"Always say no to what men want."

I never quite knew what to make of these statements. You'd think that after the molestations and inappropriate behavior I'd seen with men, and after she taught me to hate them, or at least not to trust them, I'd agree with her, but I didn't. I didn't believe that the behavior of a few meant that the whole world of men was as dark and dangerous as the picture she'd painted for me or the men I'd known.

I preferred to think the best of people. I wanted to discover who people were one by one, on their own merit. There were many men I was lucky to know—not just Uncle Maj, but also the men who were my teachers and mentors as I grew up. They gave me a balanced and beautiful view of the world, and helped to heal my wounds from the dangerous men.

Besides Uncle Maj and Uncle Willard, my other "adopted" fathers were my music teachers. These musical fathers opened up worlds of beauty. They taught me the cello and the piano; they conducted the symphony with their whole bodies and hearts, waving their arms, shouting out directions to the strings, brass, and wind sections, laughing with the joy of it all. My first musical father was Mr. Brauninger, who toe-tapped his way into my life, playing his violin like the Pied Piper, when I was nine years old. His red hair fell across his face as he bent and swayed with the music. I fell in love instantly. I wanted to follow him, to play like that, to beguile and coax sounds from a violin like he did. I already played the piano and could read music, so when he suggested the cello, it was easy for me to learn. I fitted the instrument against my heart and allowed the music and my musical fathers to change my life.

The conductor of the university and town symphony, Dr. Wehner, was a kind, smart man with a lovely wife and a daughter who was my friend in grade school. I was accepted into the youth symphony, where Mr. Brauninger taught us Bach, Haydn, and all the classics. A year or so later, I joined the town symphony, where everyone made a fuss when I played a solo, "To a Wild Rose," accompanied by the orchestra. Everyone I met in the music world was kind and had a great sense of humor. Laughter and music, Beethoven and Vivaldi and Mozart, were the lights in my life. My childhood friends Jodie, Keith, and Floyd and Lloyd, the red-haired twins, were all in the symphony, too, and there the magic happened. We practiced hard for that moment of praise when the light of the conductors' eyes would fall upon us. They'd smile and say, "Great job!" To please them was to please ourselves, proving to ourselves that we could make real music. I discovered that hard work paid off, and that when you had a goal for a recital or a concert, you'd work hard and sweat and get frustrated, but then something would start to soar away from the troubles of the ordinary world and you'd enter an ethereal world of beauty.

Mr. Brauninger met his wife, Eva, during those years in Enid. All of five feet tall to his six, she was a fireball teacher and conductor. Together, they became the musical mother and father to all of the musicians in that small town, seeding our souls with the love of music and offering us moments we'd all hold dear for the rest of our lives.

Making music was like entering another universe, another world, where there were new principles—keys and tonalities, rhythm, and the wordless language of emotion. In the symphony and at my music lessons, I was free; I was surrounded by love. Mr. Brauninger would look into my eyes, giving me his full attention, his caring. I didn't realize then that each encounter helped to balance out the effects of the unsafe men. I could be myself with my musical fathers; I could allow the music to flower within me and enjoy being invited into something fine and uplifting.

When I was thirteen, Mr. B. and his wife moved away to take another teaching job, leaving me bereft, even though I was lucky to find other symphony conductors and teachers in high school and college who offered their wisdom and inspiration. For a few decades, Mr. B. and Eva and I were out of touch. I'd dreamed that I searched for them and we had a joyful reunion, only to wake up grieving because it had been just a dream.

Four decades later, mutual friends put us back in touch, and I visited them in Des Moines. The decades melted away, and my reunion dreams came true as Mr. B. and Eva approached me, white-haired but smiling just the same way, as if no years had passed. During the visit, we had deep conversations about what they remembered from back then, especially about Gram. Mr. B. said, "I tried to get your grandmother to let you be a little girl, to sit on the floor with me and play marbles, but she wouldn't let you." I nodded—yes, I always had to be a "lady." He admired Gram, too, for her intelligence and her determination to encourage my talents in music. I told him that he'd made me feel special, that he'd helped me feel better about myself when I was young. He took my hand and said, "Linda Joy, when I looked into your eyes, I saw the face of God."

I asked him what he meant.

"You were a beautiful, innocent young girl, and I cared about you."

He saw me for what I was and took care to cherish me. His

words validated the sense I'd had that I was special to him, a wordless knowing.

Mr. Brauninger, Keith, and Linda Joy-1957

For several years, I took the Zephyr train across the Great Plains, my love of the vistas and big skies affirmed once again, to visit Mr. B. and his wife in Des Moines and they even met my children. Then the news came that Mr. B. had cancer. Already grieving, I arrived to see them for what I knew would be the last time. He had gotten better briefly after surgery but had started to weaken again. I stood by his bedside, taking in his sweet face and gentleness. He smiled at me, though I knew he was in pain. I thanked him for all he had given me and told him he was the father I never had.

He smiled and took my hand. "Yes, I think I was a father to you." We held hands, the years dissolving into a single moment of the Present, where life and death hung together on one thread.

I was heartbroken when he died a few months later. I often speak to him, say hi to photographs of him displayed on my bookcases. In one picture, he's twenty-seven years old, playing his violin into our hearts. In the other, he's white-haired and leaning toward me from first chair in the Des Moines Symphony during our first reunion, violin and bow and smile at the ready to heal my heart.

CHAPTER 7

Silences

When the truth is hidden, you live two lives. Guilt follows you around, the fear of being found out, blamed. When adults help to create your secrets, you're trapped. You don't have free will; you're dependent on their good graces, money, and food. If you are a peacemaker at heart, like I was, you will do anything, make almost any compromise, to get the fighting and conflict to stop. It means lying, it means pretending, it means that your body is split into parts. And your mind and heart.

When you live two lives, one secret and one public, you tuck things away into packages of silence and carry them with you. They begin to grow heavy, but you fear that dismantling them might make everything unravel. You might incorrectly assess your safety. It's best to be wary and keep gathering your packages of secrets—until one day, they explode.

People who knew me when I was growing up tell me I

always seemed happy, smiling, and optimistic. That was part of who I was, but it was also a way to whistle in the dark. To keep my balance, I looked for the beauty in nature, tried to fill my mind with it. I learned that the sparkle of dew on the grass and the perfection of flowers can lift you up. White pillars of clouds in an azure sky, and the grace of wheat fields in a summer breeze, can comfort you.

I tried to appear normal, drawing upon my study of what "normal" seemed to be, but sometimes I felt like an impostor. No one knew about my grandmother and her terrible rages or the darkness that surrounded our house, not even my best friend, Jodie. I dared not let anyone know, for fear Gram would punish me. She'd say, over and over again, "Keep your mouth shut!"

There were moments when Gram could be my friend, when she smiled at me with love in her eyes. I wanted to hold on to those moments, but as the years went by, the darkness that finally overran us was her enduring hatred of my father.

When I was fifteen, Gram's hate letter–writing campaign had lasted for five years, leaving me with dread when she'd get wound up and start ranting, but I had coping mechanisms, too. Studying and working hard at school made me feel good. I got A pluses in English, took French and Latin (in which I read Virgil's *Aeneid*), studied the Civil War in history class, read English poetry and Shakespeare. I smiled and played music at concerts, wearing pretty dresses. The world saw my most acceptable self, while everything else—the shameful world of Gram's smoky house—was hidden.

The summer I was fifteen, Aunt Helen and Uncle Maj appeared to be concerned about her hate campaign and its effect on me. They took me aside one afternoon when I was alone with them at their house to say they wanted to help me get to know my father independently of my grandmother. I could write letters freely at their house, and my father and I would be able to respond to each other naturally.

Shocked that they would dare defy my grandmother's rules against absolute loyalty, I hesitated. "It's like she can read my mind; she'll find out." I knew she'd mount a full attack against me if she discovered it. They assured me that we'd be careful.

For a few weeks, I enjoyed the freedom of writing to my father and receiving his responses; I had cautioned him to be careful about what he wrote privately, versus what he wrote in the letters that Gram opened at home. However, I suppose it was inevitable that she would have found out. One afternoon, she greeted me at the door, screaming, waving a letter from my father in my face. "What have you been doing? How dare you betray me! Tell me the truth!"

She demanded to know the truth, yardstick in hand, ready to beat it out of me. I told her Aunt Helen had suggested I write to him, but then when Gram asked Aunt Helen about it, she said it was my idea. My mind swirled with fear and shock. Everyone had betrayed me, and now Gram's web of hate bound me in her trap. She cut me off from all activities except summer school. No friends, no phone calls, no more visits to Aunt Helen—I had lost her, too. Gram told me that she had people keeping track of me when I was out—though I never knew whether that was true or not. Most days, I was trapped with an irrational, screaming, angry woman who used her walnut yardstick to punctuate her rage whenever she felt like it. I never knew when the blows would come, and they left me with swollen knuckles and bruises.

After several weeks of her outbursts and threats every day—now, we would say she was obsessed, perhaps even that she had some kind of psychotic break—Gram surprised me by proposing that I contact my father and ask him to visit. I looked at her suspiciously—what was she up to now? I wrote him, and he agreed, saying he was happy to be invited. They negotiated that I would go with him to Oklahoma City, where we could have our own space away from her. I had not seen my father since I was twelve, a little girl who played with dolls. Since then, though I was naive in the ways of the world, I had gained a figure, slim though it was, and had become a young lady.

The war was over! My father and I would finally be free to have a relationship of our own. I imagined a peaceful world where everyone in my family would be friends again, but I'd soon learn that hope is dangerous.

A few weeks later, we waited for his arrival. Gram was wearing one of her silk dresses and had fixed her hair. My father drove up in a yellow Cadillac convertible, wearing fashionable slacks, a yellow golf shirt, and a diamond ring on his pinky finger—flaunting his style, as usual. When he came into the house, he looked a little older and had a few more crinkles around his eyes but was still charming. As if in a dream, there he was before me, smiling and talking with Gram as if none of the fights had happened.

After a quick good-bye, I felt like I was in a movie, rolling down the prairie in the Cadillac, the wind in my hair, my handsome father next to me. I kept falling into his smile, watching his strong hands guide the steering wheel. The deep chuckle in his throat and his Southern accent made me feel secure. I had a father again. He was cheerful and full of life, and I felt safe with him, safer than I'd felt for a long time, worn down as I was from the pitched battles with Gram.

He had reserved two adjoining rooms in a motel in downtown Oklahoma City and made a reservation at a nightclub, where we would have dinner that evening. I got dressed in my room, and meandered into his. His doors were open. He stood at the bathroom sink, shaving, totally naked. I'd never seen a naked man before. Shocked to find him in that condition, a frisson of fear passed through my body. My face grew hot, and I murmured apologies. I backed out of his room as quickly as I could, worried he'd take what happened as an invitation to unwanted intimacy. I'd fought my grandmother to have a father, a regular father who would be a friend, someone who might be able to protect me from Gram's rages. I wanted that and nothing else, but I hadn't forgotten how he'd taught me to kiss when I was seven. Dread settled in my stomach.

A few moments later, he strolled into my room, wearing only Jockey shorts, his hairy chest and body a shock, a warning, stunning me into silent paralysis. Grinning and murmuring how lovely I looked, how great it was to see me again, he grabbed my hand and before I could figure out what was happening, he pulled me onto his lap. He pressed my face to his and began to kiss me the way he had when I was small. Squeamish at his wet lips and at his having appropriated me so suddenly, I pushed away, laughing to distract him, trying to get off his lap, but he pressed me close again. My mind raced: *No, I can't do this. But I can't make him mad. I just won him back. What should I do?*

His seductive voice whispered, "You're so thweet. Come on, let me teach you how to kiss. You're going to be going out with boys—you need to know how." As he took my lips between his teeth—*this is wrong*—I pushed against his chest again and tried to get off his lap, but he pulled me closer. I tried to feel nothing, though I was slightly nauseated as he pulled at my lips. My mind chattered on: *But he can't be doing this. I went through hell to have a father. I convinced Gram he wasn't bad. Was she right?*

I was frozen, the phrase *but I just won you back* repeating in my numbed mind. Then he got up and led me toward the bed, murmuring about teaching me things I needed to know, while my mind kept racing on a loop: *Don't make him mad. He doesn't want to really do anything.* My denial told me that he wouldn't really "do" anything sexual to me. Sex, body parts, and sexuality were all part of the "bad and sinful" world I was unfamiliar with, something to be avoided, according to the Baptists and my Victorian grandmother, and the morality of the 1950s. Those words and images were not in my innocent world. It was unthinkable that my father would see me as a sexual person—it was bad, it would make me bad, and he would be bad, just like Gram said he was. I could hardly breathe as everything swirled around me.

I think it was only a couple of minutes later, but time had stopped—I realized that he *did* see me as sexual. I broke through my fog of *this can't be happening* and jumped up, pretending to be a little girl. A little girl would not be sexual, so maybe he would listen to her.

"I'm so hungry, Daddy. Can we please go to dinner? Please, please, I'm starving." He smiled and got up, chuckling as he went back to his room.

Shaking, I closed the door. I stood alone in a dark cave, cleaving myself into different parts. A voice shouted as I hung my head, *You're bad, you're nothing, you're worse than shit. It's your fault—this is why all these men come after you. It's you—you're the one who's bad. You're hopelessly evil.* The last weeks of torture—Gram's cruelty, losing Aunt Helen, and now my father's throaty chuckle, being forced to kiss him, his hands on my bottom as he pushed me toward him, the choking shame of being in a motel with him, the fact that he'd pulled me into bed—all this gathered around me in a dark, heavy blanket that pressed me down, down, until I perceived myself as a small nugget of nothingness, not deserving of any good ever again.

Somehow, I managed to put on my dress and go to dinner as my mind spun out of control. I could barely hear the music or look at my father. He ordered an alcoholic drink for me, though I was underage: a Manhattan. It, like everything else, was bitter.

The next day, as we went to a museum and rode around the city in his car, I was aware of the split in my psyche. One part of me was exhausted from having fought to win my father, defending him, wanting to believe he was good and that Gram was wrong. The other part began to realize that I had no father, not really. I could see that I had to be on my own with Gram—there would be no protector, no rescue. I would be alone with everything.

The events in the motel were seared on my soul and would remain a secret for nearly twenty years. Even then, I'd keep the shame tucked away in a separate compartment in my mind. Later, in therapy, I would learn that what my father did throughout my childhood and in the motel was called incest. It would be a long time before I understood that those years of warfare with Gram and my father helped to determine how I would fall in love, how I would deftly choose the wrong partners, men who would replay the dramas of the past over and over again. For years, I was unaware of the divisions of myself into various parts, into sections separated by unconscious mechanisms that would shape my adult life. But one day I would discover that naming what you don't want to know about yourself ultimately leads to freedom. It would take a long time, and the "cure" would come through digging through fortresses of lies to find what I'd buried. I'd search through layers of secrets and silence to bear witness to a bigger truth: everything that happened does not need to define me. I would discover that wounds leave deep scars. To heal, you must open every one and shine the light of knowledge and compassion upon them. Until I learned this, I would replay the tape of my childhood over and over again.

CHAPTER 8

The Gifts She Gave Me

$\mathcal{W}$e grow up with images and impressions imprinted upon our eyelids, the sense and whisper of something that later we will recognize as a calling. This calling can become a theme in our lives. I didn't know then, when I was in my late teens, still firmly planted in the flat and stark landscape of the plains, that one day I would want to follow my grandmother's heart, the youthful, idealistic heart I think she had when she was in her thirties. Like her, I would become fascinated by England, its history and gardens, the green, rolling hills of the downs, and the chalk cliffs rising like white flags over the channel. I'd want to know more about the Dartmouth of Sherlock Holmes, the moors of Yorkshire that the Brontë sisters captured in their books, the Renaissance world, and Queen Elizabeth I.

But it wasn't just my grandmother's stories that would prick my curiosity. Thanks to my high school English classes, I was introduced to Shakespeare, Dickens, and English poetry. We were given assignments to read literature and write essays that explored the depth and meaning of the stories. Our teachers expertly guided us to discover form, allusion, and metaphor, showing us how the English language worked as art. English history was woven into the poems and novels, too. Starting when I was eight, my grandmother began my sojourn through English literature by reading to me and making me read to her. Though our town was not located in a part of the country famous for its educational excellence, I had an education that prepared me for college.

All these years later, I'm still impressed by the depth and range of what I learned, especially from my English teachers. I know without a doubt that I would not have the grammar skills that are so important in my writing and teaching now without my ninth-grade English teacher, Miss Luikhart. Thanks to hours of English homework each night, I can still diagram sentences and parse complicated tenses.

Ever since first grade, when the hieroglyphics of black marks on a white page in the Dick and Jane books bloomed into meaningful stories, so much so that I hid my library books on my lap in second grade to protect me from the tortures of math, books and the worlds they create have helped me to survive. I was seduced into worlds beyond my own and had adventures I'd never take myself. I think my grandmother must have been similarly entranced, given her passion for reading, though she was self-taught. I'd often find her reading *The Oxford Book of English Verse* or Shakespeare. She read books on historical figures in England, like Queen Elizabeth I, Henry VIII, Lady Jane Grey, Eleanor of Aquitaine, and others, who offered her another world. Each book was a doorway into realms that must have seemed romantic to her, eras when there were powerful kings and when women could rule kingdoms—roles far from her Iowa roots. Stacks of books were piled all over the house, sturdy hardback books thick with ivory-deckled pages. Important books. I would open them and randomly sift through the pages, dipping my face down into the spine to sniff, comparing the aroma of one book to another. I remain a book sniffer to this day.

It was futile to resist my grandmother when she sat me down to read *Treasure Island* or *David Copperfield* aloud. I wanted to play outside or color, but she forced me, through her will and gritty determination, to sit across from her with a heavy, thick book—a real book, not just some kid's book, which she didn't allow me to read, though she allowed Nancy Drew mysteries when I was sick. At first, I would hunker down miserably, feeling trapped, but then the world of the book would begin to draw me in. Those books were difficult to get through, but Gram taught me how to pronounce each word and had me look up the hard ones in the dictionary, building my vocabulary as the years went by. I will never forget the rainy, cozy night she read the poem "Annabel Lee," by Edgar Allan Poe, out loud to me. It has a sorrowful, singsong rhythm, a perfect accompaniment to the rain drumming on the awning. The living room was bathed in golden light, and I was curled up on the scratchy Oriental rug by Gram's knees while she read to me, her voice vibrating with her love for the poem and the emotions or memories she might have been drawing from. It's a poem about loss, but she didn't seem to think it would harm me. She loved being swept away by poetry and stories, and she wanted to share that love with me.

My grandmother was an unusual woman in our Oklahoma town. The town was small-minded, but there were a few exceptions, thanks to the presence of Phillips University, not far from our house. Scholars and musicians with doctorate degrees lived in neighborhoods around us, and Gram made sure that we met some of them so I'd be exposed to educated people. Given that she was self-educated, though she'd always told me she'd graduated from high school, she seemed determined to make sure I had a life bigger than hers. She always assumed I'd go to college—I would be the first of our family to attend. I don't know what made her so determined about my education—her zeal embarrassed me at the time—but I think that at some point, her own ignorance from growing up with uneducated farm people embarrassed her, or perhaps she saw that without a good education, your choices are limited. Maybe Blaine's family let her know they saw her lack of education when he brought her home. His family was middle-class, a cut above hers, and she would have been ignorant of their manners and customs.

But when I watched her talk intelligently about art with an art professor from the university or discuss history with my music teachers, I was amazed at what she knew. These men, nearly four decades younger, in their late twenties, she in her sixties, would light up in delight as they began discussing some theoretical matter of dispute, or talking about philosophy or historical facts. I could see the look of surprise on their faces as they listened to what she knew. In those moments, I sensed that she was in full flower, happy to share information with people who could appreciate it. I think that then she was fully alive, knowledge flowing from her in a stream of delight. It reinforced my feeling that adults were walking history books, with stories ready to share if they were invited.

Another of my favorite distractions was learning music. Recently, brain imaging studies have shown how learning music, just like reading, helps to develop the brain. I know that the arts help people express what they can't say in words, and I know for myself that books and music helped me with the secret pain I was carrying. They always soothed me, making it possible for me to move past the stings.

The arts were the focus in our house, without any distractions, until I was fourteen, when Gram finally got a television. For a few years, we'd been going to the neighbor's house to watch Liberace play his shiny grand piano decorated with candelabra or *The Ed Sullivan Show*. After we got the TV, there began another layer of things Gram and I could share happily. The TV opened up worlds to us; we'd laugh and predict the plot to *Gunsmoke*, *Maverick*, and our all-time favorite: *Perry Mason*. We'd make bets on who was guilty, and the loser had to make the coffee.

For years, I listened to Aunt Helen and Uncle Maj talk with Gram about the war—it had ended four years before I'd come to live with her. They saw it as the biggest upheaval in history up to that time, which, I've learned, was true, though the people of that era viewed World War I as the Great War until 1939, when World War II began. Helen, Maj, and Gram would come to life when she reminisced about the flapper era of the '20s, the Depression of the '30s, and "the war." Gram would weave in stories about her travels.

Gram was eager for me to learn about World War II through documentary programs. She'd narrate in the background as we watched how Hitler came to power as chancellor in 1933, and about the buildup to Germany's running roughshod over Czechoslovakia and Austria by 1938. Righteous anger animated Gram's face as she said, "That stupid Chamberlain—he thought he could trust Hitler!" She was referring to the Munich Pact When Hitler had hoodwinked Chamberlain into agreeing to "peace in our time." She'd shout at the television during scenes of the Battle of Britain, the air war in 1940 when the Royal Air Force fought with Hermann Goering's German pilots. She'd hold her head in her hands, tears in her eyes.

We watched the fiery nighttime explosions and the collapse of buildings as London was bombed every night for months. On the streets, people picked through bricks and burning wood to find their dead. Frightened families huddled in the Tube, the subway, which for months served as a bomb shelter. Gram would start to yell at the TV when "the bad guys" appeared—the English fascists, led by Oswald Mosley in England, and of course Hitler and Mussolini. She was particularly indignant that Roosevelt didn't help the Brits by bringing America into the war before the Pearl Harbor attack in December, 1941. She'd fling her fist in the air and shout, "They stood alone; we abandoned them! That bastard Roosevelt, he should have intervened sooner!"

I was surprised to learn that Hitler conquered Western Europe in six weeks in the spring of 1940, leaving England the last European country standing. Finally, Roosevelt got Congress to approve the lend-lease program: the United States "loaned" ships and equipment to Britain—this would help protect Britain from being invaded. Of course, everyone knew that destroyed equipment would never be returned. "It was too late, but at least we were helping," Gram said, looking grief-stricken.

She'd talk about how brave the British were, their courage and grit facing bombs and severe rationing. Every time the defeat of France appeared in a movie, she would be moved to tears. The German *blitzkrieg* trapped the Allies at the English Channel, and they all would have been killed if it hadn't been for the "little boats" owned by fishermen and ordinary people. When the call went out, these boats rescued over three hundred thousand men from Dunkirk. Gram pointed out that *Casablanca* was made in 1942, before the outcome of the war was known.

She'd practically start singing "Rule, Britannia!" when shy King George and graceful Queen Mary made their way through the rubble of the East End near the docks to cheer up the populace. She reminisced about England's delightful tea shops and the charm of using proper china for the ritual teatime every afternoon. I didn't know then how much time she'd spent in Great Britain, but I could feel in my bones her passion, her admiration, and her near obsession with keeping close to her heart her memories of the time she spent there.

Years later, I'd understand that through her memories and love of English literature and poetry, she would return to a world that was easier for her to inhabit than the current reality of her life by then—the dark living room where she sank into her spot on the couch, haunted by her obsession and anger at my parents. Through these special moments when she focused on literature, history, and England, I came to understand her earlier life before I knew her. She'd be transported to places she loved, whether in her imagination or in her travels, and that there she would return, inviting me to go with her. I didn't realize that her interests would become seeds that would bloom into my own fascination with England and the war. One day, I would stand in front of a castle, wondering if she had visited there; was that the castle that had inspired her time-traveling imagination? And I would bless and thank her for having shared her passion with me.

CHAPTER 9

Stars and Light

In the vast landscape of the Great Plains, you are reminded of your place in things. If you are lonely, if you are bedraggled from the affairs of the day and the endless chatter of human drama, if you are damaged by tooth-and-claw fights between people you love, if you feel reduced by the endless roughing-up you experience in the house you live in but can't call home, if you find your despair climbing up your throat, threatening to choke you, you can come to the open plains and find that the emptiness matches you perfectly. You can sink deeply into weeds and prairie grasses, and in the right season, you can merge into the sweep and sway of the wheat that fills the horizon from edge to edge, a golden sea of beauty.

You might stand there, heart beating from fear—you always have this fear, your stomach in a knot from the last beating or screaming fit or raging rant delivered by your grandmother—

and there, in that land and sky, you will find a blessed silence that marks your soul with hope. You will find a moment to contemplate yourself—your lonely, single self—but it will not be a grieving; it will be a moment when the landscape and land and sky and susurrous wind give you everything you need. The emptiness will fill you. You may begin to weep, or you may laugh out loud. But in that moment, you will be free and full of life.

My musical life gifted me sustenance, spiritual food that helped me to rise above the tension and pain in the house on Park Street. Years later, I would find out that it was the same for my cellist friends, Jodie and Keith. The kids in the orchestra with us were good, conscientious students who followed the rules of the times and the town: keep your family secrets, protect adults from embarrassing exposures, put on a good face. Smile. We were innocent children, but for our own pangs and worries and hopes.

Decades would pass before I would get to talk with Keith and Jodie about that long-ago time when we were imprinted with an abiding love of music. Jodie went on to become a professional musician in Italy, and though Keith and I didn't continue to play, our time in Enid wove deep memories, years later, that we would celebrate over phone lines two thousand miles apart.

I'd always thought Keith handsome, with his sleek black hair and dark eyes, inherited from Cherokee blood on his father's side. The first time I met him, he was wearing jeans and a yellow-and-white-checked shirt, struggling up the street with his cello in a canvas case slung on his back. My grandmother noticed the boy from the youth symphony and gave him a ride home. He was a little shy but very polite to my grandmother, and when we dropped him off, we met his mother; his two-year-old baby sister, who held on to her mother's skirt; and his six-year-old brother, who wore a pink-and-white-checked shirt just like his brother's but for the color, his grin revealing a gap where his front teeth were missing. His father and his other brother, two years younger than I, weren't home, but that brother and I would soon become friends, too, playing together in the cello section in high school.

Keith's mother and Gram chatted, and from then on we were all friends, in the same music circles. At the end of my grandmother's life, his mother was one of the few people who still visited Gram. I'd always secretly wanted Keith's family to be my own; they had a lovely home, with a mother who cooked every night and tended them; a father who was respected in town, a CPA like Uncle Maj; and four bright, talented children. When they invited me over to play board games, my sides hurt afterward from laughing so much.

From the beginning, Keith treated me as a "person," not just a little girl of eleven, and that's what made me admire him. In those early years, I was so hungry for positive attention, his kindness seemed like a kind of love. Maybe human tenderness *is* about love, though not necessarily the romantic kind. And as he went on with his life and dated girls and graduated from high school and went to the university in town, I envied the girls he paid attention to. But in symphony each week, he always acted the same toward me, smiling across his cello as our bodies vibrated to the music swirling around us.

When I was seventeen, Gram invited Keith to go with us on a trip to Kansas to see Mr. B. and Eva. One evening while we were there, we took a walk on grassy paths by a fountain. It was June, and there were the moon and stars, just like in all the songs. We looked at each other, and something went off like a small firecracker. He was twenty by then, and we'd been playing together in symphony for six years in the embrace of Beethoven, Haydn, Mozart. The complex counterpoint of Bach's Brandenburg Concerti was like an old friend. Music wove us in a tapestry of beauty. In the middle of a rising exalting phrase, our eyes would meet and we'd smile, sharing the joy. That night, when Keith kissed me, I floated with him above the pain and tension in my life. I didn't know it was possible to feel so good, so free. When we returned home, I held those moments in my heart. I never thought he would choose me as a girlfriend—I was not worth it, not good enough—but I knew that the music we'd shared through the years connected us. We'd grown up together, and now we had this gift of love.

For a while, we kept our feelings a secret. But I knew that Gram liked him, so I made the mistake one day of forgetting never to trust her. I was so happy that Keith liked me that I wanted to share my joy with her.

She shouted, "I knew I couldn't trust you! You have no morals. How dare you act like that? You're common and low-class!"

"But it's Keith—you know him. We've known him forever."

She rushed to the phone. "I'm going to tell his mother right now what you two are up to."

I begged her not to call, but she was grim, her jaw set, her dark eyes flashing danger, each turn of the dial an excruciating moment closer to my losing him. Gram told his mother we were too close, that we were on the edge of something—I wasn't sure what they were afraid of. On the phone, they made a pact that we were not to see each other, though we were allowed to continue playing together in the symphony. Apparently, now that we'd kissed, we'd crossed some kind of line and were in danger.

Gram's beady eyes bored into me after she put down the phone. She made me promise not to see him. Crying, I agreed, while I tried to figure out how we'd get around it. I went to my room, knitting my arms across my hollow belly.

At first we obeyed, out of fear of punishment and because you obey your parents when you're a "good" child. We were good, but we were also in love—a simple love based on friendship, excitement, and respect. He'd drive by the high school some afternoons to see if he could catch me, or I'd call him from a pay phone, taking the chance that his mother wouldn't answer. I'd pick him up in Gram's gold Nash Rambler, and we'd slip out of town to the wheat fields. In winter and summer they offered themselves to us as sustenance, as witnesses. On winter nights, on a side road with the sky wide and huge above us with stars, we steamed up the windows.

Our kisses were full of passion but also innocence. We didn't even consider going further than kissing and talking. Church and the strict morality of our town taught us that thoughts about sinning were the same as acting on them. I preferred being "good." I *needed* to be good, which meant that you belonged, you were normal and acceptable. Gram would tell me that I was bad, which confused me. What did she mean? To prove my goodness, I got good grades, sweating over my homework for hours each night. I practiced the piano and cello constantly. But secretly, I was "bad" in this way: I would lie to escape her control and her rage. When Keith and I were forbidden to see each other, I'd tell Gram that symphony rehearsal had lasted late. Keith and I would drive to the lake near the university and park the car. We'd kiss and talk and laugh, and the soft night would sigh around us.

After the scenario two years earlier with my father, I was on a self-survival mission: to get through high school and to endure the prison conditions of home with Gram until I could escape to college. There had been so many nights of Gram's rants, when for hours she'd raved about my mother, my father, Aunt Helen, and of course me. Sometimes the assault went on for eight hours, leaving me limp. Often there were nights when I'd stand at the front door after Gram had gone to bed, grateful for the silence. I'd look through the three bars on the window, which seemed like prison bars, since I could not leave, and gaze at the faraway moon, in a kind of worship. It shed light on everything, the whole planet. It was wise and whole and always there.

Someone once asked me why I didn't just run away, but I had no place to go. I knew what it was like to be homeless—Gram had rescued me from that—and I wasn't ready to be on my own yet. I knew my mother and father didn't want me with them. I could see that Gram needed me, and it was the only home I knew. Keith was a respite from these dark struggles; he offered me something beautiful. His arms around me gave me the most tenderness I'd ever felt in my life.

When he held me, I tried to understand why Gram kept saying that boys were dangerous. In the past two years, she had allowed me one date with a boy I liked but had no objection if I wanted to go out with boys I didn't like. What? How could she be so irrational? I couldn't figure out why she hated men so much. I'd had my problems with them—my father, my uncles—but I didn't believe those men represented *all* men.

Spring, the air was alive with flowers and the wheat fields were approaching their glory, growing tall enough to tickle your chin if you waded out among them. Keith's green Chevrolet was parked by the fields on the east side of town, the sway of the tassels whispering as the wind brushed across. His arms were tight around me, and I could feel the muscles in his body and hear the tremor in his voice as he whispered love things to me. For months we had grieved our enforced separation. Each moment apart was a prologue to the next stolen kiss, but we were still "good." His hands never ventured below my neck.

It was worth it to sneak out for our delicious make-out sessions. This was a different world. Keith had no idea what it was like at home, how afraid I was of Gram, how she acted. He knew nothing of the dark nights when I wanted to escape the house and Gram's wrath. He was acquainted with a polite older lady whose demeanor demanded respect. He didn't know that she'd stand like a harpy above me, gray hair frizzed, eyes wild, screaming, "You're a slut! All you can think of is boys. You know what they want, what they all want, don't you? They're all alike, and you're stupid enough to believe sweet words and promises of love?"

"Finally, someone loves me," I told her. "He's sweet to me; he's kind."

"Love—ha! I will not have my granddaughter marrying young and giving up on her education. I've spent too much money on you to have you throw away all the opportunities I've offered you. I've sacrificed everything for you, and you just want to go out and have fun. Get in here and do your homework."

"But we're not planning to get married. We never . . ."

Despite swooning over the romantic songs, I knew that marriage, if it ever happened, would be far in my future. And I knew that my time with Keith, and with all my music friends, would end soon, at graduation. When Keith and I played in the symphony, we touched each other's hearts without words. Didn't she know what music can do to you? It opens your heart. It makes you know people in a different way, via a subtle connection that travels through your muscles and speaks another language, one that brings light into the darkness, without words.

On those nights in the car with him, everything was magical. The wheat was all around us, the blue sky turning to rust, then indigo, as the stars popped out. I sighed with pleasure in our safe bubble of love, the pain of my hidden life with Gram disappearing for a while in the soft touches and Keith's eyes looking at me in the dark.

Over the past two years, whenever my grandmother had slipped into some kind of irrational, cruel state, I had missed the Gram who once called me Sugar Pie, the way her face lit up when she laughed, how she loved telling me the stories of her travels. Most days now, she was gray and pale and smoky, her eyes dangerous, unpredictable with rage, the yardstick too handy near the couch. She'd lock me in the house, threaten to send me to a place for delinquent girls, slap my face. Sometimes I argued back, determined not to let her beat me down. Other times I stayed silent, out of self-preservation, gritting my teeth, using thoughts about Keith and his gentle affection to comfort me. I learned to think quietly about pleasant things: the music we had just played in symphony, the melodies humming in my head, or the funny jokes my friend Jodie told, her dimples blazing as we spent a few minutes together, talking and laughing, after school.

Those final months of my senior year, as I ran errands in the Nash Rambler, hoping to meet for a few minutes with Keith, I began to remember the story Gram had told me long ago about my mother's having eloped. When she was seventeen, she had run off and gotten married to some young man. I don't know how they were caught, but Gram confronted them and made them promise never to see each other again, and had the marriage annulled. I could only imagine the horror my mother must have suffered from Gram's wrath. It occurred to me that Gram thought I was in danger of doing the same thing, but she didn't know me. She didn't know that the main thing I wanted was to get out of Enid, go to college, and learn about life on my own.

And then I remembered the fuss Blanche had made about Gram's elopement and a puzzle piece slipped into place. *Click.* The mystery of Gram's rage about my relationship with Keith became clear: *she* had run away and gotten married. *She* had gotten in trouble with her family. She was assuming I'd do what my mother had done, what she had done. I thought about all the years we'd gone to Iowa, the undertones and hints and raised eyebrows about my grandmother. Well, everyone in the family must have known the story about her. And then there was my mother: she had married without consent at seventeen, repeating

Gram's pattern. What would have become of her if Gram hadn't interfered? Would I even have existed?

Carl Jung says we inherit the unresolved issues of our parents, which live on in our bodies and our dreams. Perhaps the past itself is a dream, a saga made of all the bodies and yearnings of all those who went before us. They're silent then, after death, but for wisps of remembered stories, ghosts in photos, the line of a cheek or the shape of an eye. They mark us with their stories; they're in us and with us. But we must separate from them and create our own narrative.

Years later, I would return to those side roads on the edge of town, humble with their bumpy ruts, the wheat fields of my memory more majestic in my imagination than in real life. The wind still swept across the land, making me gasp, the air crisp and rich with the nutty scent of wheat, the fields having no memory of us so long ago as we walked there. Yet there was a kind of music, a song so rich with feeling, it nearly brought me to tears. A song from another time, when hope stretched its wings and we went forward into the unknown.

CHAPTER 10

Fly Away, Butterfly

$\mathcal{U}$nlike other mammals, human children take a long time to grow up and have a sense of their place in the world. They need a secure foundation from which to launch; they need permission to become who they are. But when you spend your efforts on survival and listen to someone who's angry at the world and her life, to hear her spew hatred and trouble on you like a disease every day for years is mental and emotional torture. You have to gird yourself against it every day, try to build walls and look for glimmers of light so you can keep your own flame alive. You have to find your own light, which becomes your banner. As in a painting where white and gold create a golden light—think van Gogh or Monet—the light from the sun. Or think about the light that emanates from the kindness of strangers. These glimmers of light helped me not to lose my way completely, though I would struggle to find myself and set a course for my life for years to come.

My first day living away from home finally arrived in the fall of 1963, when I stepped into the dorm at the University of Oklahoma. There, I found a new kind of freedom. I had a fun roommate and entered with a breath of gratitude the world that was opening up to me. Our kindly neighbor lady, May, had driven me to Norman, about two hours away from Enid, with my cello, boxes of music, books, and a suitcase.

I don't remember packing, but I do remember that in the weeks before I was free, Gram did everything she could to guilt-trip me into not leaving her. I understood it as her insecurity and fear of being alone and her habit of living through me over the years. And I knew that she wanted me to get a good education. I had no problem keeping to my course of action. If she had truly interfered, I'd considered how I might escape, perhaps with Aunt Helen's or my mother's help—I don't know. I just knew that I had to pry myself away so I could think my own thoughts and create a life of my own.

Thanks to my music scholarship, Gram didn't have to pay much, or perhaps anything for college. I don't recall the financial details, except that they were fraught with conflict with my father. She told me not to tell him I'd be going to a state school, three hours away because she didn't want him to think he'd won. He had urged me to get away from home, and to take the scholarship and go to the University of Oklahoma.

I don't remember how much I was speaking to him then. The breakdown that began when I was fifteen after the motel, the secrets, and my anger were burdens I wanted to let go of. I was sick of all of it, the fighting, the warring people in my family. Surely there was a different way to live. I hoped I could find it.

One of the final pitched battles for my wings had played out in July, during my last summer at home—I was eighteen and trying to find my own way, finally. Though I was ambivalent about some of the Baptist teachings at the church I attended as I grew up, I was always a spiritual seeker. Other than poetry and the moments that sparked magic in the Great Plains landscape, I wasn't sure how to think about spirituality, which then was viewed in the context of a particular religion. I wasn't sure that prayer worked—I'd prayed about Gram since I was young. I believed that Jesus would help us if we sincerely desired it, so I prayed for my parents and grandmother to quit fighting, but things got worse, not better. Had I not prayed sincerely enough? Where was He?

But the Bible did seem to offer some hope. I clung to the promises it made that I would be saved, though I wondered why Jesus hadn't intervened with my grandmother. I decided I'd be safer from dangers of death and hell if I were baptized. The Baptist hellfire sermons had scared me since I was small, but I believed there was eternal life and that you needed to be prepared to face God. I prepared for the baptism with my Sunday-school teacher and then drove myself alone, on a hot summer night, to the church. Gram was angry that I'd chosen a Protestant sect, and refused to give her permission. I fought her about it, determined to take action for my own soul. I knew she had some interest in religion and that she read a Catholic prayer book she kept on her night table. She'd always judged people who went to church as hypocrites who touted beliefs they didn't live day-to-day. "They think they're holier than thou," she said, "but they don't know what Christianity is." I guess she thought I was going to be a hypocrite too.

We lived in the Bible Belt, and there were forty churches in our town, so a lot of people went to church. Gram, always wanting to prove herself to be "above" or better than others, was proud that she didn't. But those last few weeks with her, all I saw was a broken-down, negative person drowning in her own hate. Some kind of spiritual path had to be better than that; there had to be some light, some hope, and I believed Christianity tried to offer that. (I had never heard of any other religions yet.)

The night of my baptism, my Sunday-school teacher stood with me in the empty church with the preacher, who was smiling, out of kindness or pity, I don't know which. My teacher was motherly in her gentle guidance. She offered me a white terry-cloth robe and led me to the small pool. The minister was kind, too. God knows what they thought of me or Gram—most people were with their family when they were baptized. I tried not to be scared as he gently dipped me into the cool water. I yearned for the past to be washed away, for the ugly tension of fights with Gram and mother and my father, and the shameful history that I carried in my heart, to disappear from me, as if all of it was an extra skin that could be shed. Perhaps I blamed myself for not being able to make things better. As I was immersed gently into the cool water, I thought about how hard I'd tried to make peace, but nothing had changed. I knew that the only way to find calm and comfort was to tear my grandmother's sticky claws away from me in every way I could. As I rose out of the water, I imagined the dove of peace wrapping itself around my heart and showing me a new way to live.

Afterward, I felt lighter. The pain I always carried in my back and shoulders lifted. I wanted harmony, forgiveness, and compassion to be the way of the world. That day, though still young and shaky in my values and beliefs, I took a definitive stand for myself. When I got home, she offered a punishing silence for days, but I was used to it. I kept my head down and counted down the days—about sixty—until I would be free.

A few weeks after the baptism, my Sunday-school teacher invited me to go with the church youth group to their summer retreat in the hilly country in southeastern Oklahoma. Gram told me I couldn't go, but I got my Sunday-school teacher involved, and I think she called Gram to persuade her. I was desperate to get away, and I wanted to have an adventure and immerse myself in a group of people with similar beliefs. Gram gave in, but she promised, "If you leave me and I have a heart attack and die, you'll be sorry! I'll come back and haunt you!"

I knew she just wanted to scare me into staying at home, but I didn't care about her judgments, though her threat stayed silently within me for years. I made an invisible concrete barrier between my heart and hers. I knew I had to take a stand, even if it meant disobeying her again. Shaking off guilt and fortified by anger, I left her and hoped she wouldn't die. I'd always wanted to go to music camp or do the kinds of things that kids did together, but she had never allowed it. I'd lived a small life there in Enid, playing music, practicing, and reading. Yes, when I was younger, Gram and I had our fun through the TV programs and her Europe stories, but when you're eighteen, there's a time bomb built in your psyche, saying, *It's time to go. It's time to grow up and find your way.* It means leaving in every way you can.

I still remember the bunk beds at the camp, girls in curlers and baby-doll pajamas, and cozy late-night talk sessions as I learned about other girls and their lives. I began to realize how isolated I'd been. I listened to them carefully, hoping they'd give me clues about how other families lived. At camp, we got up in the morning to watch lavender and pink clouds paint the sky, a brilliant sunrise from the tops of huge boulders. We sang praises for the beauty around us; we smiled at each other in harmony and the fun of being young and having an adventure together. The kindly ministers prayed with us, teaching us about peace and forgiveness. I began to think maybe there was a God, not just the scary God I'd learned about in church, but the kind and forgiving Jesus part of God whom I'd just taken into my heart to help me with the tangled mess of my life. I hoped that my new dedication to find the light and learn about love and forgiveness would help me to create a life that would allow me to leave behind the darkness I'd known for too long, a darkness that seemed to haunt our family. On the way home, I felt hope, knowing that soon I'd be free to live my own life.

The price for those few days away was brutal. There were silences and the usual attacks, hours of screaming, the yardstick on my body, but I just kept counting the days until my escape.

As I watched the sun set from my dorm window in Norman my first night away from home, I felt physically lighter, almost like I was floating. I was sorry that Gram was unhappy, but I was done squishing and silencing myself, though it would take decades to heal. Luckily, being a music major keeps you very busy practicing, and the first year especially is all about discovery. Socially behind and painfully shy, I was curious to learn about the lives of the girls in my dorm. I joined in the pizza parties and found out what "normal" life could be like. I learned about people who had two parents and who hosted fun gatherings in their home. They went sailing and enjoyed barbecues with friends. I found out about fathers who taught their daughters skills, or listened to their thoughts, or gave them a hard time, but they were there at home with their children. I found out that some of the girls had lovely mother-daughter talks and that their mothers were like friends to them. I saw how much I didn't know and how backward and dark my life really was. I was ashamed of who I was and where I came from and didn't share anything about myself. I tried to maintain my disguise as a "normal" person as I observed the world around me, and began to imitate traits or phrases that others used.

Weekday mornings, I got up at seven o'clock and walked eight blocks in winter cold and wind to my Music History class, where the world of music over the centuries opened up for me: medieval, Renaissance, baroque, and more. I studied studio piano and cello, which meant practicing several hours a day, and I played in the symphony, where the rehearsals opened my eyes to the excellence of other musicians. I'd been one of the best musicians in Enid, but here, no. I didn't mind—I preferred to be away from the pressure and to disappear at the back of the cello section.

I was thrilled to be on my own and in school, where I could decide what I wanted to eat, read, or wear; how I wanted to fix my hair; how late or early I wanted to go to sleep or get up. I'd been controlled for so long, watched every moment by beady-eyed Gram, that ordinary activities felt like a miracle. I wanted to learn about dating and boys, too, but that would take time. I was a girl who had been blessed to grow up with safe and sweet boys like Keith. I put the dangerous men in a box in my mind that was separate from my "real" life. Managing the world of boys and men out there would be its own harrowing adventure, with fun, excitement, and risk. I soon found out I was hopelessly and even dangerously naive.

Studying and school offered me ways to escape the confusion in my mind. I enrolled in literature classes and journalism. We were told there were no careers for a woman in those fields and no money to be made there, but I loved literature and writing and took the electives anyway. Besides, in 1963, your job was to get your "MRS. degree," so maybe you wouldn't need to get a real job. Being married meant you'd be loved and taken care of and would never have to worry about anything again—a legacy of '50s culture—and there was no reason not to believe it, though marriage seemed impossible to me. I was a wallflower who wore glasses and conservative clothes. I hardly knew what to say or do around boys. But I did know how to laugh and have fun, and I continued watching my peers for clues. I danced to Chubby Checker and Fats Domino and did The Twist with the best of them. They called me the Dancing Baptist, and finally I was just another adolescent girl having fun at college.

During holidays, I still had to go home to Gram. Each time

I went back, the darkness swallowed me up again. I'd lose the paper-thin sense of self I'd learned to enjoy and would struggle to find my way back to hope. More and more, I wanted a new life, one far away from Enid and my grandmother.

By my sophomore year, I needed to know who my parents were without my grandmother's poisonous influence. I was still wary of my father, and I knew Gram would hate me for it, but I decided to reach out to him, trusting in Aunt Helen's example of forgiveness. I believed that he realized he'd made a mistake when I was fifteen in that motel room, though we'd never discussed it. He was overjoyed to hear from me. On a brief visit shortly after that, he was careful about how he interacted with me, and he seemed to understand that we were starting over.

I explored the idea of transferring to the University of Illinois. I'd be an in-state student there because my mother still had official custody of me until I was twenty-one. My father agreed to pay the tuition, and helped me plan my last two years of college. I was thrilled to be accepted into the music program, this time as a music education major. I'd had enough of the pressure performing onstage as a studio major—stage fright had made me miserable for years—another secret. I didn't know that other musicians suffered from it until years later. I wanted time to expand my focus beyond music—to things I wanted to learn: art, history, English, and psychology.

When I moved to Illinois the summer after my sophomore year, I imagined lovely trips to Chicago to see my father, and even spend a holiday with him for the first time. I hoped my mother and I could become friends like the girls in my dorm and their mothers were, or that we'd have a version of it. I knew my mother was odd and difficult but I hoped for a better relationship with her anyway. It would be years before I'd understand what was actually wrong with her.

And, I would be free of my grandmother. Her ability to make me feel guilty was still powerful, despite my attempts at psychic separation. It was my parents' turn to know me, and my turn to be their child on their turf. We could finally make things right. I left behind the landscape of Oklahoma and headed north, to the state Gram and mother and my father had adopted as their own, the land of my birth. I waited until the last minute to write Gram about my decision. I predicted she'd punish me for being disloyal—and I was right. She didn't write or speak to me for a year.

When I was a child, my parents seemed to arrive in Oklahoma from a mist of dream from Chicago, the Windy City. It never seemed real to me—Chicago was a magical place in the north where my parents were eager to return. I could only imagine the city based on a few postcards I'd seen. My father would tell me his mythic story of how he escaped from the farm in Kentucky to Louisville, then on to Chicago, as fast as his career at the L&N railroad could get him there.

I couldn't wait to be a part of a bigger and more sophisticated world. I was nineteen years old, curious about Chicago. I wanted to make my fantasy come true: to see my mother and father together for the first time. They'd be their best selves, in honor of being together with their daughter. We'd all sit down and have a civilized conversation. Ever the idealist, I had stars in my eyes. I believed if people tried hard enough, the past could be put aside.

As my father ushered me into his twelfth-floor Lake Shore Drive apartment, facing Lake Michigan, I could see how proud he was to have risen high in the world—literally. It was a one-bedroom, tastefully decorated, modern apartment, well kept by my stepmother, Hazel, in colors of rust and blue and beige—a far cry from the dark, messy house on Park Street. I wondered how I would have been different if my father had raised me, but I knew that he had none of Gram's passion for art and literature. His head was in business and making money. Still, I was grateful that it seemed safe to get to know him and my stepmother better. She welcomed me and was always gracious. They'd had no children of their own, but after he died, she told me that he'd asked her not to have children—he couldn't bear the hurt he'd created with me. I don't know if that is really true, given what happened through the years. She told me she didn't mind their agreement—she was thirty-five when they married, and happy to focus on him.

I visited Chicago in early October, just after I started my junior year. It had worked out that my father would give my mother a ride to her apartment. My dream would come true— we'd all be together for the first time. I'd be able to look from my mother to my father and see the roots of my being, where I'd come from. But what followed in the Cadillac that day was a screeching, nonsensical verbal battle, each one-upping the other. My body vibrated with the storm *and* war that broke out, leaving me shaking with confusion as the tongue-lashing attacks continued. The ride lasted forever, though it was probably just twenty minutes. This was my heritage? All my fantasies broke into sad, glittering pieces, making it painfully clear how necessary my parents' divorce had been.

I carried a childhood full of hopes to Illinois, convinced I'd have a positive relationship with my parents. Reality is never as good your dreams, but that year my father and I did begin to build a new kind of relationship. For the first time, he helped me financially and taught me about bank accounts, and he encouraged me to have a practical head on my shoulders. He praised me for having been willing to work ever since I'd left for college. He worried about me as a young woman, given the negative traits in my mother and grandmother. I suppose that was understandable, but he didn't actually know me. We were strangers who'd had barely any contact for the previous twenty years. Though the shadow of his inappropriate behavior hung around the edges, he never made any moves toward me again, but the tension between us never went away, either. I just wanted him to love me as a daughter. I wanted protection and to feel special to him. I wanted to make up for lost time.

I was a little like a lost puppy, awkward in the presence of my sophisticated parents. They both loved the noisy, bustling city, having left behind the quiet farm life and small towns where they'd grown up. During a school break shortly after I arrived at the university, I visited my mother one bitter winter day when I learned firsthand about the biting cold and wind that Chicago is famous for. I also learned about another kind of sharp bite, which would forever be woven into my memories.

I was eager to have time with my mother alone, imagining we'd have coffee and talk about the past, the future, or anything that might help us heal our fractures. That morning, Mother guided me around brick buildings where gusts of wind took my breath away on our way to a jeweler's shop. She enjoyed evaluating jewelry and antiques, and liked interacting with the dealers. My main memory of that day is the wind raw on my cheeks and hands, and, after we left the jeweler's shop, how wispy and emptied out and invisible I felt. I shuffled behind my mother's clicking heels, consumed with dark confusion, trying to piece together in my mind what had just happened in the last hour.

When she went into the shop, she told me to wait at the end of the counter by the door. I obeyed her and watched her sashay over to the owner, a middle-aged man she obviously knew well. She chatted and preened, leaning close to him over the glass case while they talked about the various pieces on display. The icy wind blew in the door beside me, but I was afraid to move, worried that I'd make her angry if I disobeyed. Over a half hour passed while I tried to understand why Mother hadn't introduced me or acknowledged me in any way. I gestured to her, but she turned away. After a few more minutes, she said flirtatiously, "See that girl down there?" They both looked toward me. She wiggled and squirmed. "That's my daughter." She pointed to me.

I stood taller and smiled, starting to move toward them, but he clicked his tongue and leaned toward her. "Oh, Josephine, you're much too young to have a daughter that age."

More wiggles and squirms. "Oh, really? Do you think so?" Mother turned her back to me, and focused on the jewelry. I skulked back to the end of the counter, thinking she'd wave me toward them soon. Bright lights shone golden in the jewelry cases, and white fluorescent lights beamed from the ceiling as I waited. They ignored me for several more minutes as everything turned dark in my mind—I felt ashamed and insignificant. Time slowed down, my stomach ached, my thoughts raced. *Why won't my mother bring me over to talk to her friend? Isn't she happy I'm here? I thought she loved me. Her letters always say, "Love, Mother."* Why was she acting like this?

After she finally left with a new purchase she stuffed into her purse, we struggled against the wind on the street corners. My heart beating wildly, I finally found the words to ask, "Why didn't you want me to meet him?"

She stopped and lit a cigarette, her back to the wind. Frowning, she blew out gray smoke that whisked away in a gust of icy air off Lake Michigan then began walking quickly away. I tried to keep up with her as her heels clicked on the concrete. "You have to understand, to everyone here, I'm *Miss* Myers. I don't want people knowing my private business, or that I'm divorced. I can't have a daughter if I was never married, right? I have my life here, and I don't want anything interrupting it. That jeweler, I've known him a long time. He thought I was just kidding." Her voice was matter-of-fact, as if it were the most logical thing in the world to have kept my father's name and yet be a "miss."

I felt myself dissolving, my stomach a hollow hole in a body that seemed to disappear. *How can I be alive if my mother doesn't claim me?* My mind scrambled as I thought about the loving letters she'd sent me, the times we'd been close when I'd scratched her back; the years that I'd waited for her visits, eager to smell her musky aroma and see the few moments of light in her eyes before she lost herself in a fight with my grandmother. I'd thought she loved me. But now I was simply stunned.

That day, I kept to myself the chattering questions about why and how she could act that way, descending into a darkness that I'd spend the next thirty years trying to heal. For the next couple of hours, I pretended to be okay with her. Heartbroken and afraid, I put on a mask, just as I did with Gram. Though there were people all around us and my mother was with me, I felt alone in the world. Her rejection would be my terrible secret. I told no one for years. What had I done wrong to make her so ashamed of me? Was I a bad person?

But I felt sorry for my mother, too. I knew that she'd been abandoned, that she'd had a hard childhood. Because I felt for her, and because I wanted some kind of relationship with her, I went along with her rules. One day, I would realize that by being willing to take crumbs from her, I'd set up a pattern that would play out with friendships in the future, leaving me alone and isolated.

I slunk back to school after that visit, small and miserable. I tried to pretend I was a just a regular student as I took my finals and planned the next semester, but I felt wispy and insignificant inside—nearly invisible, half-alive. I spent Christmas break in the hospital with pneumonia.

Over the next few months, I gradually pieced myself together. As always, I drew upon books and poetry to help comfort me, and I was beginning to make friends in the music library where I worked. A couple of months later, one winter day in March, spiritual help seemed to come to me in the simple act of walking in the snow.

At the university that spring, I continued my "research" about how other people lived life—tuning in to conversations at the music library, overhearing wisps of the ways in which people lived "normal" lives. The more I heard, the more I understood how the fights and rage and abandonment patterns in my family were not only abnormal but way off the charts. I discovered other people, besides Aunt Helen, who had a positive view of life. As I traversed the plains of dark and light in my mind, things began to rearrange themselves. I began to believe that I didn't need to be so afraid.

That year, art movies by Federico Fellini and the psychological movies of Ingmar Bergman appeared in the theaters. As I watched images unfold on the screen, I saw how art took the human story and made of it something universal. I found out that Bergman drew from childhood pain to create his art. I hoped that I could find a way to transform my life through the arts, but I had no idea where to start. Besides, I was sure that anything I might try would not work out. Everyone knew there were hardly any women in the arts.

During the early morning that day, flakes of snow had begun to silently cover the campus. It was a Saturday, and I was supposed to open the music library by 9:00 A.M. At my dorm, I put on my boots and coat and walked on the deserted sidewalks, my boots scuffing up the snow. In the middle of the campus, stately trees wore their necklaces of white gracefully, and the buildings, brick and stone and silent, wore crowns of snow like winter hats. The silence was everywhere, the only sound the soft brush of flakes as they fell on my coat. I stopped, finding myself in an altered state of awe and wonder at the peace before me. I was entirely alone, and yet I felt more connected to the beauty of the world than I ever had. I felt a kind of certainty in my body not only that I could hope for a better future but also that somehow my life would sort itself out, though intellectually I had no idea how to achieve such a thing. It was as if a voice wiser than my own were guiding me to these hopeful thoughts. I felt assured that all I had to do was keep searching and seeking, keep trying to understand and make sense of things. I relaxed as I walked through the landscape in an altered state of consciousness, as the world, with all its possibilities, opened to me.

I kept walking, calm and at peace, despite the pressure on my body and mind from the past. None of that past, though, was "me." I saw in those moments that I hovered in the miraculous. The date was March 4; later, I would translate it as "marching forth" into spring, marching forth into my own life. I claimed the possibility of a new life for myself—it truly didn't belong to anyone else. Every year on March 4, I celebrate it as my spiritual holiday. I told my friends about it, too, and they began to honor their own marching forth in turn. Over the years, I would meet other people who were lost or hurt, who needed to find their way. Marching forth made sense to them. I'd come to adopt them as family, and would learn that the family you come to trust and love doesn't necessarily have blood ties with you.

CHAPTER 11

In the End is the Beginning

Sometimes things happen all at once, like one of those wild Midwest summer storms. Usually you can see them coming—purple clouds rolling in from a dark western sky, the taste of rain on the wind. You might even have time to protect your house or yourself, to batten down the hatches, as the expression goes.

If I had known of the storm to come when I was twenty-six, I'm not sure what I could have done about it. There's nothing you can do when the strands of fate gather around you besides try to ride out the buffeting and turmoil. The legacy I'd been given by all my parents—Gram, Mother, and my father—came knocking all at once that year. We're always living our lives in the era of our times. It's like the air around us, coloring our thoughts and dreams and decisions. And so it was for me that year.

Four years earlier, in 1967, it was the Summer of Love. I was twenty-one, and I believed that I'd solved the troublesome questions in my life. I'd met my future husband, Dennis, on a blind date. I discovered he was fun and interesting—he was getting his PhD in chemistry, he loved music, sang in a chorus, and he educated me about the war in Vietnam and American politics, subjects I knew little about. He was smart and could engage in deep, meaningful conversations. I preferred men who could think and talk intelligently, who read books and appreciated the arts. I was glad that he was not the typical, macho type of guy. I enjoyed his tenderness, and after a six-week courtship, he proposed—I'd made it clear there would be no sex unless we were engaged. I said yes to his proposal, excited and eager to create a life of my own and ready to find out what all those rules against sex were about. Most of the young women I knew were getting on the pill and taking the leap into full womanhood. Our generation was breaking out into the sex, drugs, and rock 'n' roll era.

After we were engaged, I decided to go to the doctor to get on the pill. I walked away with the prescription in my hand, waiting for the Baptist God to punish me, but the sun continued to shine. I looked up at the greening trees and blue sky, amazed there were no dark, punishing angels or threats of impending hell. A few weeks later, the night Dennis and I decided to "do it," I was still waiting for some kind of punishment, but it began to occur to me that those old rules were nonsense. Dennis took me to a nice dinner, and afterward we went back to his apartment. He put on a Bob Dylan record and made Black Russians to relax us so we could celebrate our first step toward being an official engaged couple.

In bed, we were shy together, and he was kind and gentle. I observed this "sinful" act mostly without guilt. There was nothing to be afraid of; there were no angry gods. I couldn't figure out what all the fuss about virginity had been about. Finally, I'd joined the regular world of adults.

A few months later, we got married, in the middle of an ice storm that was forever famous after that. It shut down O'Hare Airport and all other modes of transportation, so my parents were unable to attend.

My father was acting more like a father than he ever had before, but when he told me that he planned to move to Arizona in a couple of months, I felt rejected again. I understood that he wanted to retire and that he hated the cold Chicago winters, but I had imagined that finally we'd make up for our lost years. However, I never told him how I felt. It seemed best not to reveal my needs or deepest thoughts to anyone, safer to act strong and not made of tissue paper, which was how I felt most of the time.

Love and normalcy in the late '60s meant freeing oneself of fear and guilt. The philosophy of the time urged us to break our links to the past and jump into life with both feet, to find our voice and listen to our heart. Our generation was making new rules to create a better, more conscious, and free world, which meant protesting the war in Vietnam. The young men who were still in school were grateful for their student draft status, as Dennis was, but they were in danger of being drafted after graduation.

Dennis and I marched with protesters at the university and joined one of the marches on Washington, where we met other kids from all over the United States who believed in creating a new era of peace and free speech. The march was powerful, hundreds of thousands of young people waving signs, singing, gathering in a surge to get to the Pentagon. We were thrilled to add our voices to the protest. Late in the afternoon, as dusk fell upon the streets of Washington, groups of us were bundled up in our coats, leaning against the marble steps of the Lincoln Memorial, talking about freedom and our dreams for a better world. After the long bus ride home, Dennis and I were even more fired up against the war, determined to learn more about politics and how we could make a difference.

At home, we learned about the differences between the Left

and the Right, history, and the politics of truth and lies. We were introduced to *I. F. Stone's Weekly*, a left-oriented newspaper that explored politics and the war. We gathered with others of like mind with a bottle of wine and a casserole at potluck dinners, where we all talked and laughed and played music late into the night. Growing up in small-town Enid, I never imagined such multilayered conversations, in which people could disagree politely and part as friends.

We had a coffeehouse on campus where we listened to folk music and the protest songs of Joan Baez and Bob Dylan. We tried to keep up with the changes that were happening everywhere— in the Midwest we seemed to be the last to discover all the cool things. We sang along with the songs, we bought the albums and played them day and night, believing that every song, every protest, was bringing us closer to a world of peace and equality.

Those first years of being married were like playing house— it was legal to have sex, something I had trouble with, though I did enjoy being close to my husband and learning about his body and his thoughts and dreams. Sharing such intimacies was still something I was not used to. I wasn't sure how much of my thoughts or feelings were "okay" to share. I didn't tell him much about my past, ashamed of Gram's abuse, Mother's temper, and my father's roving hands. I didn't want to be seen as strange or abnormal because of my family. The important thing was that for the first time, I had a home of my own. I finally had a kitty who slept with us, and a life filled with home-cooked meals and guests, tablecloths in bright colors. I'd left my old life behind, but what I didn't know is that it stays with you, hiding, ready to press itself into your consciousness with the right trigger.

A music student named Steve, a drummer and Renaissance man who had been the usher at our wedding, was one of our close friends. I liked him from the moment we met in the music library before I married Dennis; his gleeful, quirky sense of humor always made me laugh. He was from the "East" and was more sophisticated than us Midwesterners. He'd already been married and divorced—unusual at the age of twenty-three—but his bubbly personality and charm were like a magnet. On wet winter days over coffee and doughnuts, we talked about religion, poetry, books, and ideas, subjects that fed me ideas and made promises about a possible future. Over spaghetti dinners with Steve and Dennis, Steve's dark eyes flashed with his passion for ideas that sculpted new worlds, sparkling with juice and creativity. As he talked, he invited us to enter these palaces with him, making it seem as if anything was possible.

After we all left the university, we three stayed in touch. Steve found work in some kind of programming job and kept us in the loop about his forays into what turned out to be the early years of computers and music. He sent us lists of the books he was reading and his own poetry. His talent as a wordsmith and the joy that bubbled out of him were a heady mix. I secretly had a kind of crush on him, but I was committed to Dennis. I tucked away my feelings about Steve so completely, I forgot about them.

Living in the middle of the cornfields of Illinois, I observed race prejudice through adult eyes. We were best friends with a mixed couple, a white woman and her black husband. They told us how careful they had to be when they drove away from the university town, that blacks had been lynched just a few miles away. This was during the 1968 race riots and upheaval following the assassinations of Martin Luther King and Bobby Kennedy, which devastated our hopes for a better new world. At our potluck dinners, discussions focused on who was going to burn their draft card. Would they go to Canada or to jail? We gave away some of our dishes and pans to a couple who decided to escape to Canada, rather than fight in a war they did not believe in.

We had our plans: after graduation, Dennis would get a

job; we would buy a home and have a baby. I wanted all the usual hallmarks of normality—husband, house, child—to prove that I'd broken my own family patterns. I also believed that all these things were the best path to happiness.

Life does not proceed quite as we imagine. Dennis didn't get the ideal corporate job he'd accepted, because he refused to sign the loyalty oath to the US government, which was one of the job requirements. We were already pregnant, happily and easily; when we heard the job was refused him, we didn't know what to do next. Luckily, he found a postdoc position in Portland, Oregon, a possible transition into an academic career.

Though I loved being pregnant until I got too gigantic to move, giving birth was not the way I'd imagined it. Dennis wanted to keep an interview scheduled on my due date. I asked him to change it, but I also wanted to support him. I knew the interview was important, but on my due date? We both looked forward to being together during labor—we had pledged to do everything important together. Afraid that changing it would create a mark against him, he kept the interview date.

Naturally, as fate would have it, a few hours after he left for the airport, my labor began. I was staying with friends who dropped me off at the hospital. In the labor room, I was shocked by a pain like nothing I'd ever experienced. I shouted and screamed until they gave me a drug that made it all seem like a dream.

Our son, weighing a hefty nine pounds, was born on his due date in April 1969, helped out by nurses who had to push on my stomach, he was so big. I watched in a daze, grateful for the saddle-block anesthetic. When they brought the baby to me, I unwrapped the flannel bundle and gazed at this wriggling being I couldn't believe had come from me—his tiny legs and toes, his fingernails and eyelashes. What kind of life would he have? Would we be good parents to him? I wanted him to be happy and secure, and said a silent prayer that we'd give him what he needed, that we'd be a solid family for him, despite my fractured past.

Three days later, Dennis joined me, grinning with happiness to have a son, and celebrating his first real job at the University of Oklahoma in Norman—oddly enough, where I'd attended college. Smiling about our healthy son, I covered up my disappointment that he'd missed the birth. But during labor, all I could think of was that I was alone—again. Abandonment seemed to be some kind of fate or curse that kept repeating for me.

Dennis's new job would also bring us back into the orb of my childhood and grandmother. Norman was only two hours away from Enid. I hoped that Oklahoma would not be so bad, but memories of the past threatened me like summer storms. As we made our way to Oklahoma across the country in our camper truck with the baby, Dennis became ill with hepatitis and when we arrived, he had to spend four months on bed rest. I would learn how to be independent in ways I never imagined.

Using time, distance, and my marriage to Dennis as buffers, I'd tried to minimize the damage Gram could do to me. I hoped her attacks were over, but I was still wary of her. During the four years since I'd left, Gram had been critical when I had heard from her, but I had kept my distance as much as my guilt would allow. I knew that though I was officially "grown-up," much of me was still under construction. My generation was living through an era of creative rebellion where you could decide who you would be, could explore new ideas and your sexuality, and could experiment with clothes and lifestyle. You might even uncover the masks and roles that propped you up and discover a more authentic way of being. I identified with the artist persona and still loved poetry, but underneath my search for happiness, the past still had me in its clutches.

I loved my husband and child, though at times I felt strangely distant from Dennis, as if I were looking at him through a mist. When we settled in at Norman, I joined the university orchestra, where Classical music still soothed my heart, but I found myself in dark moods I didn't understand. Sometimes I'd look at my husband and baby and wonder why I didn't feel happier. I kept saying to myself that I *was* happy and blessed to have a partner who wanted me, and a beautiful little boy with blond hair and a big smile. What more could anyone want? We'd never get divorced; we'd be good parents, right?

On our way to Norman to our new life, we briefly stopped in Enid to stay with my grandmother for a night. Nearly three years into the marriage, she'd never met Dennis, and I was eager for her to meet him and our son, her great-grandson.

We all arrived at the door of the house, a smiling, fat baby in my arms, Dennis at my side. Trembling, I tried to hide my fear as I stepped into the smoky living room, embarrassed to reveal all this to Dennis. Of course, I'd told him about Gram, a sanitized version, but seeing her in person made everything all too real, too pathetic. There she sat on the couch, smoking, books and papers scattered around, her hair barely combed. She greeted us, made polite chitchat with Dennis, and just gave the baby a glance. I knew she'd never wanted to be a great-grandmother any more than she'd wanted to be a grandmother when I was born, so I tried not to feel hurt when she didn't make much of a fuss over him. But I did feel sad about her dismissive attitude. I wanted her to accept me as a grown woman now, with my own life, and to embrace us as family. To create a new chapter. Couldn't she even try?

None of that was to be. The first couple of hours were okay, but Dennis went to the store and left us alone. The baby was asleep, and I'd gone out to the garage to sort out our things. Somehow a scathing battle broke out—her usual critical attacks, ranging from my choice of husband to the clothes I wore to my hair and my life. Why had I abandoned her? Why hadn't I written more or visited? How dare I leave her for my father? What had I meant by getting married so quickly? I tried to explain, tried to get her to be quiet, gritting my teeth against the waves of insanity, but she just kept on screaming. My mind was reeling; being back in that house with her was a nightmare. But it was different this time. I'd begun to create a different kind of life. I knew what it was like to be at peace and get along with people.

Suddenly, something snapped in me. My own rage grew red and hot, stoked over the years, silenced all those times when I was afraid of her, when I knew I'd be homeless if I spoke against her. This time, I shouted back, I screamed for her to leave me alone, but then I began to break down, tears of rage more than sorrow. I hated that she saw me crying.

She stood before me, crazy-looking, with frazzled hair, a gaping black mouth with no teeth, and wild eyes. I wanted to kill that creature, to stop her shrieking. To my horror, I imagined stabbing her just to find some silence. I wanted to be free of these attacks, never to live this way anymore. It wouldn't really be Gram I was destroying; it would be this strange creature.

I backed away from her as she shouted, trying to blot shrieks that tore through me, despising myself for having such terrible thoughts. I sank into a blackness that was all too familiar, like a pool of sticky oil. Perhaps it was like hell. Or it was *actually* hell. I could see that I was not free. Not yet.

Luckily, we heard Dennis coming back then with the bags of groceries. Gram quickly calmed down and put on a shaky smile. I tried to act normal, too, but I saw him look at me as if he knew something had happened. Together we carried on with fixing dinner and playing with the baby while Gram sat smoking on the couch. I asked her to open the window, not wanting the baby to breathe in the smoke, but she refused. That night, as I cuddled next to Dennis, my childhood bedroom seemed surreal, with its familiar wallpaper, my old dresser with White Shoulders perfume bottles and talcum powder, stuffed animals on the chair.

I told Dennis a little about the fight and how she had changed instantly into an angry force, but I didn't confess all my dark thoughts, afraid that one day, he'd "get it" and see how crazy we all were and leave me—so the less I said, the better. He'd already met my mother, who had outright flirted with him.

I was from bad blood—no doubt about it. Could I ever escape it? Was it my fate, this shame, this blackness? My blood family and I, were we destined for tragedy?

A few months later, the cold warning of death swept into my life with a phone call from my stepmother about my father. I picked up the phone in a room that shimmered with green light from the sun playing on ivy and trees that surrounded the windows. Her words about his diagnosis—"liver cancer, terminal, three months to live"—cut into my body. Over the last few years since our reconciliation, he and I had woven a peaceful relationship, one that had never confronted the past, but there was also an uncomfortable intimacy. The previous summer, during our vacation to his house in Arizona, he'd told me of affairs he'd had while married to Hazel. I was not happy he talked with me about it. I tried to brush aside his bad boundaries—I just wanted a regular father-daughter relationship, hoping we had another twenty years at least to make up for lost time and correct the mistakes of the past. In fact, I counted on that. One day, we'd get a chance to talk over the past and resolve it. I wasn't strong or brave enough yet.

A day after the phone call, I flew to Phoenix and arrived at my father's bedside in the hospital. He was thin and weak, his skin a sick kind of yellow. As I looked at him, I marveled that I used to be afraid of him. He was old and powerless now. One afternoon while we were alone, when Hazel was out shopping, he began to cry out that he didn't want to die, he was afraid. I comforted him, and in a few minutes, he grew calmer. He began to ramble on about my mother and how passionate she used to be. I didn't want to know this, but I didn't know how to stop him. I talked about my concerns about my marriage and my future, assuring him that I would find a way to work it out and even find a career, which was more of a possibility in the early '70s than it ever had been. Maybe I'd go back to school. Maybe . . .

He began to chuckle deep in his throat. "Oh, so you're a Myers after all," he said, looking proud.

Some kind of small stone sank into my stomach at that remark. What could he mean—"after all?" He didn't think I was his child? I wanted to ask him, but Hazel came back with the doctor. After that, there was no more time to talk, but my body buzzed with a new level of insecurity and confusion.

When he came home a few days later, I tried to talk with him again, wanting to put things to rest, wanting to ask about what he said, but he wanted only superficial discussions or to talk about money, and Hazel seemed never to leave us alone.

While I was there, the cold wind of death beckoned from another direction: Aunt Helen called to tell me that my grandmother was in the hospital and not at all well, though it was not clear what was wrong.

In the utter darkness, you might find a jewel you didn't know existed. You can't prepare yourself for such a gift, because it's out of the realm of reality, a reversal of the known laws of fate and history and "all that came before."

When I left my father's house the next day to see my grandmother, he waved and told me he'd see me later, but I sensed that I'd never see him again. He didn't want any good-byes. My father and I didn't settle things; we never said good-bye. Perhaps that was a factor in the recurring dreams I'd have for decades about him reappearing, not dead anymore, lively and chuckling, walking toward me with his arms open wide, until he dissolved in a mist. I'd cry out, "Oh, you're not dead. How could I have thought you were?" as if I'd betrayed him, and I'd wake up sobbing. So much was left unfinished.

Once I got back to Oklahoma, I went to see my grandmother. I'd had little contact with her—a few phone calls, a couple of letters—since the nightmare incident in the garage. I felt guilty about abandoning her, but she terrified me and I didn't want to be subjected to her attacks. I was still trying to find a life of my own, and by then things were tense with Dennis and me. Our distance after the baby was born was never quite mended, and I was confused about the lack of passion between us.

My heart was pounding with fear. I had decided that if she said one word against my father, I would turn around and walk out. I was finished with their stupid drama. I stepped into the room where I'd been told Gram was resting. Everything was light and airy, nothing like the dark and heavy aura that usually surrounded her. The covers were pulled back and the bed was empty. I was sure it was the wrong room. I called out her name, and a soft, lilting voice said, "I'll be there in a minute."

A moment later, she emerged from the bathroom, a lithe figure in a nightgown, and practically leaped into the bed. She had a soft smile on her face, and her dark eyes were glowing. I tried to figure out what was going on—I'd never seen her that light on her feet, and with such a sweet energy around her. She seemed lit from within. She beckoned me to come close to her— she wanted to tell me something. I went to her bedside, and she looked into my face. "I heard about your father. I'm so sorry about hating him all those years. Can you please forgive me?"

Time seemed to stand still. I was speechless, stunned to hear these words as I gazed at her face. She looked soft and sincere as she waited for me to answer. I had never thought she would ever apologize for anything. I wanted to tell her I forgave her, to give her that before it was too late, but I didn't want to lie, either. How could I forgive in one moment all that had transpired? As I stood there, I imagined the mess of the past swept under a huge rug that rose in a heap to the ceiling. So much of the mess of their lives and mine had never been worked out; so much had never been said or acknowledged or forgiven. The past I carried was huge—the history of my grandmother and what she brought to my life and my mother's, the history of my father, most of which I didn't know, though I knew all too well the years of rage and strife between them that I carried in my body, in my back and my shoulders and my belly. That past was the darkness in my heart, and it would be a few years before I could find words for it or find out that there was a way to heal it.

In the few moments it took to answer her, I could see the garbage and pain piled up under that rug but I tried to find a small place in my heart where I could tell Gram I forgave her without totally lying. I sensed that someday I would have a chance to take the mess apart piece by piece, that someday forgiveness would come. I stood on a small green square of hope for that future as I held her delicate hands in mine and said, "Yes, Gram, of course I forgive you."

Her face broke out in a beautiful golden smile that made her look years younger. "Come closer. I have something special to tell you—it was like a miracle."

I drew closer to her and held her hand while she looked up at me with a childlike face, her dark eyes sparkling with life. I used to love her touch when I was a child—her hands soothed my brow; they rested gracefully on her books when she was reading. It seemed that she wanted to tell me some kind of secret. She told me a priest had come to her hospital room—she was in a Catholic hospital—to find her crying and sobbing every day. Finally, even though she wasn't a Catholic, he offered her the Last Rites of the church so she could find peace, and in the prayers and anointing, she felt a burden lift from her and she knew she was forgiven. She grinned. "Who knows—maybe I'll live a while yet."

It was a startling comment, given that for years she'd threatened to die on me as a punishment. I gazed at her in wonder, trying to adjust to the new person before me. I allowed myself a little hope, and I was not quite so afraid. Maybe we would have some nice times; maybe it was not too late after all.

When I left her that day, I felt as if my molecules had been rearranged, and perhaps they were. It was utterly new to see Gram again as light and sweet as she once was. I remembered that once she had been my savior, the person I depended on and desperately loved and needed when I was a little girl. So much darkness had gotten in the way, years of pain and anger and sorrow. But as I looked up into the new spring leaves that day, I was reminded that at any moment, something new can happen. That hope for something fine and good is always possible, and you truly can't predict what might occur. The past can be swept away by a prayer and the finer side of a person that reappears, even if they've been lost for so long.

Two weeks later, I visited Gram in the hospital again. This time, the doctors were concerned about her deterioration; years later, Aunt Helen would tell me that most likely she had a brain tumor. I sat by her bed as she rose up in garbled confusion, talking to people who were not there. I was not alarmed. I'd read that sometimes when people are dying, they talk to people on the other side. I prayed for a smooth passage for her if it was her time. Aunt Helen and Uncle Maj were keeping vigil with me, and a couple of times they got her to laugh. We were all family there, Gram and her good friends who had taken part in raising me so kindly.

At dinnertime, Aunt Helen was helping Gram eat, when a nurse came to say that a "Miss Myers" was downstairs. Aunt Helen and Uncle Maj exchanged glances of alarm. "It's her daughter. She'll upset Frances. We don't want that." The nurse said that perhaps my mother should stay downstairs awhile, so I offered to go to her while Aunt Helen fed Gram her dinner.

Gram asked who was there, and we told her that Mother was downstairs. A soft, nostalgic look passed across her face. "Oh, my brown-eyed baby." Those would turn out to be her last words.

In the lobby, Mother was pacing and smoking and worrying about Gram, but I didn't have answers to her impatient questions. I tried to keep her calm, but finally she broke free and ran up the stairs. We found Gram resting with an uncanny stillness, covers up to her chin. I sensed that something was wrong, but it would be a few hours before the doctors realized she had lapsed into a coma in those few minutes I was with my mother. I believe to this day that she could not bear to see her daughter again, to chance another disturbing encounter, as she made her way from the planet. Later, I learned from our neighbors May and Kenny that eight years earlier, they'd had a terrible fight—they had heard it from across the street. Soon after that, my mother had left, and Gram had told Kenny she'd paid Mother $10,000 never to return until that night at the hospital.

In the few days it took for Gram to die, my mother went nuts, pacing and shouting at me and nurses and doctors and making an embarrassing fuss, talking about how much money she would inherit. On my twenty-sixth birthday, Gram died, having never awakened to see her daughter, my mother, again.

There was a funeral in Iowa, which my mother attended. She acted crazy, telling wild stories amid all the attention focused on her. Eleven days later, my father died, leaving me with confusion and grief that would take years to resolve. All that loss at once must have changed me. Shortly after that, I decided to separate from Dennis, unaware that I was suffering from severe grief and depression. I know now it was not a good idea to make such a big break from my marriage so soon after the deaths of Gram and Daddy, but the past pressed too much against me and I wanted to get away from everything. Years later, Dennis and

I would talk about how I was depressed and he was depressed, but we had no way to see that then, and no words to explain ourselves to each other. I left Dennis, though it was a wrenching decision, full of guilt for me and anguish for him. Ultimately, the break was amicable and Dennis and I agreed to share custody of our son.

Though I wanted a new life, I didn't realize that until you dig away at that big pile of baggage, that gigantic lump of crap you've swept under the rug and try to heal it, you'll remain trapped by it—not only your own mistakes but the layers of the past, a legacy that will smother you and haunt you. I would find out how powerful this legacy was in the years to come.

During that heartbreaking time, I promised myself that when my mother died, I would be at her side. I thought it was the saddest tragedy possible that she and her mother had missed each other at the end. That neither of them was able to forgive or let go. If only Gram could have left the earth with love for her daughter. But she went into a coma when she knew Mother had arrived. Perhaps she couldn't bear one more confrontation.

In the years to follow, when Mother and I talked about how her childhood was similar to mine, she would say, "You know, my mother wasn't very nice to me, either." Sometimes my mother was cruel and unwelcoming, and she never stopped denying me, but sometimes she revealed a tender side of herself. She'd grow quiet, her dark eyes would moisten, and she'd tell me how much she missed her mother. This always created a soft spot in me for her, a place where I saw us as more like sisters than mother and daughter, both partly raised by the same mother.

After Gram died, Mother went through the house and gathered up and threw away almost everything, including my childhood keepsakes and dolls—it took decades to forgive her. She threw away letters from my father and Gram's archive of old letters, documents that would have given me clues about her story. Thankfully, Mother did save and label, in her flowing, beautiful hand, some photographs of Gram, which I later inherited. In one photo, Frances is in her late forties, in Texas, amid adobe walls and Spanish architecture. Mother wrote: "San Antonio, 1946." Aunt Helen told me that Gram had fallen in love with someone on one of her visits south for the winter in Texas. I wondered if this was a picture from that time. I had the photo for years, but as I was writing this book, as I kept trying to understand what happened in our generational story, I took a closer look.

In the photo, she's smiling and looking languorous and lovely, her chestnut hair falling to her shoulders. The man, darkly handsome in a Latin kind of way, looks at her, and you can see a kind of electricity between them. On the back, Mother wrote:

Looking over pictures of my pretty mother and feeling that all the glamour fled this life with her death on March 19, 1971, at 3:43 A.M. Am desolate.

I caught my breath as I read my mother's note. Despite their fights, they both yearned for each other. Long before I joined their story, they'd been connected by love. Deep in the history of their past lay the clues to what happened with them, a story I had to know.

CHAPTER 12

Happenings

A few weeks after Gram and my father died in that momen-
tous year of 1971, I was on my own again, partly glad and
partly ashamed to be single.

I moved back to Champaign-Urbana again, and immersed
myself at my job in the main library at the university and learned
how to be on my own. Big events of the early '70s were playing
out around us—protests against the Vietnam War, the women's
movement. But I felt at home there where I'd first begun to grow
up on my own, and the uplift of the '70s gave me hope.

When we look back on the past, the person we were then hovers
like a ghost, familiar but blurry. In a fresh perspective offered by
the passage of time, when I remember myself then, I reflect on
what "she" did, that younger person who is no longer me. Numb

with grief, she didn't know how she would make her choices from a foundation of mourning, or how she was trying to escape the pain of loss lingering in the background, despite the smiles she wore.

My first month back in Champaign-Urbana, Mother came to visit. Sitting at a café table in my small apartment, she lit cigarette after cigarette, gray smoke swirling around her head as she told me about running away from Enid after Gram died, taking a bus, getting off, and being blown into a building. She lost her memory, she said, and it took her three days to get to Iowa for the funeral. I wanted her to keep talking so she wouldn't ask about me, but soon enough she started criticizing everything: miniskirts, long hair, leaving Dennis, what I felt and thought. During what seemed like an exchange of mildly opposing views, I don't remember what it was, she slapped me across the face so hard my ears rang.

Shocked, I held my throbbing cheek, trying not to cry, instantly enraged. It took all my strength not to hit her back. Why was she the parent who had survived, and not my father, who finally was ready to redeem himself? Or Gram, who had asked for forgiveness? I thought I had escaped my shameful life, but here it was again.

After she left for Chicago later that day, I needed some comfort and found a new café. The room was made of redwood and woven fabrics, homey and comforting; the aroma of brown rice and teriyaki sauce promised something delicious. Shaky as a reed, I settled at a small table, trying to return to my body again, aching with confusion. Maybe my mother was right: I shouldn't have left Dennis. I always said I'd never get divorced.

Slim, ethereal sounds filled the café; mystical phrases of poetry made their way into the wounded places in my body—I felt as if my mother had whipped me everywhere. I knew I had fallen into a familiar, shadowy pain, but the music shone its light upon me. I sat for a while, sampling new tastes, as the music wove a prayer of beauty. The music was a new recording by Joni Mitchell,

Songs to a Seagull. I bought the album and listened to it over and over again as hope crept back into my heart.

During my first weeks there, I thought about Steve—there were reminders of where we used to have coffee, where he used to live. I remembered the time he'd helped me write the orchestration for a symphony for my orchestration class, and another time when he had waxed poetic about the writings of Aldous Huxley. He'd always impressed me with his knowledge of literature and the way he used it to illuminate his experience of life. After a while, I decided to contact him. He'd been a friend to both Dennis and me, and I thought of him as a positive connection to the past.

I curled up on my living room rug with the phone as Steve's familiar voice came over the wires. We caught up with our lives: he had a job he loved, doing computer research, and a marriage that was on the rocks. We reminisced about poetry, remembering our long discussions about literature and the parties we'd had, where Dennis had brought pure alcohol from the chemistry lab and added it to innocent-looking Hawaiian punch. At another party, someone had played the trumpet while another guy read *Howl*, by Allen Ginsberg, the poet of that era. Back then, we thought we were the epitome of coolness. Steve and I talked several hours that evening, which led to conversations the next week, and gradually we were talking every night. His long, poetic letters swept me into dreams of a new chance at love.

August 1971

I was, am, and ever will be impressed by one quality of our relationship, regardless of how it may develop. We seem to be the embodiment of a perpetual motion machine. What I fed you came back again, amplified and enriched. We seemed to fit like a suit of clothes made to be worn under the skin.

My first encounter with you in the music library was like stepping blindly into a bottomless abyss and then falling up. How lucky we are to have encountered each other for the first time twice like this. I am hard put to express the degree of mutual understanding that we seem to approach astounds me. . . .

I have always seen your fragility so clearly that it was a joy to comprehend it. . . . Would that I could be so transparent and so firm. I sit here in awe of us. . . .

Nothing is preserved forever, or even for long. But we will always have a great deal to renew. I have more to say to you, but there will be time. First come the important things. Now we begin.

We decided to meet in person, to see if the magic that had seemed real over the phone and in the letters would be there in real life. A few weeks later, we danced through cornfields that surrounded the old farmhouse where I'd moved with my son and roommates. We made love for the first time, and indeed it seemed that magic swirled around us, body and soul. When he left with promises implied more than explicit, we continued our letters and long phone calls deep into the night. After a few weeks, he invited me to live with him on the East Coast. I was sure this relationship was meant to be, that he was the love of my life.

November 1971

There are days of great fullness, richness, a time when the poem of my life attains the posture of a mosaic sculpture made in many layers, some seen, some invisible from without, each tiny fragment itself alive, changing, growing in its awareness of its own textures.

The days and nights melt into a continuum of overlapping and interconnected melodies which are constantly refreshed. . . . I confide and console my innermost dreams and imaginings with the soothing

*sound of the Chinook, which is heralding the approach of
the summer of my life.*

The snag was that Steve was still married, though he said
he was getting a divorce, that the decision was in play before we
met, and that his wife knew about us. It was a big leap for me
to leave the Midwest so soon after moving to Illinois and launch
into a relationship with Steve, but it seemed right. We were old
friends—it wasn't like we had just met. I consulted the *I Ching*
and laid out frequent Tarot readings as I tried to decide what to
do. Would it be right to start a new life with him, and on the East
Coast, where I'd never been? Perhaps there was an adventure
gene in me like the one my grandmother and my father had. I
was eager to explore sophisticated New York and leave behind
the boring known world.

The final factor that determined my decision was when
Mother said she might move to Champaign-Urbana to be closer
to me. What a disaster it would be for her to live nearby! Desperate to escape her, and believing that a new life with Steve was
worth the risk, I decided to move east. I packed up a few things
and drove all day and night to a suburb of New York City, to a
new life where I knew only one person.

At first, the way Steve presented himself lined up with my expectations. His apartment was decorated with modern and classical art prints, musical instruments—a piano, a drum set, a flute,
tablas, and bongos. I liked his hardwood floors and nice carpets,
sets of attractive dishes, cloth napkins, and fancy coffeemak-
ers. He introduced me to all his friends and toured aw-shucks,
Midwestern me around the city of New York, where I was gog-
gle-eyed at everything from the Staten Island Ferry to the Empire
State Building to crowded Chinese restaurants, Indian food,
the Village, and the cool coffeehouses we'd dreamed of back in

the Midwest. He socialized with a group of friends involved in experimental music, art, and film. In the early '70s, New York was the place to be.

For a while, my escape seemed to be the best decision I could have made. We were in love; he was passionate and interesting and never ceased to surprise me with his wit and quick mind. When my son came to live with us, Steve would get on the floor to play with him. He made up games, taught him card tricks, and included him in our adventures in the city. At night, I snuggled in Steve's arms, feeling safe, protected by someone who was trustworthy, the sweet, bright guy I'd admired and liked for so long.

One day, I found him in an especially bad mood. Sometimes he was grumpy in the morning, but it would pass, and other times we'd disagree, but these moments were just part of life, I assumed. I don't remember why we argued on that particular day. We'd always resolved previous arguments after some careful listening and apologies. We were still getting acquainted, and we had come from different worlds. But that day, I watched as he changed into some kind of stranger with rageful eyes who shouted at me, and banged on the walls. It was like a storm, and nothing I could say calmed him.

Eventually, he ran out of steam. Both of us weeping, we made up, and for a few weeks, things were better again. But I began to notice a pattern—he'd be critical, often about a small thing I did or didn't do. Sometimes he'd feel I was not attentive enough to him and we'd get into a long, exhausting fight. At first, I would defend myself, but doubt would creep in. Maybe it was my fault; maybe I was careless and thoughtless, even though I tried to please him. A few weeks later, during another argument, he broke a window and threw furniture, leaving my son and me cowering and crying. Each time he lost his temper and we seemed to resolve things, I was sure things were improving, that we were "working through" our problems. He had asked me to read about "healthy conflict" in one of his favorite books, *The Intimate Enemy*. Its premise was that fighting was good for a relationship. It cleared the air and invited honesty. Truth and honesty were the currency of the era. Young people all over the country were angry about the lies and manipulations that had led to the war in Vietnam. The new ethic of the time was truth at any price, so when I read these principles in the book, I believed that every fight, no matter how edgy, would lead us to something good in the end.

These strange storms with Steve continued. As our first year together ended, days might go by without resolution, leaving my stomach in knots, my mind swirling with fear and worry. What if he decided to get rid of me? I had nowhere else to go. I knew my mother wouldn't help me—she thought I was a sinner for living with Steve out of wedlock. He became more controlling, demanding to know everything I thought and did and said. He felt easily abandoned and betrayed. I bobbed between confusion and misery and hope, except for the highs when things were great again, and I was certain we were making progress to a happy relationship.

I didn't realize that the darkness that swirled around me during the down times was a result of the fact that the relationship had begun to parallel my experience with Gram and *her* wild moods. Because of my bad childhood, which Steve knew about, we would end up agreeing that I was overreacting when I was upset. Once I admitted I was to blame, he'd return to being the caring, funny, and brilliant guy I loved. And I was very open to seeing most things as my fault. After all, I knew my weaknesses, my need for approval and peace, my sensitivity to criticism. When we passionately made up and celebrated a new level of intimacy, we thought the teachings in *The Intimate Enemy* were working.

After almost two years of exhausting struggle, I began to feel

I couldn't continue living under so much stress. I was crying all the time; I had lost weight. I got an unrelenting pain in my back and stomach, finally diagnosed as gallbladder attacks, which led to surgery. Sure I was going to die, I called my mother, rolling the dice that she'd be nice to me. She told me I deserved to suffer because I was living in sin. I put down the receiver, trembling with dread.

Luckily, the surgery went well, but I was still anxious and insecure and at the mercy of Steve's wild moods. Luckily, a series of inquiries about his career led to him to decide to go to Stanford, where he could get an advanced degree. Since the '60s, I'd always wanted to live in California, so we talked about starting over there. We promised to negotiate when we were upset; Steve agreed to control his bad moods and temper. I still hoped we could get back the love we'd had at the beginning. If we could learn to trust each other again, maybe it would work.

The West drew us to its silky, rolling coastal hills, sunny winters, and what was left of the zeitgeist of the liberal '60s. As we drove across the Great Plains, the place of my roots, the great American West beckoned me to a new life. I breathed in the huge spaces of clouds and open land, my body relaxing into the familiar call of the landscape I loved.

One morning in November, a few months after we arrived at Stanford in Palo Alto, California, I watched orange sparks fly into the autumn air as the fire in the raku oven snapped at wood and eucalyptus leaves. My pottery class had been invited to our teacher's backyard for a raku firing. As we stood in a circle around the warm fire, the leaves on poplar trees above us fluttered golden in the light. In a raku firing, you can't predict the effect the wood, leaves, or other natural materials in the oven will have on the glaze. It's all about chance, raku, which means "happy accident." I hoped it meant good things as the alchemy of fire changed the pot from a plain glaze to metallic rainbow colors.

Steve was busy with school and had made an effort to be more positive. I was enjoying a peaceful life here in this new place. As the sun melted into me, I luxuriated in the welcoming world of art, making pottery, experimenting with glazes and taking walks in the warm fall landscape. In my bones, I knew I'd finally found a place I could call home. The Pacific Ocean was only a few miles away, and on summer afternoons, the coastal hills were shaped like a woman's body misty with fog.

The spring after we arrived, we believed we'd gained a new level of trust and decided to get married and have a baby—a girl, we hoped. Steve had always wanted children and was crazy about my son. That summer, we were in love again, and I was overjoyed to get pregnant right away. One day, as I was kneading the clay in my pottery class, I "knew" I was pregnant with a daughter. As the months passed, I imagined having a fabulous relationship with my baby girl, so much better than Gram and my mother's. I'd create the mother-daughter moments I'd never had. I'd shop for cute clothes, comb her hair, read to her, play in the park. I thought that my mother would be happy if I had a girl. I'd prove it was possible to have a daughter and love her and stay with her. By having a daughter and raising her right— with her father, who of course would be everything my father wasn't—we'd mend the broken places. I'd prove I could change a heritage that had seemed predetermined. Anything was possible. Anything.

I focused on the positive, choosing to push aside the times when Steve's edgy moods returned, hoping if I ignored them, things would settle down. During the pregnancy, I pursued my love of art, moving from pottery to something I'd dreamed of but hadn't dared to try: learning to paint. Slowly, my art classes revealed the secrets of oil paint and shape and shadows while the baby made fishy loops in my belly.

Steve's moods began to occur even more frequently, and once again he grew away from us, but I kept arguing for more closeness. I wanted him to put his family first, but his attention was drawn to his studies, friends at the university, and the young women students who adored his charming ways. Night after night, he'd invite guests at the last minute for dinner and entertain them all evening while I served and watched his charm light them up. After they left, the delightful, brilliant person who invited them would turn into a dour, angry guy no one else saw. As I reacted to these mood swings with tears and anger, I worried that my powerful emotions would affect my baby.

When the fights escalated, a strange kind of silence came over me. I could hardly hear his shouting, as if I disappeared beyond the noise. The same thing used to happen when I was with Gram. Later, I learned it was called dissociation. I escaped into a soundless place in my mind, trapped in a struggle that seemed impossible to resolve. Despite our conflicts, Steve agreed to accompany me to Lamaze classes, and on a good day, he would pat my stomach and welcome the baby. Each time things seemed better, I'd pray they would stabilize and that our struggles would slip into the past. But we were in a cycle that kept repeating.

On a March morning at four o'clock, my labor began. We were excited to get to the hospital. The Lamaze coach had given husbands strict orders to trust the wisdom of the mother's body rhythms, but Steve was someone who understood the yes/no switches of his computers better than people and insisted I do the breathing his way. However, I had to breathe my own way to keep the pain under control. Finally, he gave up and sat down, irritated that I wasn't obeying him. During the ebb and flow rhythms of labor, a voice made itself known within my body: *It's over. The marriage is over.*

I sagged into the bed, knowing that my body accessed a deeper truth than my mind could grasp. I knew that when my body spoke to me like this, it was never wrong. But I had work to do. I took another breath, hoping our baby would make things better.

Labor progressed suddenly toward delivery. Nurses hurried me onto a gurney and rushed me down the hall. As I rolled along, I entered some kind of trance. I experienced a flowing away from my body, where there was a "me," to an expanded world where I did not exist as a separate person. I merged with pine trees and oceans and clouds, floating inside another kind of consciousness. I was aware of having a body and of the powers of life that were surging through me but saw myself as strangely lifted above my body to become simply a part of nature, in a wordless bliss. During birth, you are all body, bones and muscles, limbs and blood linking you to your corporeal ties to the earth, where the slipping-out of a baby reminds you of multiple worlds of soul and body and breath and life. Having experienced a transcendence of my body, I was brought back by pushing the baby out into the world.

In the photo Steve snapped just as she was born, my baby girl's legs are blue, her body pink from her tummy to her face. That image captures Amanda's first breath, her arms trembling as she felt the cold air of the world on her skin for the first time. I was recovering from that last, powerful push, which had raised me from the sorrow of my crumbling marriage to something that rose above everything—the joy of creating a new life.

I held her in my arms, looking in awe at this tiny child. I was once a baby girl—did my mother feel the same kind of fragile love for me? Did my grandmother feel it for my mother? My heart ached to feel such a big kind of love, a tenderness like the petals of a flower, beautiful, breakable.

The first few weeks after our daughter was born, we became a happy family again. We'd all sit together and hold her, entranced with her tiny fingers, smelling the baby scent of her neck, admiring her sweet smile. My son loved his sister and cuddled next to me when I nursed her, touching her tenderly. Dennis happened to visit shortly after she was born and, like an attentive uncle, carried her around, crooning to her. The three of us, Dennis, Steve, and I, still enjoyed being friends, despite the fact that we were living on opposite sides of the country. When Dennis remarried, his new wife added to our circle of family-friends, a connection that would last through the years. They would pick up my son for the summers and enjoy a vacation in the West.

For three months, Steve and I were in our happy cycle again, but the dark moods returned, evolving into physical blows as his temper flew out of control. *How could we have descended to this?* I asked myself, as I tried to figure out what to do. I knew that I couldn't live with the same kind of fear I'd grown up with. I'd been hit too many times in my life already. In my calmer moments, I still hoped that things would resolve as I kept the family going: nursing the baby, folding mountains of laundry, managing my son's school and his visits to his father. I didn't want to remember the message my body gave me during labor: that the marriage was doomed. I couldn't bear the idea of another failed marriage, but as things spun out of control again, I knew it was over.

It was then that Steve finally agreed to therapy. He charmed the therapists into failing to recognize the validity and depth of our problems—he could charm anyone who did not know him. Desperate for support and for a reality check, I found my own counselor. One day she asked me, "If you are this unhappy, why do you stay?" I had been trying to hold on to the idea that if we, if I, tried hard enough, we could get back to the love we'd had at the beginning. But now I lived in fear, in the shadowy imprint of my past. Her question gave me permission to consider leaving. After weeks of negotiation, Steve finally agreed to go, and we began to create lives on our own, taking turns with the children.

I threw myself into art classes at Stanford. Having a babysitter for a few hours a week helped me to maintain some kind of sanity. When I painted, the troubled world fell away. When I inhaled the heady scent of turpentine and linseed oil, I'd fall into the reds, yellows, greens, and blues of the California landscape beyond the easel. Lost in vibrant colors as I captured the shapes and forms of the natural world, I found a temporary peace, but even though Steve was gone, the shadows returned.

CHAPTER 13

The Past in the Present

*E*ven if you see a breakdown coming, it arrives in slow motion. In the moments when there's a glimmer of happiness or hope, you might think the hint of a breakdown isn't real, that everything is fine. But the sound of crushed metal, the chaotic turbulence of the accident of your life, makes it clear that you can't ignore it. You pull yourself out of the mess and look around to assess your injuries. The "accident" of a marriage breakdown and all its drama leaves invisible marks. No one can see them, so you can deny they exist. Just like when I grew up with Gram, I pretended, showed the public face of coping, put on a smile. Most people don't want to know how you feel anyway. But as the months passed, the personas I had to juggle became impossible and my facade cracked.

You can drink wine to release stress, to calm down and dull the pain for a while, but there's no real escape. The full truth of your disaster hits you in the silence of the night, in the moments when you are alone and the voices start shouting at you. When it seems you've made no progress ever in your life, when the ghosts of the past are real and walking around in your darkened rooms. When you are truly haunted, it doesn't stop. You feel crazy, but you can't be crazy, because then you'd be like your mother and that is the worst thing you can be.

It takes a long time for the truths of the past to catch up with you, but when they do, everything breaks down. You don't realize during a breakdown that there will be a new beginning, a time of renewal and healing. All you know, during the sadness and emptiness and darkness, is that you will do everything and anything not to feel it, to try to have some control. You'll keep pretending you're fine, that everything will somehow magically work out, while your heart falls even deeper into a labyrinth of grief.

After Steve and I split up, not happily, not amicably, I put on a smile for the world to see. I got out of bed every day, forcing myself upright, pretending to be strong, though my body felt heavy and all I wanted to do was sleep. I took the children to school and day care, I worked in a coffeehouse and looked forward to my art classes, where there was an invitation to simply Be. I didn't know that there was a name for the darkness that weighed me down, or that one day it would submerge me.

Art has become my refuge. I stand by the easel, the empty canvas open before me, a blank page where new worlds are hidden within that white space. A single black line, thick or thin, curvy or straight—what can it bring into being? Scrub in a color, look at the daubs of yellow ocher, cadmium red, thalo blue, viridian, alizarin crimson. Where will the next line or color or shape lead me? I breathe in the scent of linseed oil, pause for a moment to look at the swirls of colors ready to be mixed into shades that will create a world on the canvas. This is a moment that always excites me. I wonder how the paint will create images and lines, and what sensation might be evoked. Here, the feelings in my body and the hope in my heart rest without judgment. There's a silence that surrounds me; the critical voices—*you're a single mother, a failure, a sinner*—blur into the background. Creamy ultramarine blue suggests sky. If white and black are mixed in, an ocean might appear, vast and stretching to unknown worlds. Cadmium yellow light dances; it's cheerful, despite any darkness you might carry in your soul, inviting an afternoon in a wheat field. In art class, we review Renoir, Matisse, van Gogh, even Mary Cassatt, a woman who painted during Renoir's time. The vibrations in van Gogh's paintings are alive, tapping into universal vibrations of energy, showing his vision, seeing what "normal" people are blind to. In his lifetime, he was deemed crazy, suffering torments only his art could tame. When I paint, a sense of peace comes over me. I relax before the invitation of colors, the scent of oil and gesso and turpentine, and the fluff of brushes against my hands.

I joined a feminist art collective that was planning a woman-only exhibit in downtown Palo Alto. My art teacher, a woman who encouraged me to express myself with personal and autobiographical art, invited me to enter my painting of woman as Mother Earth. Images of the earth as mother had emerged in my work when I was pregnant, and now there was more permission in the art world for women to claim that kind of imagery. In the past, men took possession of the female form, but now women artists were developing images that offered an alternative to the classical view of the "nude," a body to be gazed upon by men. Women's images became active, claiming sexuality, bristling with energy. Hostile to the expectations of the world, the works created were often mystical, revealing, and even shocking. Judy Chicago, a feminist artist located in Fresno, began what would become a famous installation, *The Dinner Party*, which featured images of female sexuality in feminine colors on dinner plates.

For the feminist exhibit to which I was invited, I chose my oil painting of a woman's body, rendered as graceful hills of earth and trees. A golden head emerged, a spiritual being who was born into a mystical world. A quarter moon hung in the night sky. For some time, I had been adding moons, either a quarter moon or the round circle of a full moon, to my work. When I gazed at the night skies of the paintings, the darkness seemed to need a moon illuminating trees and land. I saw the moon as a symbol of my past, a comfort those years I lived with Gram. The moon was all I could hold on to as I gazed out of the prison of my grandmother's house. The moonlight painted the houses and wheat fields just beyond as I looked longingly for escape from the window of the front door. Its silvery beams seemed to be a promise of beauty and light in the darkness of my life. I imagined myself far away from Gram's control and criticism, bathed by the moon's blessing, wondering how I could ever escape. It was eerily similar to my marriage.

When Steve left, I was able to stay with the children in married-student housing, townhouses built in a circle around a center playground. A few single mothers lived there with their children, so I wasn't a total oddball, but I felt damaged and different from the normal chatter of families around me, which had a mother, father, and children living together. The fear that I was walking in the footsteps of my mother and grandmother began to whisper and haunt me, but I pushed back the unwelcome thoughts. That usually worked, but when it didn't, my mind swirled with: *You're a failure. You can't do anything right. You're ugly and will never make anything of yourself, just like Gram said.*

On peaceful nights, I was grateful to be alone again, not harassed, not criticized, not afraid. After I put my children to bed,

I'd listen to Judy Collins and Joan Baez, Carole King and James Taylor, Jim Croce, and Cat Stevens. The music eased the tension of my haunted thoughts, but the fears erupted anew, and I pictured my mother's horrified "What do you mean, you're getting a divorce again?" I imagined that friends, who had no idea of Steve's secret world, his tempers, his rage, would judge me. To everyone else, he was a wonderful guy. He was already nearly engaged to someone else, a woman who would become his fifth wife.

Restless after wrestling with my demons, I needed to escape, to talk to people and chase away the voices and guilt. Because there were so many mothers nearby, it was easy to get a babysitter for a couple of hours. I'd go to the coffeehouse, where everyone was rocking and grooving to a folk band or a blues singer, the scented evening air promising a better future, though I couldn't imagine what that might be. I began to date again, and found a couple of men I enjoyed spending time with. The early '70s was a new world, about as far as you could get from the '50s in Oklahoma. As with other women my age, I enjoyed the new era of greater freedom for women—Roe v. Wade had passed, and we were no longer locked into pregnancies we couldn't sustain. The pill and easy access to birth control changed everything and allowed us to make choices about men and sex that were not acceptable in the era of my mother and grandmother or the generations before them. It was a wild time that we thought would change the world forever.

The Baptist part of me triggered my guilt—I was bad, now I was alone, like my grandmother and mother. The conservative part of me that grew up in Enid fought against claiming the freedoms proclaimed in Ms. magazine and in the news and at NOW meetings. The new feminism proclaimed it wasn't wrong to make love outside marriage. Though I believed that I was free to make those choices, I still had conflicts about it. What if I was a bad person after all? What about my father and my uncles who took advantage of me—was that my fault? What if these new freedoms meant that we were hurting our children or ourselves? How could we know what was wrong and what was right?

I tried to understand the reasons to stay quiet and "be a lady," rules that were part of the upbringing of my mother and grandmother and women who came before them. Only "bad" girls broke those rules. My grandmother broke the rules when she eloped and when she left her daughter behind. Look at how she ended up—alone and lost in her darkness. Could I be "good"—a good mother and person—and find freedom?

Books and art had always filled me, silent witnesses to my search for . . . what, I was not sure, but I was sure I'd find something that would help make sense of life. I wanted to understand the meaning of what had happened in my family. I devoured Freud and Jung; their theories of the unconscious and inner motivations fascinated me and inspired me to understand the deeper layers of how people acted and why. I continued to explore readings from the Tarot and the *I Ching,* hoping to make the right choices. I read all the volumes of the diaries of Anaïs Nin, and novels by Marge Piercy and Margaret Atwood that were about women finding their identity. The poetry of Adrienne Rich and Denise Levertov offered ways to find a sense of self and a fresh kind of spirituality. I read *Sexual Politics,* by Kate Millett, for a radical feminist view, and Alan Watts, Paul Tillich, and Ram Dass for their spiritual wisdom. Marilyn French's *The Women's Room* and Irene Claremont de Castillejo's *Knowing Woman* offered me clues to my emerging self.

The Baptist fire-and-brimstone sermons had left me frightened of God, but spirit and soul and forgiveness seemed important for creating a path beyond the darkness and anger that were a part of my family story. These alternative spiritual philosophies challenged my traditional, fear-based beliefs from childhood. The new spirituality was less judgmental and offered compassion even for a guilt-ridden person like me. I tried to manage the holes I discovered within, like unraveling lace, as I remade myself through art.

In a printing class at Stanford, I learned the craft of mono-prints and etching. The smell of the inks and solvent, the thick, fluffy watercolor papers, the physical aspects of printmaking, led me into a world of creation where I was active, not passive, where my visions took form. I immersed myself in lines and shadows, the deep indigo representing a part of my soul. In an etching, the lines that appear light in the drawing on an etching plate will become dark in the finished print. The acid etches through the drawing on the metal plate and leaves a groove where the ink will gather.

But in life, unlike etching, it was hard to sort out what was dark and what was light. I started writing in a journal to capture images, ideas, thoughts, and dreams. Words became blessed anchors that kept me in touch with reality. In one journal, there's a passage that shows my state of mind:

There is no one, nothing. No one to hold on to, no one to connect with. I search and search and no one is there. Waves of emptiness roll through my stomach and chest, I'm nowhere, there's nothing. Loss. I'm alone, I've always been alone. Panic arises—I can't take care of myself. There is no one.

I want to hurry, run, find someone quick—to make these feelings go away. I want the pain to stop. Fill me, pleasure me, feed me anything good, anything pleasurable and soothing to help this go away. I can't stand the emptiness. There is nothing I can do. Nothing will help. The loss is too great, so much sadness, tears. The pain is unbearable.

I feel her now, the thin, pale girl that I was. I was a woman in age, but inside I was a girl, scared and lonely, scarred by abandonment and abuse. Now, after years of examining how the past had shaped me, I can see what I couldn't know then: Sexual abuse shaped my psyche, my emotions, and my beliefs. I believed that love—the love of a man—would save me. I was supposed to do whatever it took to be desirable and attractive, to get men's approval. I had to be quiet, sexy, and mirror them. I was lucky to be able to enjoy sex—not all women who are molested can—but I thought that sex *was* love. During an era when women were free to claim their power, I would feel fulfilled when a man was attracted to me. But I would choose the wrong men over and over, men who wanted power over me, men who were unkind or selfish or abandoning, though at first they seemed like "the one." It was as if I wore a sign saying, IF YOU WANT SOMEONE TO PUT DOWN OR ABUSE, CHOOSE THIS ONE. But, of course, I didn't realize it then.

One day when Amanda was two, I stared into the mirror at my still-young face, thinking about Blanche and Gram and my mother. They were young once, they were beautiful, but that wasn't enough to make them happy. My mother was beautiful and she was insane. Who was I? Would I ever be anything but lost?

The bad feelings began to outweigh the good, and the struggle made me feel old, heavy, and stupid. Why couldn't I get things right? Some nights when I was alone, I lay in bed, shivering. At night, a sense of emptiness and failure roiled in me. I was nothing. I had done nothing good. My son would stay with his father during the summer, as planned, but this time, in the depths of my despair, I had sent him early. Two children were too much. I could hardly get out of bed, and everything made me cry.

An image haunted me: the two parts of me, the dark and the light. I drew several self-portraits exploring a split self. One side of my face appeared in light, surrounded by trees and the softly mounded green hills of positive feminine imagery. That side had hope; she lived in a welcoming future and knew love and balance. The other side of my face was in deep shadow.

Behind that dark side was a desolate night landscape with dead tree branches reaching into a night sky etched with a quarter moon. Afraid, lost, terrified of death and loss and loneliness. When she was in darkness, she forgot about the light; in her despair, she forgot it existed at all. The light was on the other side of a wall, far away. Some part of me believed the light had to be there, but I couldn't find it.

There were other clues about my fall into darkness. I painted, drew, and etched images of stark landscapes, the trees leafless and alone, as if a nuclear holocaust had occurred. One night, as I descended further into the world of no light, I drew a person in black charcoal bound by cords and unable to move. She sits forlorn in a dim landscape strung with barbed wire. She is bald and skeletal, like something you'd see in postwar Germany, starving and alone in the night. The image shocked me—was that how I felt? Yet I knew it represented me. I was wandering in a scarred inner landscape. I'd expressed the truth of my darkness and my inner, silent trap, which no one knew about. It represented a person in dire distress, and I was ashamed.

After struggling to recover from the divorce while falling further into hopelessness, one evening I noticed a brochure a friend had given me. It had a striking design, a dark blue background with a white diamond in the center. The person who had given it to me had been trying to get me to contact the therapy program in the brochure. She had gone through the program and told me it had changed her life. I was skeptical and scared. The few months of counseling I'd had the year before had helped for a while, but I was still in despair. This therapy program promised to change your life. What might I learn that I didn't want to know? Would I find out I was crazy, too? In those days, therapy and psychology were for crazy people.

Perhaps I would have said yes to anything that night—I don't know. Perhaps it was just a mood, or even a deep kind of knowing. But as I picked up the brochure and read about healing the emotional, physical, mental, and spiritual aspects of ourselves, I felt called, tapped on the shoulder, whispered to. Tingles went up and down my body as an inner voice uttered truths I was afraid to know. *You have to do something. You are your mother and grandmother. You can't take care of your children; you've gone through two husbands. Look at you. You're a failure.*

Electricity coursed through my body as I listened to the powerful wisdom I was receiving, from where, I didn't know. It was true—it was all true. I *had* become them. I was doing exactly what they had done. I was the same age my mother was when she had me, and now I was alone, just like she was. My grandmother and my mother had abandoned their children, and now I'd sent my son to his father's house before his summer visit because I couldn't cope with two children. I knew that dark shadows had marked both Mother and Gram, and now I was sinking each day.

Weeping, I sat up straight, as if I'd been struck by lightning. It was so clear: I *was* repeating the past. I was not different from them after all. Shaking and panicked, I picked up the phone and called the number on the brochure to find out how to enroll. I had no choice. It might already be too late.

Terrified and yet excited about learning about psychology, a few weeks later, I arrived at the first session of this new therapy program to join a group of strangers, but before long we knew everything about each other. The therapy would challenge our beliefs and conditioning from childhood and teach us to see ourselves— and the world—through new eyes. We found out how we learned what love was—that "love" might become defined as abandonment, abuse, loss, or fear, depending on our experiences. The first phase of the therapy explored our mother's character. I had to write about three women: Gram, Mother, and Vera, since they had all played the role of mother in my life. We wrote a "negative emotional autobiography" for each one, digging for the detailed stories of what happened with each of them. For the first time, I wrote about Vera, about Gram rescuing me, the years of fights between her and my mother and my father, Gram's death, and Mother's denial of me. For fathers, we had to go through the same kind of biography. I was shocked to learn from the therapists that my father's behavior as I grew up was incest. I had no idea that incest and molestation included touching and sexual suggestions, other behaviors besides intercourse.

With years of experience as a therapist now, I understand that we were being educated about the psychology of child development. When we're wounded, we repress our true feelings and cut off our life force while staying unconsciously tied to those patterns of behavior. It was a therapy process designed first for awareness, then self-expression, then ways to create new sets of beliefs about ourselves. We were encouraged to express our anger and hurt, to shout and use batakas, foam-covered bats, to hit a mattress and release repressed anger. To understand how we inherited our patterns, we wrote about our parents' early years from their point of view, as if we were walking in their shoes. In the last phase of the therapy, we got in touch with the inner soul or spirit of who we really were—the diamond inside us that was pure and positive and full of love. They told us that all people have this pure self when they're born, even our parents. As I went through the process, hours of writing and meditating and seeing the past through new eyes, the dark clouds began to lift. The patterns of my family that I'd wondered about, but that no one talked about, were validated. I saw my parents as babies and young children; I saw through their eyes the times they'd been born into and the struggles they'd endured. Gram was born to a grieving mother, and she never had a father. My mother was left behind, like I was, and some of her problems had to do with that broken connection.

I began to see my mother and grandmother differently: I saw them as children who had been shaped by all the things that had happened to them and the world they'd grown up in. They had done the best they could to take care of me, given their own problems. I wrote Mother a letter to let her know I understood her childhood better, and that I hoped we could be closer. Her response seemed more open, but, soon enough, I would find that the mother who existed in letters was a different person than the one who lived in Chicago. That mother was tough, angry, and still rejecting.

The therapy process had the biggest impact on the relationship between Amanda and me. During the times of strife when I was still with Steve, I had distanced from her emotionally, taking care of her physical needs but protecting my heart. Once I went through therapy and wept for all the losses and felt the anger that I'd been afraid to feel, my heart began to open. I started a new ritual with her to reclaim our closeness. Every night I'd put on her footie pajamas and fix a nighttime bottle. Though she was nearly two, I held her as if she were a small baby, rocking her in a rocking chair. As she drank her milk, I whispered, over and over again, "I love you. I'm sorry I closed my heart. I love you. I'll make it up to you, I promise. I will try to learn to love better." Each night, I rocked her for a long time and stroked her hair. I saw how my ability to love had been tarnished by my own past, by depression and the strife of the past few years, but finally I was on a path to discover new ways to live and to be. I promised myself and my children that I'd do my best to wake up, to become the person I was meant to be and the mother they needed. I had begun the long path to healing.

interlude

Be remembered; involved with past and future.
Only through time time is conquered.

—T. S. Eliot, *Four Quartets*

The Way It Was

As I learned about the stories and genealogy of our family, a story about the generations came to me, an epic tale of American migration, of settlements in the West, characters in long dresses and bonnets, the swirl of dust, huge harvest meals, women slaving over wood cookstoves. I could see a grand sweep of time and history embedded in the land and the people who came to settle. Blanche was born in 1873, three years before Custer's last stand. Her mother and grandmother arrived in Iowa when the Indians, the Sac and the Fox, still lived on the banks of the Mississippi River. I see myself as a pearl on the long necklace of this family, connected to branches of other families woven and broken by life, and I had to know more about them.

The story has the tone of a fairy tale. It begins with the wind and the land and can't be separated from the migrations of people from Europe. We are all wanderers, meandering lost and searching for home.

A covered wagon. Big sky, thick clouds.

Miles of grasses. The moccasin prints of Indians on river-beds.

The hoot of an owl.

A Brief Guide to the Generations

❖ Thomas Dickerson (1757–1827) and Margaret Davis, Virginia—the first in the family to migrate to America.

❖ Joseph Dickerson (1783–1832) and Sally Daily. Joseph is the son of Thomas. His son is:

❖ Jesse Dickerson, born 1814, Ohio. Marries Frances Godfrey, his second wife, in Ohio, 1846.

❖ Josephine Dickerson, daughter of Jesse and Frances, born 1850, Ohio. Moves from Ohio to Iowa. English-German descent. Marries John Peter Stineman. Josephine is the mother of Blanche Dickerson, born 1873, on the Island, near Muscatine, Iowa, a piece of land cut off on one side by a slough, the other by the Mississippi River. She is the oldest of six.

❖ Lulu Frances, born 1894, on the Stineman farm on the Island. Only child of Blanche and Louis Garrett. Louis, age twenty, dies seven months before her birth. Blanche marries again, has six more children. Lulu elopes to marry Blaine Hawkins, son of a newspaperman.

❖ My mother, Josephine Hawkins, born 1915, Wapello, Iowa. Has a half-sister, Jean, her father, Blaine's, second child. Josephine marries Emerson Clifford Myers, of Louisville, Kentucky, in Chicago, 1944. He's gone when I'm eight months old.

❖ Linda Joy, born 1945, Chicago, Illinois. Only child.

❖ Amanda, born 1975, Stanford, California. Only child of Steve and Linda Joy. Has two half-brothers.

❖ Zoe, born 2006, Fairfield, California. Brother, Miles, born 2003, San Diego, California. Father: Frank.

❖ Ten generations, 232 years, of maternal family history.

A Body of Land

The prairies are lonely, with a loneliness
of which tears are no alleviation.
—William Quayle

This is where we came from, a land so flat it looks like the horizon is drawn with a ruler. Where sky and land meet, you can see a silver shimmer of possibility, a lake of illusion. A mirage.

Mirage: the merging of boundaries, an irregular line between two separate worlds seen from a distance, a meeting of air and dirt. Human bodies are the embodiment of soil and earth and breath and water. Rooted, the grasses of the plains plait together, weaving the land into a blanket of memory and time fractured in dirt, rock, effluvia. Millions of years of memory.

A body of water. Sixty percent water, our bodies. Gristle and meanness, the other part.

On the Great Plains, the wind tugs at your clothes; it tries to topple you over. It gets personal, you and the wind. The wind in your face on a gusty day can stop the breath in your chest. You have to turn your head to catch air in your lungs; you gasp like a fish on land.

The memories of bone and muscle take us back to our origins, not only of this life, but that of our forebears. I capture memory, paint pictures of eras and places that will blow through the sands of time when I'm gone, when we're all gone. But for a brief time, our history will leave its mark, ink on paper, black marks on white paper, like bird wings etching commas into the wide-open sky.

When you are driving across the big spaces of the Great Plains, birdsong wings its way to your ears, crystalline notes resting on the five lines and four spaces of musical bars, or perhaps they rest on the barbed wire that separates land parcels. The Indians never understood that white men thought they could *own* the land, that they could break it up into parts.

The Great Plains was an inland sea; the land from the Mississippi River westward was tallgrass and shortgrass prairie. The early explorers and soldiers would marvel at the endless inland sea of grass that reached higher than the heads of men on horses. Imagine the beauty and terrible loneliness of that vision, also full and rich with life: animals, wildflowers, the grasses undulating, clouds painting shifting patterns of dark and light across waves of grain.

The wheat was crisp at harvest, it smelled like hot straw, and it spoke with a whisper as the wind swept over the fields at dusk, the sky burnished red-gold, as if a painter had swiped a brush across the deepening blue. There was a kind of silence that almost no one knows these days and that perhaps you have never heard—the silence of a grand space. Yet in that silence, small sounds—crickets, the whir of a bird, the crisp sound of wheat dancing in the wind—you are offered the hope of redemption.

The woman of the plains stands upright, feet planted in the red dirt, eyes on the shimmering horizon line, wind tugging and pushing against her bones and flesh. Her feet are planted in the dirt of eons, the nautilus from this inland sea fractured into dust. Wheat grabs hold of time with its roots, feeds us bread, cycling the seasons of time in our bodies. This is a place of knowing, of heart, of solidity, even as the red dust blows, mingling with azure sky in a cloud of unending possibility.

In the Beginning . . .

They came, they came from across the big waters, the ships carrying them to the shores. Joseph begat eleven children, and Jesse was one of his sons. Joseph's children begat children, and the generations sifted through the lands, pushing the natives from the land of their ancestors, land shared with all—air and water and land shared freely with the living creatures who needed those gifts.

Westward the white men pulsed, the zest of adventure and greed driving wave after wave from New York to Ohio, from Ohio to Indiana, and to Iowa by the 1830s. The Great Plains was millions of acres of virgin land, prairie grasses of bluestem and panic grass an undulating sea fluttering high above the heads of men as they surveyed the prairie, boots clamped into horses' stirrups. Mississippi River bottomlands were ceded from the Sac and Fox tribes who had moved down from the north, forced from their original lands by French and British in the 1700s. The landscape was beautiful, red and amber in the autumn, high, trilling green leaves of hickory, maple, sycamore, and elm trees. In an area rich with black soil, the corn grew nine feet high, cultivated by native peoples for centuries. Rivers burst with catfish, bass, and trout and all manner of life.

The land changed its moods in the sweep of seasons, and wind blew fluffy white seeds from the cottonwood trees. Eagles and egrets coursed above, heartbeats pulsing under feathers. Snow drifted in graceful pillows, and black tree branches crackled and groaned with ice. The tribes wore the skins of animals, hunted wild turkey, coon, hare, and quail. Humbly, they loved the earth in its magnificence, coded in cells and blood.

The earth and its covenant—to remember.

The earth husbands its people, watching over its comings and goings. Blood bears all it has known and seen unto the following generations. Those who tread the earth leave the scent of memory, registered in cells. They live even now, drifting through the dreams of descendants. You can hear them calling. . . .

1873

The land by the river remembers every creature, every footstep across powdery dust. It remembers sweat beading in soil, blood growing dark and relentless on the ground. It remembers the originals, strangers from the north lands pushed south by the French, forced to leave the land of their birth. In this new place, they made offerings and bowed to their mother, the earth, as they worshipped the Great River.

The wind blows across the plains, hollowing, eddying through the Mississippi Valley, stirring the soil, sifting through blue air. It sweeps over crops and animals, knowing minutely each cornstalk, intimate with the rustle of wheat.

In the dim mists of the history of the land, the Mesquakie moccasins left footprints on the soft mud of the riverbanks. Their young rested against cradle boards, crying out, as children do, in the pale morning air. The land remembers these people who disappeared, exiled from the land to the Indian territory by the white laws, tearing the fabric between the mother and her children. Many trails and tears marked unnamed paths, no longer visible, across the land; cries wafted through wind, if you could hear them. Destiny was not the inevitability of birth and death, but the power of the many over the few.

The corn, with its crisp leaves and graceful tassels, towered against the immense, magical azure sky. After the prairie grasses were plowed under, the land knew the corn. The land exhaled and lifted itself, the tentacles of the four roots of the corn took hold, the soil nurtured the young plant as it rose toward the sun. The earth took pleasure in the sound of green leaves whispering on a summer night, and the color of blond corn silks, like a woman's hair.

Joseph begat eleven children, and the first of these was Jesse. Jesse came with the wind and waves of people speaking a babble of language: German, Swedish, and French. West from New York to Ohio, and west from Ohio to Iowa. He planted the land that was taken away from the People with corn, sorghum, and tomatoes and saw that it was good.

These new people, Americans, put harnesses around their own necks, pulled wooden plows, their backs aching with endless labor. Death, birth, rain, blizzard, and drought—the glad burdens of Christian soldiers, the fathers and mothers of the Future. Their eyes gazed into deep, clotted furrows as sincere prayers wafted skyward. These were Christian prayers, the Great Spirit worshipped in the name of a trinity of gods.

Perhaps a spirit blows across the land.

Josephine, daughter of Jesse, granddaughter of Joseph, gave birth on a strip of land near the river. The Stineman farm, it was purchased for three hogs, the corn in a silo, one horse, and $10 by her husband, John Peter. He came from Germany; his feet gathered the dust of America in his hand-me-down shoes when he was five. Now his fingernails were black with the grit of his own soil, as if soil could truly be owned. Now he was called "farmer." All of nature was his to work with, he believed, and today was the birthday of his first child. The apple orchard erupted in full bloom. The sun brought forth the nectar. Honeybees burrowed deep into the flowers, sucking out the centers, wove the honeycomb, made honey, and fed the queen. The bees followed their destiny: nectar, endless work, and obedience, swarming in their abundance to his barn, where the honey was given as a gift.

Josephine's child would be named Blanche. In the spring, this girl child pressed her way into the May morning. First light spilled through an upstairs window, its eye staring across the plains to the southeast, an ever-watchful eye viewing the Mississippi flowing, enriching lush bottomlands. The house was itself a sentinel, built with wood from the felled forests, built with John Peter's hands, with its own memories still buried in the grain.

The land unfurled like a woman, fertile, its breathing slow, still, and silent. The wise farmer would put his ear to the ground and listen to the moods and whispers of the earth. The farmer knew he must wait and watch the moon for the proper moment of planting, and wait again for the time to harvest the fruit of the seed. All things, their time and season. All things with their cycles of birth and death and flowering.

So it was with this birth. The midwives guided the birthing. It was woman's work—weaving the web of mother, nurturer, bearer of the seed. Hours of wrenching labor. Josephine yanked the knotted sheets, pushing against the veils of her mind. She pushed her past behind her; her future swam before her eyes. Did she imagine the progeny she would bring to this earth, the generations that would owe their lifeblood to her? Generations would remember her, and they would toil, too, on the land, but she would not know them. Still, on a silent evening, you can go to where she breathed and loved, where she made bread and dreamed. On a quiet evening, you might see her return to where the house stood on that land. Now the corn sweeps across a field where the house used to be, but she is there. Forever.

Josephine cried out, the bones of her body ratcheting open, as with all birthing. Blanche was formed in the womb of her mother, formed from the blood and sinews of two people, her mother and father, but her soul was her own. She came from Somewhere. She was Herself.

The growl in Josephine's throat harkened the initiation song, as for all women, breaking through the barrier between girl and mother. Her entire being was focused on one thing: the passage through which life came to be. She was No One. She was vessel. When the cry of her child seared the morning air, Josephine knew peace. She was Mother.

This child, Blanche, was the first of the generations to be born on the land by the river. The first of the Stineman line. Blanche: a promise. Blanche cried out, slippery, falling into the light, hands opening and closing like starfish, sucking air, lungs like butterfly wings.

A girl.

They would have sons.

Next time.

Such loneliness of the plains will drench you, as
I have been drenched with the falling waves of ragged
seas. The spaces laying hold on you like an iron hand,
spaces speaking to you in a husky whisper.
—William Quayle

The land made its demands on the family, out there under millions of stars, the kerosene lamps' golden glow in the night striking long, lanky shadows in the corners where ghosts of memories lingered. Coal stoves heated rooms in blustery winters of blowing snow, the winds raging horizontal against men, cattle, and horses. The wood cookstove filled the kitchen with warmth, the wood gathered and split with an ax, brought in from outdoors and piled by the stove, selected by weight and thickness for the kind of fire needed: frying bacon or making coffee, or perhaps a pie; on special occasions, frying a chicken for Sunday dinner. Dank cellars protected the glass jars of fruit and garden riches that Josephine and her sisters and neighbors canned in the thick heat of August.

The mothers arose at five in the morning to fix breakfast for the men, who milked the cows, slopped the pigs, tended the horses, mended the fences, sowed the seeds, harvested the hay, corn, sorghum, alfalfa, soybeans. The mothers churned butter from the fresh milk, gathered the eggs, fed the chickens, kneaded bread, made pies, cakes, and full meals three times a day. They washed dishes in a dishpan with handmade lye soap, water pumped cold in the kitchen and heated in a teakettle on the cookstove.

The wash was done on Mondays, boiled in a kettle in the yard, hung on clotheslines with clothespins, except in winter, when the clothes froze solid on the line. Irons to smooth the clothes were made of heavy iron, heated on the stove, lifted and plunked down on the thick material and pushed back and forth by the strong arms of the women, who worked sixteen hours a day, veins in their arms and hands standing out, sweat gathering on their faces even in winter.

Fireflies on velvet summer nights. Did the mothers rest on the porch long enough to see them wink on and off?

Blanche grew to know the rising of the sun each morning and the darkness of night, the songs of birds in the spring and the deep-voiced lowing of cattle. She knew the nose-wrinkling smell of horses and pigs, the mud that stuck her shoes to earth, quick summer storms. Her world was the farm. The land was lush with the creation of new life: hanging globes of red tomatoes, squash,

potatoes hiding like secrets underground, and beans with surprising round balls inside. Fields rippled with corn and sorghum.
Orchards of peach, apple, and cherry trees stretched far to the
horizon and produced sweet blossoms in spring. Their scent
cleaved to her on the first day of her life, and the memory stayed
in her soul always. She was part of something larger, a weaving of
land and sky, earth and blood. The farm carried on its life from
the bowels of bitter dust, nurturing a multitude of living things,
even the lowly ants and spiders and kittens that scampered among
the cows and hay. Each creature had its place.

As a child of two, Blanche carried kindling to the box by
the cookstove in the kitchen and helped to snap beans. Her hand
would slip into the flap of her mother's blouse. If her mother was
seated, sipping coffee, she would unbutton and allow Blanche to
play with the folds of her soft dress, to suck the familiar comfort of
the breast. One day, a burning slap on her hand and her mother's
sharp words made her stop. Her crying brought more slaps, so she
learned to press down her sorrow.

A few weeks later, Blanche's world was pierced by what
sounded like fighting upstairs. Afraid, she crawled toward the
frightening sounds. One lady filled the bedroom doorway in a
blue checkered dress and an apron with red smudges. She told
Blanche her mother was all right and to go downstairs. The
door clicked shut. The bees and flies buzzed, discussing the
birth of another life. The horses moved as one body through
the misty dust of the corral, noses flaring. John Peter slopped
the pigs. There was a cry from the window that overlooked the
river. Blanche waited, pulling at the threads of her red gingham
dress so it tickled the tops of her small, dirty feet. The women
exclaimed, "A boy, the eldest son. A boy—finally a boy!"

John Peter's boots drummed on the stairs as he rushed to
see his son, his creased face open with hope. A heaviness grew
in Blanche's chest, a new kind of sorrow. They had forgotten
about her as they celebrated the birth of a son. He would carry

their name into the next generation. It began in the house, with joyous laughter and the stomping of J.P.'s boots. In the barn, men with large mustaches and hair sprouting like spring shoots from the dirt-filled crevices in their necks sucked down whiskey. Women in long, swinging white aprons rustled through the kitchen, bearing pies, cakes, potatoes, and pork chops in juicy heaps to the table for a feast.

Blanche smelled the sweet milk and the sour, musky smell of blood. The intruder lay next to her mother's heart. Blanche wanted to lie on her mother's warm body, feel the rise and fall of her chest, suckle the breasts the new baby possessed. She must have become invisible, because no one looked at her, spoke to her. She was a ghost.

The Mississippi was moody. On a soft day, it was aqua, placid, reflecting the blue sky. Other times, it took on the mood of the black thunderheads. Great streaks of lightning ripped apart the heavens. Rain poured down, filling the low areas, the slough, the ruts in the corrals. Filling the ditches along the road, rinsing dust from green, living things. Mud careened stubbornly along earth too full to absorb any more. The river groaned and rose up like a giant, tossed its weight, tore trees from the earth. Roiling water hurled pieces of iron, wood, sticks, logs, and serpents into the lines and squares laid out by man, the lines and squares marking civilization—this and that, theirs and ours. The river knows no such language, it has no logic, only the demands of the earth, the rain, the swift current as it rolls to the Gulf of Mexico.

1885

A tornado of dust whirled from down the road, the rattle of harnesses and loud voices. Blanche observed the defeated wagon, its white covering split and gray, the haggard-faced women and children staring as if in a trance. Men with tattered beards and clothes pulled the teetering wagons into the yard. She saw gaunt faces and bleeding feet as the people looked around with flat, dazed eyes. Men's hard voices ripped the silky air. Different voices, angry and sorrowful, murmured as the women lifted down the smaller children. "The drought—we almost starved to death."

"Couldn't bury him—the dirt was froze . . . The coyotes . . ." A gasp, the woman's face wrinkled. The women's lips were slits across leathery, disappointed faces, their deep-set eyes staring. Golden light from the kerosene lamps of the Stineman house was a beacon to the weary, lost creatures. The women whispered about how wonderful the cornfields of Iowa were, so high. Listen to their sweet rustling, look how thick and green the garden. Enough food. A miracle.

They told of how they staked down their lives at the edge of Kansas territory in sod houses. The blizzards and grasshoppers, Indians and dust storms, fires and pestilence tore at them. After three years, they decided to return to civilization, grateful to live in full standing homes, grateful for neighbors, barns and fields already fertile and furrowed, planted and watered by the rains. They wanted doctors, churches, and real coffee. Blanche watched the cracked and hungry faces of the children, listened to the men talk by the barn. Children scampered in the dirt, their feet reddened with the color of the plains they had come from, as they chased chickens. The hunger ran deep. They'd lost a baby to the greedy plains, and their eyes and hearts were not the same as when they'd headed west.

A chicken was sacrificed for that special night, a smoked ham from the smokehouse, a feast with bread and cake, pie and cream. Baths would be drawn, and clothes offered to the needy, who would camp on the land until they were healed and could start over. They had come home from the West, the terrible, uncivilized West.

Blanche reached a lanky twelve years, hard-muscled, her dark eyes serious. She was the "other mother," eldest daughter in charge of young'uns. In the kitchen, the fire snapped as if it were a live thing, the music of the wood soothing her. The iron lids covering the fire seemed barely to contain it, lusty power leaping orange and feverish several feet above the stove. There was an art to adding the right wood, the length and breadth. Every young girl by the age of ten read the language of the fire, its moods and needs, reading it better than any book. Sparks flew, and she slammed the iron lids, as if to silence the fire's demands. She listened to the magic of the wood's sounds, its crackling wisdom and poetry. As a young lady, rounding and filling into womanhood, she learned to be practical, the sense of wonder folded into the tough, forming muscles of her body and bones.

On the cookstove, the teakettle hissed and heaved, droplets dancing on the black stovetop. Blanche peeled the potatoes and set them to boiling. She sliced tomatoes, yellow seeds spilling out. Blanche ate two slices, the red flesh tart and sweet all at once, seasoned with sugar and vinegar, as was the German way.

In the warming oven, the daily bread rested. Her quick fingers had already formed the loaves, aromatic with yeast and sugar. She watched the life of the bread rising gracefully into soft pillows. In the pantry were her six pies, golden-brown crusts fluted high, stained black-blue with juices, thick-crusted pies, blackberry and peach from the abundance of August-ripened fruits. The heat and dust of summer burned her lungs. Bees were buzzing, butterflies guzzling last bits from the flowers before they shriveled into parchment and fell into the dirt, compost for next year's field. Seeds from the bounty of the harvest were blueprints for the next generation. Blanche inhaled the great odor of earth rot, leaf, and seed, readying for her own planting and ripeness.

The countrywomen have their secrets from the men. They keep these secrets; whispers sing across rooms spread with cotton and stitches from the quilting that fills their lives with pattern and meaning. The quilt for the new baby, the quilt for the married couple, the quilt for the young virgin girl, and the quilt for mourning. Other secrets, too: how the boys learn to turn away from the sweet-faced children they once were into tough men who can take the slap across the head, who can bear the horsewhip. The women turn their heads away, even as they dress the wounds, teeth clamped down in silence. It is the way it has always been—this discipline. Even girls, if need be. The horsewhip is in the world of the farm, and all must bow to its power.

There is no radio, no telephone. The newspaper is far away in town. Schools are distant, down muddy, dusty roads. You don't go to school because it is too far, you are needed on the farm, you are a girl, why go to school, you are to birth the babies and feed the husband, all his appetites, you are the woman, you are unclean, you must not speak, you must obey, bow down, feed the men. You are to work inside the house, work outdoors, you are the helpmeet, you are the mother, the womb, the bearer of the fruits, you will bear the fruits or you are nothing. You are vessel.

The man and his son met Blanche at the New Island Methodist church. She took the buggy there with her Aunt Jessie, her mother's sister, who was her own age. There, Bernard Garrett, with his black-and-white beard, looked like a version of God. The gaze of his single, fierce eye—he had sacrificed the other one to the Civil War—made her feel small. He forged farm equipment in his smithy shop behind the barn; he tried to keep up twenty acres of corn and sorghum near Grandview. All Bernard's other children had died—Gabriella at six months, Martin before his first birthday, the baby at birth. And Louis's mother, Genoa, born Vaughn, died a week after birthing the fourth child. Bernard had stood at the cemetery in Lettsville too many times. He'd built three small coffins and one large one, built them himself, pounded his grief with each nail, hitting hard, hammering the wood as if he could break down the wall of death between himself and his loved ones. The light in his wife's eyes, gone. How could he go on? But he still had Louis, his youngest son. Before those deaths, he had watched men lie in twisted agony at his feet in the Civil War. He looked to Louis now. He must carry the family forward, bear the burden of his father's hopes. He would be the one to lift the family over the line into the twentieth century. His name was Louis Garrett. His hands were strong. He wanted to work. And a young man of twenty-one needed a wife. His large, dark eyes shimmered, his face delicate, without angles.

Wedding, New Year's Day, 1894

Harnesses and bridles sang in the crisp, thin air, wagons of cousins, aunts, uncles, and neighbors, everyone dressed in Sunday best for the wedding. January air clung to the lungs, a sticky, icy substance, breaths gasped and released in cloudy puffs. The guests came from miles away, a heated brick at their feet, wrapped in coats and wool blankets. The eye of the house looked toward the frozen Great River.

Today, the ice was so thick that people crossed the river from Illinois on sleds. The blades skidded across frozen roads, chips flying. The horses' hooves tapped melodies on the ice; their nostrils snorted frigid air in steamy puffs. Frost adorned the trees and bushes like sparkling candy. The first day of the new year, the beginning of new things.

Blanche was ready to be a wife, ready to move into the world that waited for her. Home was under her feet, and she would not go far. No one did.

The parlor stove was filled with coal, and the heat blasted away whirls of icy air that circulated through the house. The aromas of the wedding dinner—roast ham, a side of beef, gravy, coffee, bread, chicken, potatoes—filled the house. The large walnut dining table was decorated with the best Sunday tablecloths, and pitchers of milk. The wedding cake, pies plates, silverware—the family had made a feast for the ceremony and put out all their best for the neighbors. It was customary for the farm families that were less endowed with money to share the bounty of the farm's produce freely.

"Dearly beloved . . . till death do us part." They pledged their troth, joining hands, fingers resting lightly. Blanche and Louis married in the house where she was born, surrounded by neighbors, family, and friends, a few smiling in a group of serious people. Life was serious, to be gotten on with. His kiss was light, a brush against her lips. They separated quickly. The tips of his ears were red.

No liquor was consumed at this German Protestant wedding, but the men gathered in the barn for a nip. The men got Louis outside and offered him a taste, but he waved them off.

That night, Blanche lay in the bed, the glow of the moon on the snow shining into the bedroom, the room where she was born. The walls had watched her take her first breath. Blanche lay with her eyes open beside her husband, Louis, who slumbered, seemingly without thought or trouble, beside her on the featherbed. She had shared this bed many times with her sisters and cousins but never with a man. This was her first night as a wife, and her body refused the beckoning tug of sleep. It seemed foreign to her. It was not her body—it was her husband's.

The husband must appeal to his wife's affection for him, desire to please him and make him happy. She will appreciate his tenderness, words of love, promises about their life together. He will begin with kisses, tell her how beautiful she is. She will bear the fruit of his loins; he must help her to want to merge into his soul. It's good in God's eyes that they become husband and wife. He must be prepared for her feelings of fear, or even tears. The husband is not to be concerned about such expressions, as it is normal for a woman to express many different feelings.

Blanche found herself desiring his touch. She watched the light movement of the pulse in his neck, fluttering like a moth against light. She touched it with her lips.

A mystery. Blanche now understood why marriage was sacred. She had been innocent, and now she was awakened, with no words for this change from girl to woman. Then sunrise, the magic of a new moon, Venus tipping it like a jewel.

February 1894

From two, one is formed in the silence of the dark depths, the whoosh and flush of blood, the snap of bone. The flare and crackle of life's fire forms cells into layers, skin, nerves, fingertips that will draw and point, lips that will sing in the new century.

The round full moon rises over the snow, a white world. The temperature plummets to zero. The wind blows drifts against the stubble of crops, peach trees in winter repose.

Blanche's body throbs with an invisible force. She has no idea what fate will bring next.

March 3, 1894

Louis breathed no more, dead of twenty-four-hour pneumonia. Blanche had little warning, only his deep cough on a few icy mornings, the kind of cough that brings concern, but no one expected this. The doctor said to keep him warm; heated bricks were slipped into the featherbed. He sweated, he breathed hard. In the night, silence overtook him.

Blanche stood rigid, her lips sealed against her cries in the Letts Cemetery, the black earth slashed open in white snow. The minister droned on, Bernard, Louis's father, vacant-eyed across from her, there to bury the last person left in his family.

It was too soon to know for sure, too soon to trust in life. Blanche held her suspicions in her heart, as if she could stave off the loneliness of bearing a baby without her husband. She looked down, unwilling to see the pitying eyes of her neighbors, the sidelong glance of her mother. She drew her shoulders up and clenched her jaw against the bitterness.

Newspaper clipping:

The funeral of Lewis Garrett, youngest son of B.H. Garrett, occurred at the M.E. church at 11 A.M. Monday. The remains were interred in Lettsville cemetery. The deceased was about 22 years of age and had been married since Jan. 1. A large gathering of relatives and friends was in attendance at the funeral.

Louis and Blanche's baby was born Lulu Frances Garrett. Blanche was twenty-one years old. What were those months like for her between Louis's burial, in March, and November, when her daughter was born? Did she wish for a son to carry on Louis's name and lineage? Did her sorrow enter into the blood and bone of her daughter? How did the loss betray itself in her cells? And what about the name Lulu? Girls were named Lulu in those days, but did Blanche find a name to remind her of him? On November 7, 1894, Lulu was born in the bed where her own mother was born, in the bed where her father died.

There is a sepia photograph of Blanche and Lulu when Lulu was eight months old, from 1895. Blanche was usually serious in photographs, but in this one, a hint of a smile plays across her youthful face. Lulu wears a white dress and leans against her mother, Blanche's long fingers delicately holding the tip of one of Lulu's little fingers. You can see her soulful brown eyes staring straight at the camera. A mother and a fatherless child, five years left in the nineteenth century.

Blanche and Lulu-1895

The next photograph of the child called Lulu: She leans against her mother, Blanche, who has a grim jaw and hair in a tight knot of hair atop her head. Fierce eyes gaze out at the camera, as if she uses her entire will to look forward, as if the world will work only if she urges it into being. Is she aware they are posing in the style of the Renaissance painter, a Madonna and child? Blanche and Josephine are the mothers now in this lineage. A lily in a vase frames one side of the picture.

In the child's eyes you can imagine the shape of the past and the future. Her lips are full and ripe, sentences waiting to tumble out. In her face you can see Louis—his face, big eyes, a dreamy look.

A resolute light shines from Lulu's gaze now. She feels her father, and sometimes she sees him, but no one knows this and she does not yet have words to tell them—the grown-ups wouldn't want to know such things. They would tell her she was imagining things, or lying. And children are to be seen and not heard. The horsewhip rests in the barn, and all the children know of it. They keep their silence.

part two

This is the use of memory.
For liberation—not less of love but expanding
Of love beyond desire, and so liberation
From the future as well as the past.

—T. S. Eliot, *Four Quartets*

CHAPTER 14

From Lulu to Frances

$\mathcal{I}$ tried to discover the missing pieces of Lulu's life between
1920—when she's listed in the US census with her daugh-
ter, my mother, living on their own in a boardinghouse—and
the late 1940s, when her history began to link up with my life.
And then there were the stories she'd told me about traveling to
Europe. I wanted to know more about those trips, but I had no
idea how many times, or exactly where, she went. In terms of
the details of her life, I remember her making vague references
to having worked at a glove factory and having been a secretary,
but when? How old was she? I wanted to know things that, of
course, "facts" could never tell me: How did she feel, and what
did she do in her single life before she married her second husband? I didn't know when or where she found him, Mr. Hurlbut,
who was from New York. I didn't even know the date of their
wedding or when he was born or died.

My biggest questions had to do with when Lulu left my mother and where she went afterward. These missing pieces bugged me. I refused to believe that their hate and fights and anger were all that existed between them. There must have been times when they were close, perhaps when Mother was young, when they had coffee and talked about fashion and acted like normal people. I believed that once, before they had been wounded or lost, they had loved, or wanted to love, or had dreams of a beautiful life. I can see it in their eyes in the old photographs, the glimmer of future waiting for them.

For over thirty years, I have researched my grandmother's and mother's lives, and finally I have been able to put together their stories. To tell these stories, I view them through my own eyes and imagination and recount some of the most significant moments of my research. I have found myself standing in their shoes, looking through their eyes, speaking for them as best I can, and traveling with them in my imagination, to burrow into their psyches. My background in psychology naturally led to questions: Who were they in their hearts? Who were they before they became the bitter and frantic women who were so often upset and angry? Who were they when they were young? What were their hopes, what did they want out of life, and how much of a chance did they have to find it?

I began my research with Gram. It took years of therapy for me no longer to be terrified that I was in danger of "being" her as I get older. Being raised by an angry, bitter, older person left its imprint on me, but I knew even then that she had to be more than just that lost person. That once she had been unmarked, or nearly so, by life, like all babies and young children are. I remembered the way she'd spin the stories of her travels and her life in Chicago. She'd sit up straight, and her dark eyes would flash with the pleasure of her memories. She would transport me on a magic carpet to her past. It is that person I hold now in my heart, the woman I knew as my grandmother, who started out as simply Lulu.

The photographs of Lulu when she was young are the ones that stop my heart. She looks like Princess Leia, her light brown hair parted in the middle, smoothed into sleek folds, and worked into coils on the sides of her head. In one photograph, she appears to be a teenager. She's holding a baby, one of her half siblings—perhaps it's Edith. Her long, beautiful fingers help the baby stay upright as her soulful eyes look directly into the camera. She wears the kind of dress typical of someone in the early part of the twentieth century—white, with a tall collar around her neck—and there's a big bow on the back of her head. I feel a little weak in the knees when I see her innocent and young and smooth-faced, her lips in a delicate half-smile.

When you put her picture next to Louis's, you can see his beauty in her, his gift to all of us. Lulu's beauty in early photographs always makes me feel tender toward her, for they seem to expose her original self, who she was before she was hurt or disappointed or so lost. Maybe she was lost even then—I'll never know—but she was already more gracious and lovely-looking than her siblings. I'm sure they noticed how fair she was, how different she was from the rest of them.

Photographs tell the story of how she shaped her identity, how she went from Lulu—a farm girl living with Blanche outside of town, a girl who worked on a farm and babysat her younger siblings, as every girl was expected to do—to Frances, the sophisticated city woman and world traveler. She became the person she wanted to be, someone who others might admire and look up to. But I have to wonder—what did she lose?

Another photograph when she's a young woman, perhaps in her early twenties, shows her wearing a fancy dress, lounging like a movie star—before there were movie stars as we know them now. There is no date on the photo, and I inherited it after my mother died. In this photograph, Lulu is wearing a decidedly more sophisticated dress of silk and lace—I wonder if the photo was taken near the time she married Blaine. And that, of course, was its own dramatic story: her elopement, which led to what's embedded in our family history and talked about in whispers sixty years later: the sense that she was unacceptable still, an outsider.

Lulu, young

But, as we all do, she lived her life forward, from one thing to the next, until many years later, in a photograph of her in her seventies, you see a broken and lost old woman with only a few teeth and straggly gray hair, looking weak and fragile, in a sorrowful state that would lead to her death at seventy-five. She spent so many years threatening to die, saying it would be my fault because I didn't mind her or that I'd left her (to live my life), but what did she really feel about her own life at that point? What sense did she make of her past? What did she remember? What and whom had she loved, and when?

The photographs of Lulu in her early teen years with her brothers and sisters make it clear that they were all together some of the time on Blanche's farm, but I know that Lulu wanted more than what the usual rural education would offer. Most girls went to school only until the eighth grade, if that far, and boys often stopped in grade four or five so they could work the land. Gram would say, "*People won't respect you if you don't speak correctly. The more educated you are, the more you'll be accepted anywhere. Don't sound ignorant—if you do, people will have nothing to do with you.*"

Manners were important to her, too. She flipped out once when Aunt Helen licked her knife, afraid that I would imitate her rough country ways. At eight years old, I already knew how to manage silverware so I would not appear ignorant or low-class.

The "right" clothes meant that you would be accepted into the proper circles. She took care that I had a "classic" look and, according to the rules of the 1950s, that nothing jiggled or moved, not that I had much to jiggle—mostly I was all knobs and elbows. At all times I was to look ladylike and not "cheap." The rules in her day were that a woman should never be seen out of the house without makeup, after makeup became acceptable, and without the proper clothes for the time of day and occasion. She had a strong belief that you should never, ever wear pants in public, though they were popular in the '30s. The first time I wore pants in public, I was married, a mother, and twenty-five years old. It was 1969, and everyone was wearing wild stuff, but not I. My pants were not wild yet, but soon they would be, with paisley patterns and bell bottoms and colorful sashes. I was eager to taste the freedom of the times, to throw off the strict rules that Gram had ruled me with for years. But I had to break out of her strict teachings first.

It didn't occur to me then—and wouldn't for many years— that she might have won her place in the world by fighting for it, by breaking boundaries and rules. When I learned about how life was for women on the farm through Blanche's stories and through visiting my Iowa family through the years, I noticed the unspoken "rules": Women were to wear housedresses and aprons every day, unless company came. Dressing up required a special reason, and women who got "gussied up" too much were viewed as too fancy and full of themselves. They were not to be trusted and didn't "know their place." They wanted too much and were greedy and flirtatious. They were "bad."

That was the world Lulu rebelled against, the world she left behind, and in so doing, she had to pay some price for that. As I learned more about the times, the '20s and '30s that were her heyday, and about the role of women in the patriarchal world of the small towns and farms everyone she knew was from, I saw what she'd been up against. I began to understand how much her origins and her separation from the Iowa farm world had shaped her and cast her fate in the direction of the outsider. Her family secretly made fun of her for being different. If she was an outsider, so was my mother and so was I. Years later, I would feel the sting of this heritage, and ultimately it would break me away from people I thought of as family.

I don't know exactly what happened, but I believe that Lulu decided, or persuaded someone to allow her, to go to high school in town for the love of learning she might have had even then, but I imagine it also had to do with getting away from farm life—something she would share with me later. "I saw all those farm women, old and tired before their time, and I wanted something different."

To attend high school, she had to live with her grandmother Josephine, Blanche's mother, who lived in town with her husband, John Peter, and their two youngest children, Abner and Nina. There was a fluidity between the farm and the town. Blanche and her parents, aunts and uncles and cousins, all of whom lived either on a farm or in town, gathered for lunch or tea frequently. Living in town, Lulu would have seen along the bluffs by the Mississippi River, a middle-class or upper-middle-class set of people living in their stately Victorian houses with large gardens and maids and store-bought clothes, a cut above the ordinary people who lived on the flats, or the farmers, the lowest working class, though they were respected for their hard work.

When Lulu went to town, she would have seen the mothers and daughters who lived in those fancy houses in the shops in town, when they weren't ordering their clothes from upscale shops in Chicago. She would have noticed how they dressed and spoke. They owned pianos and violins, and graceful velvet and lace curtains would hang in their windows. They enjoyed fine dining and food, and would eat with genuine silverware from delicate china dishes.

Lulu imagined herself in that life but didn't know how to reach it. Her heart ached every time she thought about those people and their lovely things, a life she was not living and could not possibly attain by wishing for it. The contrast between what she dreamed and what was supposed to be her fate was especially obvious when Lulu visited her mother, Blanche, on the farm. She hated the stink of it, the diapers and muck and endless chores. Blanche had to give her a whack alongside the head to get her to stop dreaming when she sat still, gazing at the sky, forgetting her chores. As Blanche's daughter, she still had to contribute to the household chores, but no one could control her mind. She'd shuck corn and dream, iron clothes and dream. And when the chores were done, she'd escape to the books she loved to erase the ugliness, embracing other worlds as if they were real. Sometimes they were more real to her, these dreams, than the grit and mud. She would create stories in her mind from the stories that fed her imagination.

There were times when the energy of the sun and a summer day, perhaps a Sunday when there was a lull in the work, ignited a soaring energy that seared through her body. She could hardly contain the excitement. She shook her arms and hugged herself; she ran in dizzying circles in the barn, where no one would see her. On an August day, the cicadas thrumming, the sound of the mourning dove, or the call of a distant train made her mind leap with colors of ecstasy that flashed in her mind, moments that made her feel deliciously alive. She snuck out to the fields and rushed between fat leaves of corn that slapped her arms and legs and face, laughing for the pure joy of it. Afterward, she covered up the red welts where the sharp leaves hit her, thankful that her mother was too busy with the children to notice. Blanche, the practical earth-woman, did not understand this dreamer girl who did silly things, who seemed to live in another world.

I know that Lulu was a dreamer girl. That girl was still alive in my grandmother even in the later years. She'd come alive, sparkly and amused, when she'd tell me about believing there had to be more than the small, ugly world she'd been born into, about how she'd run through the corn, free.

I don't know how she met Blaine, but I imagine it this way: He was a well-known jazz musician in the area, and his band played in the hotel in town, a fine hotel that looked upon the Great River. Lulu was sixteen or seventeen then, going to high school and learning about history and language and numbers. She sat in classrooms with the girls who lived in the fine houses on the bluff. She watched them, learning how they spoke, imitating their gestures. She convinced her grandmother Josephine to copy some dress patterns and sew her up some dresses that looked like theirs. Blanche would come to town and ask her to come back to the farm and help with the children, but Lulu resisted as often as she could. It became even clearer to her that the farm life was not for her.

But what kind of life was available to a young woman who had been born in the Victorian era and lived in America in 1911? It was understood that even if you could escape the farm, your goal still had to be marriage and children. Single women, unless widowed, did not live on their own. A man would take proper care of you. He would set you toward the goal of children and keeping a proper house. If you were lucky, perhaps you could find a man who was not a farmer, but nearly all the men were, and your fate would be decided by your social status and education.

Blaine was the son of a newspaperman, R. G. Hawkins,

whose own father, Jasper, was an attorney and had served in the legislature in Des Moines. The family was of the professional class and was well known in the Wapello and Burlington area. Jasper's brothers were all teachers, so education was taken for granted in the family—for the men. Young Blaine already had the credentials that would lift Lulu from working-class to middle-class, but she would find out that kind of leap exacts its penalty.

Apparently, Lulu and Blaine were in love, though there's no way to know exactly what happened between them when they were seventeen years old. What we do know is that both families were angry that they broke the rules when they eloped—it was in the newspaper article and in Blanche's accusation all those years later. Lulu lied to her family, borrowed a dress from a friend, and snuck away with Blaine, who made up his own story. Some families might have been glad to see their daughter "marry up," but in Lulu's family, people who advanced to another station or class were "uppity" and thus open to judgment about having designs above their station in life. The term serves to cover any jealousy or envy they might have had.

Lulu and Blaine married without permission—she was not of age—and when the family found out the details, none of them was pleased. I assume the newlyweds were out of reach of punishment, though they could not have entirely escaped the ire of their parents and the taint of scandal. Perhaps that is what I whiffed in the air when I first met Blaine, when I was eight years old. Those intense and rebellious events of so long ago were etched on their psyches—you can't escape the history that lives in your body and soul. Lulu and Blaine had shared time together as young people that no one else knows about, but years later Blaine's daughter Jean told me that she'd heard from her mother, Bernie, Blaine's second wife, that Lulu used to make sure that Blaine came home for lunch—an intimate lunch. Perhaps passion and even love had ignited these young people. Or perhaps Bernie was jealous of Lulu and what she and Blaine once must have had together.

When Lulu and Blaine eloped, everyone would have assumed she was pregnant, that it was a shotgun wedding. Blaine's father was known to have a big temper and didn't hesitate to show it. Lulu had risked everything. Her family might never forgive her. Forty years later, Blanche and Lulu still fought about it.

In 1911, when Lulu and Blaine married, the Edwardian age in England ended and King George V's reign began. In America, Taft was president; he succeeded Theodore Roosevelt in 1908. Woodrow Wilson would be the next president, and World War I, called the "Great War," would begin in 1914, the year Lulu had her first child at the age of twenty: a son, Harrison, stillborn on January 29.

To understand anyone, you have to breathe yourself into their body and mind; you have to turn back time and forget everything you know. You have to forget how the world is now and take yourself to what it was like then. What were the buildings like, the colors of that world? What were people wearing, and what were the details of their everyday life? What kind of imagination could someone who lived at that time have had? What was possible for them, as far as they could imagine it?

Lulu could know only of a world based on what was before her eyes, her everyday life, or perhaps on what she might have read in the newspaper. Perhaps there were radios, but not everyone could afford one, or a telephone, for that matter. The endless work of the farm was how most people lived then, unless they were in a large city or were part of the small percentage of people who had a profession. Small towns had a professional and a middle class—teachers, attorneys, nurses, and doctors—but there was little for a woman to do besides stay in an expected role. Lulu did not know the world was about to change with the upcoming world war and bring about new opportunities for women, until it did. Her decision to leap away from her family and put herself in another world was either stupid or brave—and once it was done, it could not be undone. Even if she had regrets, at that time divorce was not an appealing choice. It was a desperate and extreme move for women, as thereafter they would always be seen as damaged goods and not marriageable. In 1911, perhaps because of a combination of love and desperation, Lulu made a choice to marry Blaine, and that set her on a new path, the consequences of which she could not predict, a path that, more than a century later, still bears investigation.

For years, the only knowledge I had of Harrison was Gram's story about how he died with the umbilical cord wrapped around his neck. The headstone at the Wapello cemetery is marked with his name and the date: 1914. My research in Wapello led me to the record of Harrison's birth and death, which I found in the Louisa County courthouse basement, where musty, leather-bound volumes are shelved from floor to ceiling, decorated with silvery spider webs. The stately granite building in the center of town holds facts about my mother's birth and the boy, Harrison, who would have been my uncle had he lived. It's amazing what you discover in original records. On my mother's birth certificate, there's an added inscription in Blaine's hand, a correction to her birth date, previously written as May 9, instead of June 9. The reason for Harrison's death was written out in graceful cursive: "prolonged labor." What did that mean? I had so many questions: How much did Lulu suffer? Did she sense that she might lose the baby, or was it a surprise, a terrible tragedy?

I have tried to imagine Lulu then, pregnant after three years of marriage, giving birth at home. Was their child conceived in love? What was their life like for those three years? Were they happy?

I wondered if she had a midwife or a doctor, and if her mother was with her, or were they estranged still, given the strain of the elopement? I tried to imagine my own daughter at that age, in the crisis that Lulu faced, strong but tender and vulnerable, engaged in that adventure called life, her hopes for a happy family dashed when she saw the look on the midwife's face, the baby blue and still. It must have broken her heart; she would never be the same. I could never know who that young girl of twenty was. Though people heal, and though she went on to have my mother, I remember my grandmother saying, "He is the one who should have lived." I felt the tick of the time bomb that would go off decades later. Did my mother realize she was a poor substitute for the boy who died? One time in the Wapello cemetery, she flew into a rage when I took a photograph of Harrison's grave. Was it because she was always made to feel as if she was a substitute, and a poor one at that?

I suppose the research to learn more about my family has been a search for identity, for belonging. Whom did I descend from, and what layers of history might help me to sort myself out? I carried the lost child I was within me for many years, trying to understand the lost-girl archetype that I believe my mother and my grandmother carried all the way to the end of their lives.

The sense I had that traits and feelings are borne through the generations has been validated by recent studies that show that we retain in our cells the genetic imprints of the traumas our ancestors suffered. These new theories and studies affirm what has always lived as a truth in my body: I carried my grandmother with me in my shoulders, stomach, and back. I carried my mother with me in the form of loneliness and sorrow that rose up unexpectedly. Sometimes I couldn't settle down, as if something irritated me, like an itch I couldn't scratch. I carried her rejection and whatever love she could muster. I carry the legacy with me now. I see its imprint on my children, in their moodiness, their tendency toward depression. I feel it when my body suddenly crumples in grief, when I'm caught up in the emptiness of loss for seemingly no reason, etched by endless images of darkness and worry as my nervous system tries to fend off an attack. I surprise my friends with my startle reflex at loud noises. It triggers shame that I can be this old, as old as my grandmother in the later years, and still have a body that reacts to anxiety and fear. But I'm luckier than Mother and Gram. I came of age at a time of great change, in the '60s, when opportunities for insight and healing peaked in layers of permission to create a life that could be lived with satisfaction and happiness. I was blessed with choices they did not have.

Finding objective "evidence" about Lulu's early life has freed me to stand on the platform of my family's history and look around at the landscape. Objective facts can't give you the inside experience of a person's life, but if you can find factual evidence, you're gifted with something that begins to create a real picture of how they might have lived. The records present an outline of events, a record of our steps on Earth. Woven in with those facts exists the story, the subtleties of mind and heart.

For years, I was driven to find out what happened to my mother when she was young. Blanche had said years earlier that my mother was left "when she was a baby," so I spent a long time thinking Gram had left a baby behind, but I had pictures of Mother as a baby and a toddler, and Lulu was in some of them. I wondered, though, about where my mother was living and who was taking care of her. I was driven by more than my curiosity about my mother as a girl. As a developmental psychologist, I believed that learning more about her would help me find a way to the heart of my mother and offer me insight into my own life, to understand the roots of what I was carrying in my own heart. And I might even find some peace for all of us, and pass that on to future generations.

Over the years as an adult, I would stay with Edith when I visited Iowa. We'd host a lunch or dinner that included whoever was still alive from the original Iowa family, and I'd also find a way to get to Wapello for my research about the family. I loved visiting that quiet village, where I treasured good memories of my time with Blaine and Bernie, and where Mother was born. I'd always visit the silence of the cemetery to say hi to Grandpa Blaine. Nearby were cows and fields of corn shushing in the wind, tassels waving against the blue sky. I'd plan my research, much of it in the Wapello Library. There, in the microfilm archives, I discovered that the newspaper that Blaine's father owned, the *Wapello Republican*, had a social section where you could read about the day-to-day lives of the townspeople—who came to town, what they wore, and whom they visited. For an hour or two each year, I forged my way through rolls of microfilm of the weekly paper and gleaned some answers. The evidence I found in the paper and census record answered my most burning questions and revealed the timeline of Lulu, Blaine, and Jo'tine, my mother. As if in a fairy tale, they all lived long ago in the early part of the last century. I tracked them year by year as I turned the wheel of the microfilm machine, the years whirring by in fuzzy black-and-white images, headlines from 1914, the year World War I started. I saw ads for clothes, grocery specials, and household items. The newspaper offered evidence of the reality of the everyday lives of that era, writing about people I would know fifty years later.

Mrs. Wm. Thompson is Blanche.

Mrs. Blaine Hawkins is Lulu.

J.B. Hawkins is Blaine

Mrs. J. P. Stineman is Lulu's grandmother, Josephine, Blanche's mother.

From the Wapello Republican *newspaper*
1914
Mrs. J.P Stineman of Muscatine, and Mrs. Blanche Thompson of Muscatine Island, came to this city last Thursday,

called here by the death of the infant son of Mr. and Mrs.
J.B. Hawkins and the illness of the wife mother.
(The baby Harrison was born and died on Thursday,
January, 29.)

1915

Mrs. Wm. Thompson (Blanche) and two children visit with
her daughter Mrs. Blaine Hawkins. Blanche and two children visit Lulu three months before her new baby is due.

June 10, 1915

The editor of the Republican *is feeling quite important*
today, having attainted the title of grandfather, by rea-
son of the birth of a daughter to Mr. and Mrs. J. Blaine
Hawkins last evening, June 9. Mother and child are doing
nicely. The announcement of Josephine's birth is made
by the editor of the paper, Blaine's father.

June 10, 1915

Mrs. J. P. Stineman of Muscatine came Monday to visit
at the home of her granddaughter Mrs. Blaine Hawkins.
Lulu's grandmother Josephine visited Lulu and her
newly born great-grandchild, who was named after her.

March 1916

Blanche Thompson and two children, Celia and Peter Reu-
ben, visited from Thursday to Saturday her daughter Mrs.
J. B. Hawkins.

May 1916

Note in paper: *The title "Woman's Suffrage" will not be*
on the ballot. Instead the ballot will say "Constitutional
Amendment Ballot."

July 1916
Mrs. J. B. Hawkins (Lulu) and daughter visited relatives in Letts, Muscatine, and Clarence.

August 10, 1916
Death of Avonella Kinkead Hawkins, Blaine's mother. Later, I will trace her genealogy records all the way to the fifteenth century in England.

From September 1916 through October 1917, there are eight references to Lulu and Josephine's having visited relatives.

April 6, 1917
The United States enters the war with Germany.

June 5, 1917
Draft card: Blaine Hawkins (Lulu's husband; Jo'tine's father).
Managing editor at the Wapello Republican. *Has wife and child.* Jo'tine is two years old.

February 7, 1918
Josephine Stineman and her son Abner visit Mrs. J. B. Hawkins.

April 4, 1918
Misses Grace, Edith, and Celia Thompson of Muscatine Island visited a few days the latter part of last week with their sister, Mrs. J. B. Hawkins. These are Lulu's half-sisters, the relatives I visited in Iowa with Gram when they were all middle-aged.

June 3, 1918
Blaine Hawkins, who is working on a paper at Rock Island,

spent the weekend at home. Has Blaine already separated from Lulu, the reason for his job in Rock Island?

July 4, 1918
Interesting detail of the era: *"Let the women do the work, do the work, do the work" is now an established fact. When they demonstrate they can develop manpower, it will place them on equal footing with men in every respect.*

August 1918
Mrs. J. B. Hawkins and daughter Josephine spent Sunday in Muscatine with the former's grandmother Mrs. Stineman. Lulu and Jo'tine stay with Lulu's grandmother.

October 3, 1918
Mrs. J. B. Hawkins was taken to the university hospital at Iowa City Monday for X-ray and Tuesday taken to the St. Francis hospital in Burlington for treatment. Lulu has an appendix attack. Josephine is three years old.

December 5, 1918
Mrs. J. B. Hawkins, (Lulu) and Josephine went to Muscatine Saturday to spend the week with relatives. Jo'tine is three years old and they are still together.

February 6, 1919
Mrs. Blanche Thompson of Muscatine Island visited her daughter Mrs. J. B. Hawkins last Saturday. She was accompanied home by her little granddaughter Josephine Hawkins. Josephine, Lulu's grandmother, and her mother Blanche, pick up Jo'tine, four, and take her to Muscatine to stay with the older Josephine.

February 20, 1919
Mrs. J. B. Hawkins (Lulu) returned from Mercy hospital,
Burlington, on Monday evening, having recovered from an
operation for appendicitis.

For a while, the story I discovered ended there, leaving me
unsatisfied. Years later, on Ancestry.com, I found information
that began to answer my questions about what happened to Lulu
and my mother, information that was not available before.

January 6, 1920
US Census
Lula Hawkins, divorced, lodger, stenographer, age thirty-one.
Josephine, age six and a half, lodger.
They live in a boardinghouse in Burlington, Iowa, ten
miles from Wapello. Lulu is working as a stenogra-
pher. Jo'tine is actually four and a half years old.

The next clue is about Blaine's marriage and his new daughter, Jean.

February 19, 1921
Blaine Hawkins marries Bernice Williams.
Lulu's ex-husband, Blaine, marries wife number two.
I know her as Grandma Bernie.

November 11, 1921
Blaine's new daughter, Jean, Josephine's half-sister, is
born. Later, there will be raging battles between these
two half-sisters, and a total cutoff that lasts until my
mother's death.

1922
Des Moines, Iowa, City Directory
Lulu Hawkins
Works in the traffic department of Bell Telephone.
Lives in the YWCA, Des Moines.

I'd always believed that Lulu had gone to Chicago immediately after leaving my mother behind, but I see that she worked first in Des Moines. She had told me about working for the telephone company, but I didn't know where or when. In 1922, she was still Lulu Hawkins. Soon she would make the leap to Chicago, where she would become Frances and create another chapter of the story.

I think it's useful to consider the context in which Lulu recreated herself. It was the 1920s, which some called the "first wave" of feminism and women's rights—women having gained the vote in 1920, after decades of fighting for it. When I was growing up with my grandmother, she was not political and would not have appreciated the word "feminism," but it's interesting to me that, however she might have considered her break from the "normal" reality of the farm girl's life she was supposed to live, she did rebel against the expectations of her family and her culture. First, she eloped with Blaine. I believe she saw herself as a cut above the rest of her family. She wanted more, she wanted to *be* more, than the roles offered to women.

The next act of rebellion and self-definition was that she left her daughter behind when she went to Des Moines. To be fair, mothers did leave their children with grandparents to go to work if they were single, and who knows if and when she intended to raise her daughter again. She did retrieve Josephine was she was thirteen, when Lulu married her second husband, Mr. Hurlbut, but by then the years Josephine and her mother had lost set up a pattern of disengagement and resentment that I observed as I grew up. It was never resolved, all the way to Gram's death.

As I searched for them in the newspaper microfilm, when the family names appeared, I felt a visceral thrill like electricity go through my body. Finding them affirmed my identity—I'd always carried the taint of being a semi-orphan. The reality of their lives before I was born affirmed our family history as real— there it was, in black and white. There once had been a family that had welcomed into their lives the little girl who became my mother, and Lulu, Blaine, and Josephine had once been together. When you grow up in the ashes of a world that no longer exists, it seems impossible to imagine another kind of life, but finding them in my great-grandfather's newspaper gave me what I never had before: an objective record of the place and people I'm from, and a feeling of being finally connected. When you know the truth of the past that has been lost in the fog of time and memory and find truths that no one else has claimed, you become more solid and real. You are who you are, and there's no shame. History affirms you and lifts you up.

As I traveled through time those afternoons in the Wapello library, I remembered the gentle embrace of my grandfather and Bernie, the soft, lazy summer days when I was a child. Even then, I could feel my family as invisible ghosts hovering on the dirt streets. I didn't know that the apartment where Lulu and Blaine lived was on the main street, across from the newspaper office, and that my mother and her brother had been born there. When I left the library, my head spinning, I realized that the names on gravestones marked not only the dead, but the living. And there in Wapello, just outside the library framed by leafy trees and the sound of cicadas, two blocks from where Blaine lived as a young man, is where I reunited with my heritage.

CHAPTER 15

Jo'tine, Her Brown-Eyed Baby

She was the baby who lived, born a summer baby in June, 1915. I don't know whether the love story of those young people, Lulu and Blaine, ages twenty-one and twenty-two, had already begun to fade by then when my mother, called Jo'tine, was born. No matter how many facts I gather, or how many photographs from that era I look at, or how many times I launch myself into the imagined past, I can't find her as a living, breathing person. She seems stuck in two dimensions, a girl who existed over one hundred years ago in photos. I can't find the real Josephine.

My mother took her first breath in Wapello, a town named for Chief Wapello, known for the Blackhawk Indian wars in the nineteenth century, Wapello's history a ghostly presence on the banks of the Iowa River, which lazily wound its way through town. The river invites your dreams as it rolls softly toward the Mississippi. Now, the remodeled funeral home is located on the riverbank. I imagine the souls who are trying to find rest looking upon the green water, with its birds and fish and bubbly chorus, and finding peace. Perhaps my mother found peace, as she was brought there after her death, traveling from Chicago, where she died, to Wapello, where she would be buried. I was lucky that the Hawkins family had one more space in the cemetery and that they were willing to allow me to bury my mother there, in the same plot with her father. I appreciated the symmetry, and that I could honor the arc of time that was the shape of my mother's life.

In the '70s, during that first therapy program, the leaders asked us to find photographs of our parents when they were young. We brought in pictures of wide-eyed, vulnerable kids. I think all of us were a little amazed by how young they looked, how innocent. We were told to write their emotional autobiography, to imagine their lives from the beginning all the way to the end, to inhabit their psyche, to get inside the skin of people we had feared or hated or clung to, made up stories about, or needed or cried over. To get past our need for them and our conditioned responses, valid though they may have been for our survival, we were to imagine them as they grew up, using what we knew as part of the story and imagining the rest.

I did the exercise for my grandmother, but it proved more difficult for my mother—she was still alive and had a silencing power over me, and she still scared me with her anger. I was still stinging from her rejection of me when I was twenty, twelve years earlier, when she made it clear I shouldn't call her Mother. She would yell and scream or hit me if I didn't agree with her, but there were times when she could be soft and affectionate. Her letters were always signed, "Love, Mother." She was immensely powerful in my psyche, the person I most feared and at the same time the person I most wanted to love me. It's more accurate to say I wanted her to look into my eyes and say, "You're a wonderful person and I made a mistake. I love you and I want everyone to know you."

To imagine her as a girl, I closed my eyes and imagined the "brown-eyed baby" Gram cried about, the young girl who'd lived in Wapello, who'd lived somewhere—I didn't know where or with whom—during her childhood. In the old photographs, there she is, a small baby in her father's arms, a little girl in a frothy white dress, holding her grandfather's hand. She's skipping, holding his hand, almost smiling. There's another image of her, a year or so later (she was around four), in a formal portrait, her chestnut pageboy hairstyle framing her lovely but serious face. She was beautiful even then, her deep, dark eyes staring solemnly into the camera. I imagined myself with her then, wanting to know how she felt, wanting to comfort her in advance for what her life would bring. She had no idea her mother would leave; she didn't know what fates would befall her or the trajectory of her life. No one can, of course, but I have to wonder, if she had been treated differently, if she'd had more of a chance at a "normal" life, would she have been so wounded and angry? How much of what was to come was the result of what happened to her, and how much was chemistry, depression, or other mental and emotional problems? We know more now about how a mother's trauma affects a child in the womb—Lulu, her mother, had lost her first baby eighteen months before my mother was born. There is good evidence that Lulu's relationship with Blaine was volatile. Every time I looked at Mother's photos of her as a little girl, I'd touch the outline of her face, wishing I could hold that child in my arms.

I know my grandmother felt tenderness for Josephine. I saw it throughout my childhood, in moments when I would watch Gram break down and cry about her daughter. At the end of her lament, she'd say, "My brown-eyed baby." She would get angry and/or cry about her daughter's wild moods, her inability to manage money, her demands for more money. I sensed other things about their history, but I would never know exactly what happened between them. I imagine that when Josephine was born, Lulu was grateful for the new baby, though in her era boys were preferred. A boy would have had a higher status and would have carried the family name.

I wonder how her early years shaped my mother. I imagine Lulu and Jo'tine together at the beginning. It's summer, when Jo'tine is just a few weeks old. The green-leafed trees whisper softly in the July breeze. The trees and birds and voices in her head tell Lulu to be careful with this new child—everything could end in a second—but the steady, wise gaze of the baby's dark eyes soothes her.

Josephine Elizabeth is named after Josephine, Blanche's mother, and Blaine's mother, Elizabeth. Through the lace curtains, Lulu can see the summer blue of the sky and patches of white clouds as they move across the window frame. She looks closely into her daughter's eyes, noticing a white, round bump on her dark brown iris. The doctor will later reassure her it's simply a birthmark. Lulu examines each pink toe, the creases behind her daughter's knees, the umbilical cord. The baby nuzzles and stretches, relaxing into her arms. The first person she smiles for is her father, Blaine.

Lulu feels lucky for the ordinary days as she washes her daughter's soft body, her belly, the folds of her neck. As the baby vigorously sucks Lulu's breast, her uterus aches, her body returning to what it was before, though she will never be the same. She's a mother who's borne a live child. Everywhere they go, people admire this beautiful little girl.

Blaine comes home from his work at the paper to cradle the baby in his big hands. He whispers how pretty she is, how lovely. Lulu marvels at her delicacy, how loud noises make her startle, her strength as she learns about her body and the world. When the child's fingers tug Lulu's hair, tingles rush through her. She feels the invisible threads connecting herself, her child, and her husband. In those moments, relief pours through her like rain on a hot day. She's not alone—she and Blaine are married. Surely one day he will slow down the drink, but she thinks he's away too often, more interested in the newspaper and the tavern than he is in his family. His mother suffers to have them over twice a month for Sunday dinner. Now that Lulu has produced a living child, she's proven herself useful. Maybe they'll finally accept her, but still they have that look in their eye—disapproval, disdain. She's had to learn about manners and dinner rules, but sometimes she forgets which fork to use. When she returns home and sees her brothers lick their knife, she flushes, knowing now how educated, refined people behave.

Another sepia photograph shows a spring with leafy trees and a picnic. Lulu stands beside one of those wicker carriages you see in old pictures. The dark-haired baby lifts her head up toward the person clicking the shutter—perhaps it's her father. The snap of the camera echoes in the crisp afternoon. Lulu wears a kerchief around her head and looks down, as if she's lost in thought. She seems to have found herself outside the regular web of the world, as if she were looking into a window where other women are engaged in normal things, like cooking, ironing, washing, cleaning—things that bore her to death. I wonder if she was trying to escape the domesticity that bored her, or would that come later, as the marriage broke apart?

In another picture, there's Blaine, a slim-faced young man with a strong jaw who wears a workingman's cap. He cradles his daughter. I wonder what kind of life he's having as a new father, but who can penetrate the mysteries of photographs? Their images solidified in the silver process of the film are the only testimony that this was once a family. I wonder how Lulu and Blaine felt having this baby after the loss of their son. Did they talk about him? Did they visit his grave?

There are no photos of the family after Jo'tine is past babyhood. The summer day carries the sound of chirping birds, the lonely whistle of the train at the Wapello train station.

Lying in the carriage during the blessing of her babyhood, Jo'tine lifts her head, capped with hair the color of chestnuts. Her eyes are turned up at the edges, her cheeks are fat, and white teeth glitter in her mouth. She lifts herself onto her forearms and smiles.

Later in Jo'tine's life, the years with her mother will fade. She will tell no stories of her idyllic country beginnings. When I ask her about her childhood, she won't remember, or perhaps she had no language to talk about it.

But I could imagine her looking for her mother when she was a little girl. She would wait by the gate at the edge of her grandmother's yard to see if she might have a visitor—she would have been about seven or eight. She'd gaze down the walkway to see if her mother was coming up from the train station. Steel-gray clouds hovered over the brown earth; rumbling clouds flickered with lightning. When her mother visited, the little girl watched her—she seemed like a dream—wearing perfume, lovely clothes, and too soon, would disappear back into dream.

When Jo'tine was three or four, her hair was cut short and bouncy, tickling the inside of her ears. Her dress had a ruffle at the hem, her legs in cotton hose, three-button shoes. During summer nights, she waited on the porch step at her great-grandmother Josephine's house, listening to the cicadas throb, the low murmur of adult gossip inside the house. She waited for life to be more interesting, waited for her father to visit, but most nights he did not come. He lived in Wapello with his new wife and their little girl, Jean. He was a quick figure who weaved in and out of her dreams.

For the most part, the older people she lived with were kind: a caress on her cheek, someone crooning a song to her on a night she woke up screaming. But there were sharp words that criticized her, sharp voices that hurt her, and then there were the hands that sometimes made their way under her dress. She tried to be brave, but it was hard to smile, even when people put cameras in front of her. The photos from years later show a shy girl, her face held still and neutral, her big brown eyes solemn. I can't tell what she might be thinking. I wonder what secrets she held even then.

Josephine on the left, 1926, at her grandmother's house

"There's your mama," Blanche told her one day when she was in town from the farm, showing her a photograph of a beautiful woman in a fancy coat and stylish hat. She remembered her mother, but she could not imagine what she could have done wrong to have been left behind.

Photographs tell a fragmented story about my mother's life. Some came to me from family members in Iowa when they found out I was trying to piece together our history. I was lucky that Josephine Dickerson, Blanche's mother, had many siblings and cousins. As the twentieth century progressed, some of us in later generations managed to connect over our interest in genealogy.

We shared our finds, and the Internet gave clues to the answers we didn't have. Someone gave me a photo of the farmhouse that faced the river where Lulu was born—the house I'd seen as a child with Blanche and Gram, the house that got them to whispering as they imagined a past that was long gone. I learned that Blanche's mother took in children of one relative or another at different times; in one photo, Jo'tine is about nine and playing on a scooter with one of her cousins.

My favorite photograph shows my mother, around age seven, in a crowd of family members that includes Blanche, wearing an apron, and her sister Dell and her daughters, standing by a black Ford, with Josephine's aunts and Blanche's chickens in the picture. They are all wearing their Sunday clothes—perhaps they stopped by Blanche's farm after church, or took a joyride in the new car. This must have been in the early '20s, given how small Jo'tine was. Her dark hair is blowing in the wind, her face innocent and sweet as she gazes at all the commotion around her.

Jo'tine eventually lived near Des Moines with Blaine's sister June and her husband—I don't know when or why this happened, but my mother wrote me once: "I loved living with them. They were young and more fun than those older, boring people. June and her husband surprised me once by bringing me a puppy!"

She must have been a bit older by then, around ten or eleven, according to another photograph. In this one, she's standing by some trees, stark, dark shapes in winter. Snow is on the ground, and she's holding a striped tabby cat. Her face is solemn, and she still has the straight, dark hair of her earlier pictures. That photograph, which I later lost, so entranced me that I did a painting of it, moody with swirling winds and blue and brown colors to suggest the darkness in her expression. At that time, she would have been without her mother for several years. I don't know how often Frances, as Lulu would have been known by then, visited. Was it once a year, like my mother visited me?

I finally found a listing on Ancestry.com for Josephine, age fifteen in April 1930, when she was listed as living with her mother, Lulu-Frances, in a boardinghouse in Chicago. The next listing, in July, shows that Frances had married her second husband, Burt Hurlbut, and they were all living in an apartment on Hermitage Avenue on the North Side of Chicago, not far from Lincoln Park.

I know little about these years, other than that my mother took piano lessons. She told me she hated them, but she was skilled enough to play *Liebestraum,* an advanced-level étude by Franz Liszt, for me years later, when I was a child in the 1950s. Every time she visited, I begged her to play it. I'd sit next to her, breathing in her scent, feeling the warmth of her body as her fingers flowed over the keys, happy that she was playing a "Song of Love" for me.

Even after all my research, I've been able to put together only a few puzzle pieces about my mother's life. Besides the "facts" in the Ancestry.com records about her, my knowledge about my mother is based on a few memories I have of her in Iowa with her father when I was young, and on conversations with relatives over the years. In the years when I spent time with Bernie and Blaine, my mother sometimes visited at the same time. There were some treasured moments there—we'd sleep together in a bed in my favorite room, the front bedroom, where the sun spilled through the gauzy white curtains and the open windows inhaled green grass and flowers. If there is an ideal image of summertime happiness I hold dear, that's it. The air smelled sweet, and the aroma of my mother surrounded me: her musky body smell, her makeup, the throaty murmur of her soft voice as we scratched each other's backs at night. When we'd go to sleep, I would curl up against her body in bliss, breathing her in, wanting it to last forever, holding her gently close, like a fragile flower.

Those ideal moments were short-lived, however, and being in Blaine's house was another place where I witnessed parental struggles. She was angry at her father—I don't know why, but the tone was familiar, rising up and down the scale in levels of upset as she paced and smoked, storm clouds above her head. His tone would harmonize with hers as he argued back and forth with her, keeping pace. Bernie would wring her hands, her brows furrowed, her smile forced. She'd take me aside and we'd do a project, like make doll clothes or pick flowers in the garden, the voices of my mother and Blaine haranguing in the background. I could see it was hard for Bernie to listen to them argue.

One Sunday, we all went to church together to hear Blaine offer his testimony about being saved. He and Mother had already had a fight that morning, arguing back and forth, room to room—it was a small house, and their voices ping-ponged in familiar, irritating cadences. Finally, all dressed up for church, we got into the hot car, where we immediately started sweating. Everyone was miserable, faces tense, the car full of unsaid words that just about choked us all. I just wanted everyone to be happy and stop fighting.

I took my mother's hand to try to comfort her, but she grabbed it back and folded her hands together in her lap. I watched tall cornfields swirl by far above my head, as if the car were traveling through a green tunnel. When we arrived at the church, everyone greeted Blaine and his family. Since his other daughter lived in Wapello, I'm not sure they understood who Mother and I were, or maybe the stories had preceded us—the daughter and granddaughter of that first wife, Lulu.

That day, I was happy to sit beside my mother in the small church. The aroma of polished wooden pews and Grandpa's gravelly voice declaiming Bible verses mesmerized me with a memory I would never forget. I snuggled next to my mother, who was gazing at her father with a wistful, soft look. In this quiet moment, they had become entirely different people than

Josephine, my mother, at Grandpa's

they had been an hour earlier, when they argued. Mother even sang a hymn then sat down quietly. The expression on her face seemed sad, or maybe she was moved by what her father said in his testimony. I couldn't understand why they yelled so much and why they couldn't just love each other.

My curiosity about what had happened with my mother to make her so angry at both her parents would later fuel my drive to try to parse each element of the story, the parts I remembered and everything I could find that offered a clue to the mysteries of the past. Even now, I know that I don't have the whole story. I can only imagine that Jo'tine missed her mother and father, and that she got lost in the breakdown of the family. Perhaps she wanted the past to be different than it was. Maybe she simply wanted an apology, an acknowledgment that things had not gone well for her when she was young. That she had been abandoned by both of them.

I do know that things did not end well for my mother and the two people who brought her into the world. The last time my mother saw her father alive was when I was twelve years old. By then, Bernie and Blaine had moved to a suburb in Davenport. When I visited, my girl cousin and I had plenty of smooth concrete where we could ride bikes. We played endlessly in the backyard, which was next to a cornfield. I loved the smell and sound of that field and would stop playing just to look at the shape of the fat green leaves, or listen to how the pretty golden tassels rustled in the wind. That year, Gram and I had made our yearly trip to Iowa, and the plan was that I'd meet my mother at her father's house. My stomach clenched as it always did when I prepared to encounter warlike conditions, and, as usual, my fears were confirmed.

The ranting between Josephine and her father went on for hours that weekend, Blaine red-faced and enraged, Mother desperate and shrieking. I don't know what it was about, but it seemed to be one of those "summit" battles, where important things were at stake. Later in the afternoon, after the heat of summer descended upon the house, after hours of fighting, Mother rested in the bedroom we shared, the heat making us limp and exhausted. We all felt raw from the conflict. I was scared to see that people who were so closely related could yell and wail and not be able to let it go or forgive or stop the crazy back-and-forth. I still believed that something else was possible, that things shouldn't be this way between a child and a father. Because I had been trained in the war trenches with Mother, Gram, Blaine, and my father, my true nature was to be an inveterate peacemaker.

I slid into bed beside Mother for a few minutes as she rested, wanting to comfort her. She'd been crying. I forget what she said to me, but I tried to soothe her, encouraging some kind of truce. That evening, Bernie begged them to forgive each other. She said,

"The Bible says that we should not let the sun set on our troubles. You two need to forgive each other." But there is a smudge of movie footage in my head of my mother's quick and anguished departure the next day. It left me ragged with feelings I couldn't name, my whole body aching as if I had been the one fighting.

They never forgave each other. They resolved nothing. The next time I saw my mother with her father was a year later. She was pressing a red rose into his dead hand, wiping her tears, as he lay in his casket. I secretly made a pact with myself that day: that I would never let that happen to me, that sad end to life. That I would try to find a way to forgive. Or at least to understand.

I was grateful that I had known Blaine and his "other family." Some of my fondest memories of the Iowa summers of my childhood are of playing with Jean's daughter in Wapello on lazy days. Jean was my mother's sister, and I had no siblings, so I observed her closely, trying to understand these sisters. Was Jean like my mother, or was she different because she had a different mother? They both had a temper, and either or both of them would fling themselves noisily out of the house after a big blowup. But we had fun times there. Jean's daughter and I were almost the same age. We played dress-up, made doll clothes with Bernie's help, and sold lemonade by the road. On hot, sticky days, we cooled off with a hose in a tin tub, squealing with joy. Blaine and Bernie believed, even said out loud, that I acted too grown-up for a child and encouraged me to be carefree and to play. I heard them whispering that I shouldn't have to worry so much about practicing my cello, that I needed to have more childlike fun.

After that last, epic fight before my grandfather died, I didn't hear from that side of the family again. Decades went by, leaving me wondering if I had done something wrong to offend them, but I suspected my mother's crazy behavior had tainted me. After all, if your mother is nuts, what does that say about you? I figured the "bad blood" curse had marked me, but there was nothing I could do about it but feel ashamed.

Fifty years later, when my mother was dying, Jean found out about her condition from another relative and contacted me. She apologized for having cut me off. "It wasn't your fault. Jo and I just couldn't get along. I hope you will forgive me."

I paused, wanting to forgive her, knowing that my mother could be impossible to deal with. I thought about how much I liked Aunt Jean, her warmth, the good times I had in Wapello so long ago. I told her that I forgave her, but in my heart I was sad that the strife in the family had isolated me from them, and that we'd all lost a lifetime of connection.

Our tumultuous history was all there in the tragic fragmentation of the family: the fact that Lulu left and Blaine drank, the silent jealousies between Blaine and Lulu and Bernie, my mother's nasty disposition. There's violence in our family story: his alcoholism, everyone's bad temper. Jean told me once that Bernie drew blood in response to one of Blaine's attacks. She stabbed his leg with a knife, according to Jean, who'd witnessed their fights and violence back when he was still drinking. Finally, he was saved and converted to Christianity, and from that point on, he was religious, attended church, taught Sunday school, and tried to control his personality and moods with prayer. I thought about that moment in the driveway when I was young, when he was kneeling at Bernie's feet, troubled by what might have been temptation to drink or guilt for what he had done in the past. It began to make sense.

As my mother was dying of a brain tumor, I gathered more puzzle pieces of my mother's life through Jean's phone calls and letters.

In one of the letters, Jean wrote:

The time when your mother was nice to me was when she was twenty-one and I was fourteen. I visited her in Chicago.

She treated me like a big sister who accepted and loved me. How I admired her! She was patient, thoughtful, and happy to show the sights of Chicago to me. We rode the largest roller coaster in the world, and Jo was fearless. Some of her behaviors were strange, though. She insisted that one of the young men with us open and close the car door for her, and she wouldn't budge to enter or exit until he did, but it was the long lecture afterward that left the young man defeated and embarrassed. That day, though, was to be the one and only congenial experience I ever had with Jo.

For several days after, I tried to act like Jo, sound like her, and imagined that I might resemble her a little, but down deep I had no illusions. She was and remains in my memory one of the most beautiful women I've ever seen. Why wouldn't I tell her she was pretty when she asked me? I would have happily volunteered it before she began attacking me. . . .

She seemed to need affirmation of her looks, her capabilities, from everyone. She sought approval constantly. . . .

Blaine and his father loved a good argument. Dad (Blaine) would often present an opposing view of any subject just to get a rise out of other people or set them to thinking a little deeper. . . .

Blaine loved you, Linda Joy. I wonder if you brought to mind the years lost with his own little girl whom he affectionately called "Jo'tine."

The story of the past began to weave together as I got more information from Ancestry.com. Around 1920, Lulu and Blaine must have separated. Josephine was five. Jean's letters told me that he met Bernie in a fancy hotel in Wapello in 1921. They soon married and had their daughter, Jean. By 1922, Lulu was working in Des Moines as a telephone operator and Josephine was living in Muscatine with her grandmother, and after that she lived with June, Blaine's sister. When she was thirteen, she went to be with Lulu, who had become Frances, and her new husband in Chicago.

I'm guessing that Lulu wasn't going to stick around to witness Blaine with his new family while she lived alone with her daughter. When she left to find a new life, she couldn't have known that the results of her decision would haunt her to the end of her days, that it would be a part of my mother's anguish, and my own, and even touch the lives of my children. But the way I see it now, Lulu Who Became Frances was simply trying to find her way.

I don't know how my mother and father met, or what my mother was doing between 1936, when Jean visited her in Chicago, and 1944, when she met my father. Perhaps she was taking courses to learn her trade as a legal secretary. Perhaps she was falling in and out of love, wanting to be married. She was working in Chicago during the '30s, when Frances was traveling to Europe. There's a gap in their histories between 1937 and 1944.

In 1944, three years after WWII started, my father, Emerson Clifford Myers, called Cliff, was a captain in the US Army, using his career in the railroad to route trains across the United States for the war effort. He'd worked for the L&N Railroad since he was a teenager in Louisville. He loved trains, the early-twentieth-century equivalent of today's tech industry. He was intelligent and had some college education and enough ambition to rise up in the world from his humble farm origins in Kentucky, the baby among six children. At the age of forty, he still cut an attractive figure.

Josephine was twenty-nine when they met. According to my father, she was beautiful, and they had a quick courtship of six weeks. When I read between the lines, I detect a powerful sexual connection. They married before he knew about her mercurial moods and spoiled personality. One of his sisters said that my mother acted offended when my father tried to get into the Pullman bed with her on their honeymoon; he told his sister during that trip that he'd made a mistake in marrying her. What a start!

I was conceived a couple of weeks after they got married. When I was in my twenties, they both insisted that they didn't "do it" before marriage, but I didn't care if they had, and I was not sure I believed them anyway, given how defensive they were about it. I learned from my grandmother that during the year they were together, my father hit my mother once, no doubt in the middle of some powerful disagreement. Mother may not have used physical violence, though she was capable of it with me. But her words were daggers skilled at hitting their targets, leaving you so enraged you wanted to destroy something, desperate to shut her up by any means necessary. They both had a temper and were prone to hysterical outbursts, though I think my father's leaving her broke her heart. My mother never spoke unkindly about him and didn't like it when my grandmother did. I knew that I could never tell my mother that my father had acted inappropriately with me. She would have defended him and said I was making it up. She would have defended him, not me.

Photographs of a March day in 1945 show my petite mother huddled in a fur coat outside a brick building. Standing next to her, my father is wearing his captain's uniform. It was the night before I was born, three weeks early, six weeks before the end of World War II. She told me I was born quickly and would say in letters that my arrival was the best thing that ever happened to her. Little did she know what a saga was ahead of her. Too soon after I was born, she would be alone with me. I imagine she felt lonely and lost, though she tried not to feel anything at all.

There are a few photographs of Mother holding me when I'm small, and only one of me with my father, when I am a baby of about six months. He left when I was eight months old. In one photograph, when I'm about two months, Mother's beauty shines, her dark, curly hair falling to her shoulders. It's not a Madonna-and-child picture. I lie loosely on her lap, her gaze beaming toward the camera, not her baby. But I'm smiling.

I lived with my mother in Chicago until I was four. When Frances recovered from the shock of being a grandmother, which at first she resented, according to Aunt Helen—she didn't want to be "old"—Frances tried to help my mother by giving her money and setting her up in the apartment on Hermitage Street where Josephine had lived with Frances and Burt. By then, Burt had died and my grandmother spent most of her time staying with Aunt Helen in Enid, according to the phone-book listing I found on Ancestry.com. Aunt Helen told me that when the telegram came announcing my birth, my grandmother threw it down and said, "The brat is born."

This is the heritage that's tugged at me for as long as I can remember. My mother married someone she hardly knew, had a baby, and then was on her own, carrying within her the inheritance of grief and trauma and brokenness, unaware of it except for what I believe was anxiety and a deep kind of loneliness. Able to care for me for fewer than five years, she returned to Chicago and left me with my grandmother.

We're full circle to where we began this saga, where the seeds of our brokenness were sown, the roots of where we came from deep in that plains soil, and in our hearts. I believe that for all of us, there existed a vision of something better, something called happiness.

CHAPTER 16

Not a Hallmark Mother

All my adult life, from when I was twenty-six, after my grandmother died, until my mother's death, my mother haunted my life. As I look back on how things evolved, the fallout of my mother's rejection of me as her daughter sparked a rebellion. I was going to "show her" she was wrong. I'd prove to her what a good person I was, and I'd find the perfect husband and create the happiest family. We'd show my mother that I was not just the product of what she and Gram had created.

It follows, given the confusion, the secrets, and my low opinion of myself, that I would have looked for love in all the wrong places, as the song goes, unaware that parental rejection and the wars between everyone had burrowed deep into my psyche, leaving me unsure of what "love" was. I'd choose men who themselves were broken. At first, it would be a dream relationship, exciting, and wonderful, but then a sense of déjà vu would come over me.

I'd become haunted by feelings I'd had in my childhood, uncertain whether it was because I imagined them or because something was wrong in the relationship. I'd feel betrayed by my partner, get confused about what I believed or wanted, and terrified of being abandoned. I'd charge onward, still hopeful about love.

After the period of breakdown and discovering the healing that was possible through the first therapy I'd done in the '70s, I continued on that path learning how to face up to unbearable feelings. In our weekly sessions, my therapist would nail me when I grew numb. He'd confront my defenses, my denial, and the fantasies I would use for survival, tactics that of course never worked. I'd had only a year of therapy when another promising man appeared, three children in tow. By the time I began to doubt the viability of that relationship, which was eerily similar to my last husband, I was lost "in love" and accidently got pregnant. We went forward with the marriage, despite doubts that I kept to myself. I wanted a family so badly; I dedicated myself to learning how to be a mother to all the children, despite being an only child myself.

Our son was born at home with three midwives assisting. It turned out we needed all three—he was ten pounds! When he burst from my body, a deep maternal energy filled me. Perhaps it was the hours of labor I managed to breathe through, or that I'd had the courage to have the baby at home, but when he was born, I felt motherly in my whole body, without reservation.

While I juggled the children, my challenging husband, and school, I discovered another career—as a therapist. The desire to learn about how people functioned psychologically, and how I could help others as I had been helped, tapped me on the shoulder in a powerful way. The courses the psychology program offered made me hungry to learn as much as I could. As a therapist, I would be able to develop a career that could support me—this was in the '80s, when therapists were still able to build a practice and get paid for it. I was eager to give back to the world the healing and compassion that therapy had offered me.

The marriage ended, and over the next few years, I built a therapy career slowly. I took care of the children and created a home for us until they grew up, but I always I considered it a failure that I was alone, terrified that being alone made me like Gram and Mother. By then, though, I had the sense to be cautious about marriage.

By the time I was in my mid-forties, I tried once more to give the story of my mother and me a shiny new chapter. I wanted to introduce my children to her: my fourteen-year-old daughter, who'd met her once as an infant, and my nine-year-old son, whom she'd never met. Mother never visited us, which was probably a blessing, but sometimes I visited her when the children were with their fathers in the summers. Now that they were older, I wanted them to know the joys of train travel, so we rode the *Zephyr* from California to Iowa, a wonderful three-day trip where they saw the country, from the mountains of California to the Nevada desert, and which followed the Colorado River for 234 miles, then led into the flat Great Plains landscape I loved. We stayed at Edith's house, and from there made plans to see my mother, a three-hour car trek to Chicago.

Hope is a strange drug. It resides in your heart more than in your head, and it makes pretty pictures of how you want things to turn out. It's so clear now, nearly twenty-five years after wrestling with my mother over her cruel and irrational attitude about me and my family. There was no way to change her, but I tried. I hoped that when she saw my daughter, whose face had the look of Louis and Lulu, Mother, and me, that she'd have some kind of maternal or familial "aha." But my children were way ahead of me in figuring out that something was off kilter with my mother.

"Tell us why we can't say we're her grandchildren, again?" they asked me, as I let them out in front of her apartment building. I was dropping them off and then searching for a parking place. Mother had given me strict orders: "Tell them not to say I'm their grandmother. I don't want anyone knowing my business." I knew my children—they did not blindly follow rules, which made life hard at times, but also I wanted them to have a voice in the choices of their lives, unlike me. I had told her they couldn't be perfectly controlled. "Just make them mind! That's all there is to it." I knew what that had meant to her: hit children, and they will submit out of fear.

After I parked the car, I arrived in the lobby. I was trembling, nervous about what Mother might do or say, worried that she might attack my children verbally if they disobeyed. My daughter had gone right up to the desk, asked where Miss Myers's room was, and told them she was her granddaughter, visiting from California! She bounced out to greet me with this information, proud that she'd made her own introductions, unaware of how dangerous my mother could be, which of course was a good thing. She wasn't carrying around fear like I was. Luckily, Mother didn't react when she heard about this—I was surprised. Perhaps she was trying to be kind, but I knew that at any moment she was capable of some kind of unpleasantness.

After some small talk in her apartment, she took us through the basement and out the back way to a café for lunch. My son whispered to his sister, "She doesn't want anyone to know we're hers." I looked at them and then at my mother, clip-clopping in her heels down the sidewalk, her face forward, not talking with us, not paying attention to the three people behind her. I felt deeply ashamed that she was treating all of us that way. And angry, but I didn't want to create a scene. I would be playing out the Mother-Gram scenario if I did. I had to exert all the self-control I possessed not to scream at her, *Just look at us! We're your family! Stop your ridiculous denial! I'm sick of it!* It would do no good, so I seethed silently and tried to smile.

Later, my daughter told me that she had found it interesting to meet her grandmother. She understood more now, after some of the stories she'd heard about Mother and my childhood. Mother was odd, she was strange, but my daughter agreed she was very pretty. When Mother smiled or spoke softly, in her smoky voice, I was brought back to the mother of my childhood, the moments when I loved her.

I know more now about how damaging hope as a drug can be. I also know how helpful it is when you need it. It's a basic survival mechanism that can save you from collapsing into endless darkness. Hope keeps you going; it seduces you away from despair and promises better times. It wasn't until the veil of my illusions and hopes about my mother was pierced that I could see objectively how my hope had saved me and hurt me. I learned that you aren't healed until you break down your illusions and false beliefs and face the hard edges of reality, no matter how painful it is.

Two years after that previous visit, my eleven-year-old son was the one who put the truth so simply that I was unable to deny it any longer—it was a moment that changed everything. This visit was similar to the first one—Mother pretended we weren't related and made us go down the back stairs. After my son put up with my mother telling him how to act and talk, I observed how she affected him. He grew limp and laid his head on the table when she left for a moment. His eyes were half-open, and he looked like he'd been beaten. Shocked to see him lifeless, I shook his shoulder and called his name. Finally, one eye opened and he looked at me, dull and empty, different from his usual bouncy self. "Why do you bring us here when she doesn't want us?"

I stared at him, holding my fist against the pain in my chest. Everything I'd imagined about my mother one day recognizing me, claiming me as her daughter, claiming my children, shattered into pieces. A psychic explosion of nuclear magnitude took place. My voice shaking, but with steel behind it, I said to him, "You're right. We're never coming back again."

When my mother returned to the table, I carefully arranged my face into a mask to keep her from seeing my deep distress. Inside me, I put up a wall so no one could reach me, particularly her. I was used to walls, I was used to pretending. It was a useful technique for escaping from Mother without some kind of fight. I was sick of fighting, sick of the whole damn stupid story. We walked to the car, and as I said goodbye, I knew I would not see her again for a long time. I kissed her on the cheek, tears already flowing deep inside my body. I was hardened to her. I would never beg for her love again.

Under green oak trees lining the sidewalk on the North Side of Chicago, not far from Lake Michigan, not far from where we once lived together before we moved to Kansas, I told her good-bye.

CHAPTER 17

Full Circle

You can feel that wind when it whispers, feel the edges start
to fray. That wind whispers of endings, of finality; it licks
at your murky dreams. When it's your mother, the DNA starts to
hum. It taps your bones in a subtle tone—softer, more delicate
than a tuning fork. It's the melody of life on an edge, a preci-
pice. When I parted from my mother that last evening in Chicago
after my son's "out of the mouths of babes" comment slapped me
awake, I felt as if I were shedding skins, ones that had perhaps
been psychic blankets of hope to shelter me from her rejections
through the years. By the time I entered the end game with my
mother, I was fifty years old, and years of therapy had helped
me to understand my family dynamics. I knew that abused and
abandoned children take a long time to heal, but surely I was on
the slow side.

When Mother told me she didn't want people to know I
was her daughter, I took it in the stomach, where it would live

for a long time, vibrating through my psyche and my life in ways that would take decades to sort out. And yet I gritted my teeth and plunged forward in my determination to prove her wrong. I suppose when you have a dedicated mission to change someone, the energy it takes to push forward through all obstacles can blind you. Over the years, every time she tried to pretend I didn't belong to her—it was always on her turf in Chicago—I would suffer the blow, but after I recovered when I got home and back to my own life, I'd redouble my determination/belief/fantasy that one day she would open her arms to me. The idea that I could create a different outcome than Mother and my grandmother did was primary in my mind. I was sure that if I stayed steadfast, I'd erase the shame and sorrow of our family curse of angry mothers and daughters.

Every year or two, I'd visit Mother in Chicago, and sometimes she'd come down to Iowa with me to visit the family at Edith's, where I would watch them observe her with a "you've got to be kidding" look on their faces as she obsessed over which men in her office might be in love with her, her voice rising and descending in a familiar, irritating cadence. She was clearly not living in the same world with the rest of us, though she functioned well as a legal secretary and worked until her late sixties. During these visits, I'd go to the bathroom and splash water on my face to manage the aggravation she caused within me with her mooning over a married man, or with her ongoing critiques of my clothes and my life.

That day in Chicago after my son asked me why we kept coming to see her when she didn't want us, I drove away, holding back the urge to scream out my rage and pain. I wanted to empty myself of grief for all the times she'd scurried me out of sight as if I were something to be ashamed of, but my son was in the backseat and I knew I had to protect him from any more of the craziness that was my legacy, and therefore his. I turned the radio to a rock station and turned up the volume loud, then barreled down the freeway to a motel a couple of hours away where we would spend the night.

As I drove into the sunset, blue skies and golden fields of corn spread out before me, I felt a dim kind of comfort in knowing what I finally knew. Here in the plains I'd always loved, my body softened, as if it were tuned in to the vibrations of earth and sky, the place my family hailed from, the rooted earth where my ancestors were buried close to the Mississippi River. Sorrow and loss were laced into the feeling I had as I encountered again the vastness of the landscape, my body telling me I'd returned home. But I didn't belong in Iowa; I didn't belong in Chicago or even Enid, Oklahoma. I didn't belong to my father or my mother. I was overwhelmed by the sense that I'd come into existence on a chance moment, as if I existed only accidently on the earth. In California, I'd created a home and a family life with my children, and I had a therapy practice where I helped others who were suffering. In that life, I'd found meaning and purpose, and I had friends who'd become family to me. I'd learned that not being blood relatives offers you the possibility of true family—chosen, not inherited. I was still finding myself in that life, late bloomer that I was.

The sun set before we got to the motel that day, and I could see that my son was grateful just to have dinner and go to bed. He'd been lost in books and games on the ride. I hoped he'd missed my distress, but probably he hadn't. After dinner, I kissed him good night and put him to bed. I turned off the lights, went into the small bathroom, and filled the bathtub with water. I shivered while I waited for it to fill. I was always cold when my emotional life crashed.

The bathtub bubbled as it filled, blocking out some of the sounds of sobs I could no longer suppress. Shaking uncontrollably, I got undressed and sank into the warm water. I stuffed a towel in my mouth to mute the sounds that were erupting from me, animal sounds beyond tears and crying, roars of rage and grief coming in waves, on and on. For a long time, I lost track of time as my mind went through movie clips of the visits when my mother had rejected me.

One memory that came back that night was a visit to see Mother when I was thirty-two. A few weeks earlier, I'd completed the Quadrinity therapy. It had revealed many deep patterns in my life that were causing pain and confusion, but I needed much more help. A friend referred me to Ron, a therapist, mentor, and spiritual guide who would show me a path to true healing, though it would take decades. He offered himself as a compassionate witness to my chaotic and crazy family, and gave me a way to hold the complicated mess of our story.

I was just a few weeks into starting therapy with Ron that summer when I stopped in Chicago to see my mother on my way to Europe. After a couple of hours visiting with her pleasantly enough in her apartment, we were on the elevator to have dinner in the building where she lived. I noticed her gazing at me, looking me up and down, a half-smile on her face. I started to smile back, thinking she was going to compliment my hair or my new outfit. Instead she said, "You look like me. I hope no one thinks you're my daughter."

I was too stunned to speak. I shrank back against the elevator wall as a pain seared my stomach. I sank into confusion and shame. I knew I couldn't let her see my vulnerability, or she might attack me again. She would certainly be defensive and remind me how she needed her privacy, how her life was no one's business, and the whole litany I'd already heard too many times before. I stumbled behind her, and we sat down to dinner. Somehow the subject of Vera came up—the woman who'd forced me to call her Mother when I was five. Mother's face softened a bit, and she asked, "So was she very cruel, really? Those things Gram said they did . . ."

In moments like these, I wanted to protect my mother—
the lost girl I knew she was, an abandoned daughter, like me,
almost like a sister—from her pain. We'd both been raised by
Gram, after all. But that night I wouldn't let her off the hook. I
assured her of Vera's cruelty, rather than trying to ease her mind.
I implied that what had transpired there had marked me forever,
and then watched for her reaction. She could not, at least in that
moment, deny what I'd said, deny the past. I knew I was being
cruel to her, getting back at her for the stab wound a few minutes
earlier. I felt both ashamed and proud of myself as I picked at
the food I couldn't bear to eat. At least I'd fought back, but that
meant that I was just like her and Gram.

Even though I went on to France and Italy for the next
couple of weeks and enjoyed seeing Paris and Notre-Dame, the
boats on the Seine, and the impressionist paintings at l'Orangerie
museum, part of me stayed frozen with my mother in the elevator until I got back home to my therapist two weeks later. Ron's
soft blue eyes were tender as he listened to what I told him about
that moment in the elevator. He began to do something he'd
need to continue to do as the years went by—to validate that my
mother had hurt me, and to try to get me unfrozen from my state
of trauma. We discussed possible diagnoses for her, how she was
unlikely to recognize her effect on me. He told me she probably
wouldn't change, but that still didn't stop me from trying to win
her over. He would hold a safe and tender space for me, acting as
the mother and father I'd never had. He gave me a place where
I was free to say anything and everything, a place where I could
cry and rage. I'd relive the moments that gave me pain as they
arose, until I didn't need to return to them any longer. He taught
me how to say no, too, and about self-care. From him, I learned
about compassion and nonjudgment, though I would remain my
own worst critic for years to come.

That night in the bath, as I continued to absorb the truth
about my mother's rejections, I became frozen again. Other

moments when she turned me away from her erupted in my mind like a movie on fast-forward. Memories I'd pushed down so I could live my life almost normally arose from my body as if they'd been buried in my very cells. Today, we know more about PTSD and how the nervous system works to create traumatic memory, memories that recur as if on a tape loop. It's clear that memories lodge themselves in our bodies and need to be released. All I knew then was that I had to allow whatever was happening to come out of me. I grieved the mother who was tender when I was young, the mother who would come and leave on the train, the mother whose dark eyes reflected her own hurt and anger when she and Gram fought. I couldn't line up the rejecting mother with the letters she'd sent through the years, signed, "Love, Mother," many of them saying how proud she was of my work as a therapist, telling me she was sure I was a good mother to my children. She'd ask me questions about where I was living and what was I doing, details that I often kept from her because she might use them to criticize me.

As the rage subsided that night, grief poured out of the hollows of my body, grief for all the times I missed her when I was little, the times when I hoped she'd change her mind and decide to come back to Gram's house to be with me just because I was her daughter and she missed me. Grief for what I finally knew would never be. Finally, there was nothing left. The bathwater was cold, and it was time for the blessed darkness of sleep.

Four years after that last visit, letters began to arrive from my mother and her attorney about her will. I had not written or contacted her since that afternoon in Chicago. My therapist's prediction was true: he'd told me I'd gain strength as time went on when my mother wasn't regularly tearing me down. During those four years, she might have written once, and I wrote not at all. I had nothing left to say.

When I got the letters about her will and her affairs, I wondered if she was ill. I never forgot the promise I'd made when Gram died twenty years earlier—that when my mother came to the end of her life, I'd help her if I could. I knew I had to create a different ending between my mother and me than she had with Gram.

A few weeks later, she called me with terror in her voice and left a message on my office answering machine. She had a spot on her lung, and demanded that I come right away. My heart beat rapidly. I was afraid of seeing her again, afraid of what was happening to her. She was seventy-nine years old.

I flew to Chicago, and by the next afternoon, my mother and I arrived at Rush Memorial Hospital for a biopsy of her lung and started to settle her in her room. An elderly woman was in the other bed, receiving dialysis, her nurse sitting on a chair in front of me. Mother was perched on the edge of her bed, still wearing her street clothes. Though she'd stopped smoking her Marlboro pack a day, she fiddled with an unlit cigarette. I stood back near a curtain as the welcoming committee came in—an efficient woman with her clipboard, and her assistant. Smiling, she looked from me to Mother. I knew what was coming and adjusted my posture to take it.

"You look alike. Are you related?"

I answered quickly, "I'm her daughter."

Mother shrieked, her voice filling the room with electricity, "Don't you tell them you're my daughter!"

The clipboard lady's jaw dropped, and I heard several gasps. I took action to shed the light of reality on this bizarre scene. "Mother, you know very well I'm your daughter."

Everyone took a breath, and the clipboard lady graciously went on to discuss hospital details while I slipped a little farther behind a curtain nearby. I knew what my mother would do, but to have her reject me publicly and loudly again was another blow, no matter how much I'd prepared for it. I pulled the curtain across my body to hide my shame—for my mother, for our family, for

being part of this strange drama. In spite of my rational mind telling me that she was insane, that I just needed to accept all this, I
found myself crying silently. There were no tears, just a few caught
breaths. The nurse monitoring the dialysis machine a few inches
away, a woman whose eyes and heart missed nothing, whispered,
"It's all right. It'll be all right."

This time as my mother denied me, I wasn't alone—there
were witnesses. The woman next to me seemed to understand
everything. Her compassion in that moment helped me to return
to myself.

That evening, there was a tender moment between us as I
tucked Mother into bed. She looked up at me with a childlike
vulnerability and softly said, "You do tuck in very well. How do
you know how to do that so well?"

"I have children, Mother."

Her doctor told me she might have three months to live, but still
it was a shock to hear it officially after the lung biopsy. But the
thing that would kill her was a brain tumor, metastasized from
the lung cancer. My mother kept saying, "That's silly. I'm not
going to die!" I couldn't blame her for not wanting to believe it,
but, true to form, despite any inkling her life was in danger, that
it might be a time to reflect or take stock of herself, she remained
her crazy, mean self with me and the hospital staff. Nurses would
rush from her room crying. The doctor in charge was alarmed by
her behavior and asked if I thought the brain tumor was causing
it. I assured him she'd always acted that way. I silently celebrated
when he ordered a psychiatric examination. Finally, maybe we'd
get a professional diagnosis.

The next day with the psychiatrist, I felt my face grow hot
with shame as I watched my mother do her seductive moves-
with-a-man routine. The psychiatrist's eyes registered every
flirtatious movement aimed at him as she sashayed around the

room, fingering her unlit cigarette, her hand on her hip, her high-pitched laughter raking across my skin.

I'd introduced myself and asked to meet with him after his assessment. I still remember the warm compassion in his eyes an hour later when we met to discuss what to do with Mother. I told him the history of our family: Gram and Mother's abandonment, my mother's rejection of me when I was twenty. His dark eyes grew soft, and I realized that for the first time I was talking with a professional who had assessed my mother in person. He put her on the bipolar spectrum, and when I asked him about Gram's rage and darkness, he nodded, agreeing that she most likely had the same illness. "These things run in families," he said.

At that moment, time seemed to stop, while all around me I could hear beeping and nurses' voices and the bustle of a hospital. The thing that had haunted us, me and my family, had a name: depression; mania. The moments of chaos and pain that flew through my mind. The crazy things that had happened through the generations could be viewed through the lens of mental illness. My body relaxed, while at the same time I noticed tears on my face. The psychiatrist gently held that space with me for a few minutes, and then it was time to go.

Names and labels don't solve it all, though. There was one more fight to be had, and it was about me, my existence. Mother was having "friends" come to visit her at the hospital, including a young attorney who was helping her. "I need you to leave before they come. They don't know about you, and it would be awkward for them to find out that I have a daughter after all these years."

I was angry to be shoved away again, but I agreed to leave, not wanting another fight. On that spring day, I comforted myself with the landscapes of Monet, Renoir, and van Gogh at the Chicago Art Institute for a couple of hours, but my rage built, despite the calming effect of the art I loved. How dare she push me away like that! I'd left my son, my business, and my life to be with her, and here we were again: "No one can know I have a daughter." It was ridiculous.

With a full head of steam, I returned to the hospital to find her stomping up and down the hall, looking for me. She started yelling, "Where were you? I couldn't find you."

"I left, as you ordered, Mother." I practically spat out the words.

From there continued a primal struggle that had begun thirty years before, when she hadn't wanted me to call her Mother. Though the exact words we said have faded, I know we entered a struggle of wills. She defended her right to have her privacy while I said the words I'd never said before. Truthfully, I shouted them: "I'm sick of being rejected, pushed away, and denied!"

Mother defended herself again, but I kept at her. Everyone on that wing heard our struggle at full, shrieking volume. Finally, I could no longer protect her from what I needed her to hear. "Mother, you've been rejecting me all my life!"

She grew quiet then, her voice soft, the fight gone from her body. "When did I do that? I don't remember."

We were standing side by side in front of a window in the hospital lounge, watching the rain fall on the greening poplar trees outside—a soft, Midwestern spring scene. I realized she was just a dying old woman. She didn't realize or remember the barbs and stings she'd inflicted, and there was no point in telling her. We were in the end game of our story now. I put my arm around her, surrendering to the softness of the rain outside, feeling how small she was, how fragile, how close to death. She was sick, mentally ill, and always had been. But finally I'd had my say. I claimed my right to be her daughter.

For the next three months after I'd gone back home, Mother kept denying me and didn't want me to return to see her. She denied me all the way to the end of her days, until finally, on the last day she could talk, she agreed to allow me to come back to Chicago.

As the plane took off, I knew that, no matter what, I was going to be with her in her last days and try to undo what had happened with her and Gram. To break the pattern that had been seeded so long before: broken hearts and broken connections for three generations.

When I arrived at the hospital room, I found an emaciated creature with no hair, thin arms rising and falling randomly. I was sure I was in the wrong room, and checked the number, but it was correct. Gingerly, I tiptoed in and finally recognized the dark eyes of my mother, who suddenly noticed me. It was not a human voice that called out to me; it was a wounded animal who raised her arms to me, wailing, weeping, with no language. Shocked, I stared at her for a moment as time seemed to stop. My mother, with her beautiful hair, always gowned and dressed in style, was no longer there. My body registered the blow, my heart aching as I went to her and folded her in my arms, our tears mingling on our hands. My mother's hands were still beautiful, like Gram's hands.

I don't know how much time passed, but as I wept with her and stayed by her that afternoon, my mind swirled with the images of the generations. I thought about Blanche in the feather-bed, telling me stories, and how the generations before her had left their silent imprint upon us. My grandmother, suffering alone, lost in her memories and regrets, and now my mother, dying. I saw her getting off the train when I was little, knitting sweaters for hours, silver smoke swirling around her head. I remembered the softer moments when she caressed my back and sometimes looked at me as if I were some kind of miracle. Those moments were fleeting, and there were so many other times when I yearned for them again. But now I was finally her daughter.

I talked to her as you would a child, and she broke down again, moaning and crying, so I held her, feeling her chest move as she breathed, the small bones of her shoulders against me, knowing she was not long for this earth. I showed her pictures of her grandchildren and told her what they were doing and who they were. I wiped her mouth and made sure she wasn't alone, except at night, when I had feverish dreams about her disappearing, about missing her at the train. She didn't arrive, or she left before I could see her. I'd wake up sobbing, and remember she was indeed leaving—the dreams were true, and the loss was all true, and this was our story. It was almost over. I grieved more for the fact that she did not live a full life, this broken person, than for the fact that she was dying. I thought about the photos of my mother as a little girl with a pageboy haircut, and then as a young woman, always so beautiful. But I knew she had suffered deeply most of her life, and that her heritage from Gram and who knows what else was part of her suffering.

My vigil lasted for ten days. After she died, she was buried next to her father, Blaine, in the Wapello cemetery, in the town where she came into this life. She was interred next to the brother she never knew, Harrison. The stories of her father, Blaine's relatives who were buried there were over, their lives marked only by names and dates carved in granite. I stood by the grave, bathed by the August sun, the time of year when I'd visit Iowa, in the warmth of summer, when the cornfields by the cemetery buzzed with life, when the aroma of grass filled you to the brim with the joy of living. Today there was life all around, the birds calling out over the fields, placid cows that gathered just over the fence. The summer skies were bluer than blue, and the grass smelled fresh as the earth was opened up to receive her. She was home now, and I felt the tug of this land, a place where I felt at home, though it was not my own. My body always knows when I am in the Great Plains, in the great expanse of earth and sky and huge clouds that go on forever, to a horizon that never stops. My body feels rooted and connected, as if recognizing the call of the land deep in my cells.

The imprint of the past can be changed if there is an opening, a new way to feel and to see ourselves in our life. Death is one
of those openings when the tap-tap of fate rings in a new tone.
I felt the possibility of something new the next day as the train
chugged its way westward across the Great Plains, the great sky
spread out from end to end, comforting me as it offered me the
landscape that was woven into my dreams.

Amanda, now twenty years old, came to pick me up at the
train station in California. Coming home to her, I remembered
the small, lonely station in Perry where I used to meet my mother.
Now I was meeting my own daughter and would feel her arms
around me. I'd cling to her for the first time, my heart broken
open, my body soft with hers, as if it recognized it was time to
let go of any kind of disconnection, that it was our turn to start
something new in our generational heritage.

As the train pulled up to the station, I got off the train and
went to meet my daughter as she stood, smiling, her dark eyes
compassionate for what she knew I'd been through. She clung to
me, and I wrapped my arms around her. We swayed back and
forth together, skin to skin, in the warm California sun. Something, perhaps a new sense of freedom, had released me toward
her. As we walked away hand in hand, I felt a new openness in
my heart. Was I now freer of our past heritage? I began to realize
I'd been afraid to love her without reserve, I'd always kept part
of myself distant, though I hadn't meant to. The damage of the
generations of mother-daughter traumas had made its mark on
us, but it was not too late to start anew.

"Welcome back, Mommy," she said, smiling, and squeezed
me again. I leaned into her welcome, grateful, so grateful. We
were the new mother-daughter pair now. Now we could set our
course for the days to come.

CHAPTER 18

Writing to Heal

*I*t's silent in the room, except for the scribbling of pens. I gaze out on the group of writers, arrayed in a semicircle, who have joined my workshop at a conference. The pens scribble and papers rustle as they grab a memory or two and wrestle them to the page. Twenty years later, after working so long with memoir writers, I know that finding memories may mean taking the chance that a painful one will surface and surprise you, or you might remember the exact contours and shape of your mother or father's face and break out in tears. As you write, you might be tempted to suppress feelings and truths that bubble up, but, as one student said, "You can try to push them down and ignore them, but they will just stay with you, like they have all these years. You may as well write everything down, as none of it will just go away."

I know how true that is. When I wrote about my struggles with abandoning mothers and our fragmented family in my first memoir, *Don't Call Me Mother*, I struggled with revisiting painful memories, but every time I wrote about how it was for me, I felt less ashamed, less like hiding. I've seen these kinds of results of writing truth for everyone I've taught over the last two decades. The death of my mother when I was fifty marked a new beginning in my life, when for the first time I became a "regular person." I used to tell my close friends, "All those years, I was abnormal and different because my mother rejected me. After she died, I was like everyone else. Everyone's mother dies." For me, it represented a new beginning, a new definition of myself. I was letting go of an identity that I couldn't release until her death: the unwanted girl, the failure.

There were other positive things then as well. A year or so after she died, I was able to buy my first house—affordable thanks to the money Gram inherited from her husband and passed on to my mother and then to me. The children had left home by then, and for the first time I had a home that was entirely my own. Home was something I'd always yearned for but never felt that I had. Certainly, I didn't grow up in a "home." It was always Gram's house, and I was a guest.

Once we're settled in our place, the right place, we can develop in ways that are impossible when we're lost. The wounds of the past, which I continued to work on in therapy, had left me half-focused, wandering a bit, my compass not clearly set. For the first fifteen years in my house, I would sit in my living room, my purring kitties on my lap, and close my eyes, deeply grateful for the silence and the space and the freedom to simply *be*. My PTSD from living in my grandmother's house began to fade, leaving me at peace.

After the students finish writing their stories, we begin the process of sharing. Voices and hands tremble a little as they read. "I've never told anyone that story," says one woman. "I always thought I should write this story, but it was too scary," says another. "I'm so worried about what my family will say if I write the truth—they always tell me that I'm wrong, it wasn't like that." She closes her eyes for a moment. "But it was *my* truth."

Everyone nods. I know how important finding the truth is—I have searched for it all my life, even when it was elusive. My body carried layers of truth and lies, an uncomfortable fit. It's a challenge to write about our lives and search for truths that are buried, but if we dig them up, we can see them from a new perspective. Sharing our stories with others can be one of the scariest parts of the journey, but it is healing to be witnessed, listened to, and respected.

In the workshop, we discuss the issue of writing the truth—finding it, bearing to know it, naming things that have never been named—and how writing helps to heal us. Writing: a magic way to enter another time and place, a way to travel through time and learn something new about ourselves and our lives. Writing gives us a voice and helps us break the silence. The group talks about courage and determination, and as we do, I feel the depth of these truths within myself. I tell them about the fifteen years it took me to write my first memoir, how I wrote because I had to, and stopped for months at a time because I couldn't bear the memories, and because voices in my head shouted at me and shamed me for writing about what really happened in my family. In that book, I tell the stories from the point of view of a young child who gradually grows up. I tell the stories about Gram and Mother and the train, Vera and my father and his busy hands, and the times when Gram's darkness swirled around me—stories birthed with both pain and relief.

Reliving our stories hurts at first, but writing takes the sting out, perhaps not at the beginning, but later and as time passes. As narrators shaping lived experiences, we become witness-storytellers. We discover there's a heady power to shape our lives into stories. As we continue through drafts, we craft our tale into something that's universal, with an inspirational message for others.

During the next writing exercise, while my students are

writing about moments of meaning and transformation, I think about how I discovered what's become my life's work: writing and teaching memoir. But then I realize that my work with writing and healing began long before I started memoir-writing groups. It began when I first found words for my own story, during my therapy process in the '70s. And after that, I put words to the long arc of healing I'd embarked upon through the decades with my therapist and mentor, Ron. My passion about the power of literature to give hope to the wounded continued during therapy sessions with my clients. I'd bring poems to those who had trouble finding their own words to talk about their trauma and pain. I discovered bibliotherapy, a healing model that incorporates literature and movies as stories that can heal and inspire.

As I developed my work as a writer and mentor, I joined the National Association of Poetry Therapy, a group that integrates writing, healing, and poetry. Since the '70s, when I started doing art and journaling, I had seen how the arts made a difference in my life. As a musician, I found that music was a way to transcend loneliness, and then I explored images in paint and ink. Finally, I discovered that I needed the precision of words and stories to help me understand the past and the histories that pressed upon me.

I had created my autobiographical story using art in the '70s, first on my own, then in art school at UC Berkeley, where I got a second BA, in art. I would Xerox old photographs of Mother, Gram, and Blanche and color them with watercolor and ink and oil pastels. I'd create overlays and transfers that left ghostly images that seemed to whisper their secrets to me. I would gaze at them, as if, by taking in their images in diverse ways, I might know them in a new way. I did a large oil painting of Blanche and Lulu in which Blanche was twenty-one years old and Lulu was a baby. I copied photos of Lulu as a beautiful young woman and my mother as a little girl, made photo etchings, and put them in gold picture frames joined together so mother and daughter would be face-to-face, perhaps peaceful at last. I imagined them conversing in the spirit world. Perhaps they were seeking forgiveness. Or each other.

I placed them in paintings, collages, and photo-sculptures, too. In the photo etchings, their faces from childhood to adulthood were burned into a metal plate, etched deep. I learned that I had the power to change the images, to twist and tug them into different forms. The image and spontaneous expression elicited new angles and insights. Images seemed to be animate and changing before me. I listened and looked, honored and sketched. I tried to find the core story through art, but in the end I discovered that I had to find it through words.

The writers are on a different prompt now, and I can see that some are struggling. One woman is crying and asks to talk with me. I take her aside, and she tells me that it's too painful to write about her childhood. I ask her if she has some other, positive memories she can write, and tell her it's okay to leave behind something she can't bear right then. That's how it goes with digging into the past—we need to hold the stories and ourselves delicately. We need to be kind to ourselves and trust that things will evolve.

I think back to when I first started offering memoir-writing groups, in the '90s. It was because of Blanche. As a therapist, I had attended a self-development workshop where we were to answer questions that would reveal our heart's desire. We were supposed to dig behind our inner critic to search for a creative path in our work life, something new that would sustain us in the long term. The questions I posed to myself were: What do you love to think about? Where does your mind wander? My answers were: Memories. Reminiscing. Nostalgia. History.

I asked myself: If I were to create something having to do with memories, what could it be? I had an MFA from Mills College in creative writing, and I'd thought about trying to merge writing with healing, but I wasn't sure how to do it. As I thought about memories and reminiscing, I thought about Blanche and her stories, the featherbed, and the histories that she shared with me over the years. It was through stories, true stories, that I became who I am. I grabbed hold of our history and used it to make sense of my own. Memoirs? Could I really develop something with just memories, something that could turn into valuable work?

Memoir then was a form that seemed reserved for famous people, though there were a few writers who had ventured into that territory: Mary McCarthy, Margaret Mead, Virginia Woolf. It was at that time that Tobias Wolff's *This Boy's Life* came out, but no one knew then that a memoir movement with Mary Karr and Frank McCourt and so many others was about to be born. I knew that memoir was the form I needed, and perhaps other people needed it as well—have a voice. To explore who we are through writing.

I put an ad in the paper about the group I was starting and was thrilled when three people answered. They became my first memoir group, and we continued on Saturday mornings for sixteen years, with people coming and going. Then there were two groups each week, then trainings for therapists on how to use writing to heal clients. During those years, I learned from my students about the power of stories to transform their lives. I was deeply moved when they shared their profoundly emotional and powerful stories. We were all changed for the better as their work illuminated joy, love, trauma, forgiveness, and compassion.

Transformation through writing, through art—that's what made me happy. It seemed to be the most important thing we could do in life—to use our words, our ideas, and memories to shift energies, to become more whole. As the years went by, I began to realize that I had created a method, an arc, if you will, in my workshops. People would start writing turning-point moments, as I had done for my own memoir, and would dig deeply to find more truths, building upon the power of the stories as they emerged. It was a tool that opened up the valuable ore of people's lives. Seeking authenticity, seeking truth—the keys to freedom. To becoming oneself.

In the workshop now, I can feel the energy of that arc building. There is a palpable shift in the room: breathing increases, the pen moves faster, there's a deepening into the experience. My sense of this shift is validated when people tell us before they read, "I have never written this before; I have never told anyone this." The supportive nods and attentive eyes all around signal the reader that it's okay to be here with their burdens. This is a safe space. A place where you can unravel your unsaid words and unwritten sentences, where you can fall into that realm you've always been afraid of. Here, it's okay to travel into the labyrinth of yourself—your words will lead you out.

Based on the workshops I had been doing and the transformation I observed with my students, I wrote my first book, *Becoming Whole: Writing Your Healing Story*. I knew nothing about book publishing, or writing, for that matter, and I was still working on my memoir, but I felt it was important to share with the world what I'd learned from offering these writing workshops and also by sharing with others the amazing stories generated there.

I returned to art for the first time in decades to create the cover, based on the image I had made in the '70s: a split self, one side in darkness, the other in light. This time, it was a self-portrait painted by a very different person, one who bathed the light side in a golden glow. On the dark side, the moon now illuminated darkness in a new way. Before that first book was published, I suffered anxieties about what I'd revealed about my early life, as I used my own story in the book as an example of how writing helped me heal. Writing about my family, even in that shorter form, terrified me. It was not a full memoir yet, but my inner critic was alive and well.

To my surprise, the book was well received and cherished by my colleagues who use writing to heal, and by my students. Like an evangelist, I wanted to spread the word about the ground-breaking research by Dr. James Pennebaker, who's written extensively on his work in several books. His research and the research of others demonstrate how writing expressively about trauma and deep truths heals people physically and emotionally. Writing through trauma changes our relationship to it. Writing opens up voice and authenticity in unique ways, as I believe all the arts can do. Since then, many more studies have been done about how the body-mind wants to get well, wants to heal our wounds so we can find the light and embrace our whole selves.

At the end of the workshop, there's a buzz of joy and hugs, smiles of satisfaction and inner "ahas" that we all take with us. We started off as strangers and three hours later ended as close friends, blessed confidants with whom we shared our lives and secrets and truths. Every time I teach, I'm reminded how we are connected by our stories and our williness to share them, and by our vulnerability, which is actually strength. Each time, I see that stories change the world. At the end of the workshop, we embrace and look into each other's eyes, exchange cards to keep in touch, and say goodbye.

By 2005, my memoir had been published, and I was told that it helped people, that it was valuable especially to those who had suffered loss and abuse, or those who had mental illness in their family. Having discovered that I could survive that kind of vulnerability, publishing a memoir, and that I was actually the author of two books, I found myself yearning for more connection with others and wanting to have a voice in the writing and creative-arts world. By then, the Internet was turning into a place where a lot of outreach was possible, where people were starting businesses and connecting with others in a bigger way. I realized that through that medium my reach could extend beyond local workshops.

I took a course that focused on creating an association that would gather people into community, which was like jumping off a cliff from the very private work of doing therapy to being public in a bigger way. Long story short, I launched the National Association of Memoir Writers in 2008. I knew nearly nothing about the Internet or running a business, about websites or PayPal, but I was excited to learn about how to connect with people. I love that there's a home on the Web where memoir writers can gather to talk, share, cry, write, and learn how to develop their craft and publish their books. I enjoy reaching out to people to join our teleseminars and roundtable discussions, teaching classes and asking experts in publishing, authors, and workshop leaders to share their wisdom with us. I enjoy creating new angles of teaching for writers, and I have made many new friends along the way. I look forward to learning more about how writing memoir can create positive change. It seems clear that over the last twenty years, a grassroots movement that shows the importance of writing stories, creating personal history, and leaving a legacy has begun. It was a trend that no one could predict in the early 2000s, when the pundits and critics decided memoir was dead.

Not only is memoir far from dead, it's flourishing for both writers and readers. Readers are eager to enter the lives of others. Perhaps we are all voyeurs, but I believe it's more than that. Through reading stories about how life is lived by ordinary people, we learn from each other. We know we are not alone in trying to make our way through the challenges that life delivers. We all participate in the wisdom, pain, joy, and knowledge that help us live our lives and grow. We are not alone when we read about a joyous event, the loss of a child, the challenge of an illness. My colleague Jerry Waxler, part of the NAMW teaching community, discusses the evolution of this movement in his book *Memoir Revolution*.

In 2012, I was thrilled to join forces with my colleague Brooke Warner and begin to teach memoir together. As of 2016, we've graduated over two hundred people from our Write Your Memoir in Six Months Intensive, a course that combines craft, process, inspiration, and support, and it's still going strong. It gives me joy each week to teach that course and our *New York Times* Best Sellers short courses, where we teach techniques best-selling authors use to craft their amazing books. We celebrated the occasion of a Mary Karr book event in Berkeley when Brooke interviewed her—we'd taught her memoir *The Liars' Club* the year before. We were surprised and thrilled to be interviewed for a *New York Times* article about memoir writing. We are still at it, cranking out new classes every year.

For me, memoir speaks a language that expresses the depth and meaning of life and offers hope and healing to everyone who is willing to step into their truth.

CHAPTER 19

A New Kind of Grandmother

For most of my life, the word "grandmother" shivered with energy. The word itself conjured up complicated, mixed feelings about my grandmother and my mother, the reluctant grandmothers. Words have images and energy, and the picture I had to accompany "grandmother" was of slightly crazed-looking older women who were rejecting and acted as if children were a nuisance. I knew it was an irrational fear, but still I was afraid that when I got older and became a grandmother, I would become them somehow, perhaps through our family's "bad blood" curse. Logically, I knew very well that I was not them, that I was myself, someone who had worked in therapy and writing and art for many years to heal as much as I could, but, again, the fears were old and long implanted in my body-mind.

When my daughter got married, I knew that she and her husband wanted children, and I welcomed this event. It seemed that new possibilities were evolving in our family—a new healing. For the first time in years, her father and I were not only civil but somewhat friendly. Steve was dealing with the breakdown of his sixth marriage and had two other children by then, so my attitude of "let's all get along now" was timely and probably a relief to both of us. The layers of darker memories I'd carried about him fell from me; a physical weight lifted, seemingly without effort, though I'd tried to let it go for a long time. I credit my ultimate success to my desire to live free of old grudges. I had been using writing to heal the past, and perhaps it had worked. One day, it simply seemed natural to view all those years ago as truly over, and to let go of my anger at him for the sake of our daughter's happiness. And our own.

In the third year of her marriage, Amanda became pregnant, as planned, and she invited me to be with her during the birth. For several years, I had supervised interns at a therapy center that focused on birth, and I'd learned about conscious birthing when my last child was born at home. I was ready to be a new kind of grandmother, a welcoming Nana. As the time came, the worries I'd carried about being a grandmother seemed to melt away. The present was a more pleasant place than the past.

That February, it rained and stormed as Amanda's husband, Frank, and his family gathered with me at the hospital while the slow hours of labor went by. Finally, it was time, and I watched my daughter go into that zone when the baby is about to come out but everything is a blur, and even with an epidural, there's pain. She breathed and sweated, and I counted her through some contractions. Debussy's "Clair de Lune" was playing, and then Miles was born, a beautiful, fat baby boy. Frank's family joined us in the room just after he was born, and we all smiled, hugged, and wept from happiness, the way a family should be when a new child arrives. The joy of sharing Amanda with the family she married into was part of healing from a past that made no sense. It was a memorable day when Steve and I stood together in

Amanda's house, holding our grandchild together in harmony. He was still charming in his way, and life had pummeled him into someone with more perspective.

Three years later, Amanda was about to have a baby girl, and of course I got weepy when she told me that the baby would be named Zoe Joy, that she would have my middle name. Blanche had named me Joy, and now we were passing that name on. I tended my daughter again as Zoe unfolded from her body like a flower. Coincidentally, three weeks after that, my oldest son's child, Seth, was born. This baby, too, was welcomed by both sides of the extended family. My son had tears running down his cheeks as we held his newborn baby boy together.

I am happy to say that I have been with my grandchildren at holidays, special school events, baseball games, and vacations, and these moments of ordinary celebration are always miraculous to me. I'm the only one who knows of the broken connections that live in my past. No one else can see them, and for that I'm grateful. My mother's and grandmother's reluctance to have had the joy I experience with these young children is a mystery that I'll never understand. The children know nothing of the darkness that I held and the fragments of that darkness that my own children experienced early in their lives. Joy lights up their faces, and they're surrounded by many different relatives who love them, taking for granted the tightly woven connections of family. Silently, I celebrate their freedom from the past I worked to heal.

CHAPTER 20

Looking for Em

*O*ver forty years after my father died, I discovered members of my father's family and met a first cousin and his wife. I learned that the family had called my father Em, for Emerson, which was his first name. I knew him as Cliff, for Clifford, his middle name. It's interesting to reflect how your relationship with someone who died forty-five years earlier can change over time. You discover that you continue to know the person after they die. It's a different kind of relationship, without conversations or hanging out, or watching TV. But because you have known them, they've marked you with their love or hate or protection or whatever transpired, connecting you always. Not only do you have emotional links and memories, but you're also connected through DNA and the blood of your ancestors. We can't escape from these links in our bodies, even if we want to.

I've wondered if we connect with the dead through our dreams, or is it all in our own mind, these emotional transactions while we are asleep? I dreamed about my father for my whole life. Our relationship was imprinted by sexual abuse, abandonment and denial, and something that I called "love" but learned much later in life was not exactly that. It was a need to have a father, and a normal desire to be cared for. But we didn't know each other. And then there's that motel scene and the kissing. In therapy, it's understood that you can "work through" pain and abuse even after someone has died. They can't apologize, but you can try to understand their life and struggles; you can try to forgive. Healing is a loopy path, not linear, not even logical. Something that you have worked through can still come back and hit you in the heart and double you up on the floor.

The legacy I inherited from my father was that I would long for someone who was not there. It was hard for me to realize that I wasn't longing for "him," someone I hardly knew. I was longing for *a* father, the father he might have been. Half my DNA came from him, and I knew that some of my problems with men had to do with my confusion about love and sex.

Trying to parse out the story of my father as a younger man, I wrote to a female cousin on his side of the family and told her about my father's inappropriate advances. I asked her what she knew about the family—my father's siblings were much older than he was.

Her letter was long, perhaps a chance to unload family gossip. She had always wondered about Maude, the sister who, I remembered, threw herself sobbing on my father's coffin at his funeral. Maude's worship of her brother seemed unnaturally close. I remember Maude from when I was young as an aunt who got angry if I did not send a thank-you note soon enough for the moth-eaten things she dug out of her closet and sent to me for presents.

My cousin said not only that my father's father was controlling and patriarchal, like most men of that era, but also that there had been rumors of his affairs, and that she thought my father's mother had put up with a lot. Most of the children in the family, my father's siblings, had either no children or only one. She told me that after I was born, my father told his family I was not his child. As much as this devastated me, I finally understood better the carved-out, abandoned feeling I'd always had, and the clue to my father's comment when he was dying—"Oh, you're a Myers after all." My body had always sensed a ghostly, half-real presence, instead of a real father. My body was wiser than the part of me that made up a father out of wispy dreams.

Why would he deny I was his child? Was it because of my crazy mother? When he got to Louisville to visit his family during the honeymoon, he told them he'd made a terrible mistake, but I was conceived soon after their wedding. Perhaps my existence was simply a not-so-happy accident that left me as a problem for both of them, though my mother told me in a letter that I was welcome. There's no way to know the truth. After all, most families have to deal with their half-truths and secrets, the stuff that doesn't make sense. That's why we sometimes just want to go back to a moment and ask them some questions—not that they would tell the truth.

Daddy with car

During my art-school years, I'd gathered "evidence" about my father's life from the photographs I inherited when Hazel died, three years after my father's funeral. I'd never seen most of the photos before—there he was, a tall, slim young man, apparently charming and seductive. In some photos he was called "the Sheik," and the family stories painted him as some kind of lothario. The photos show a man who looks like George Raft or Humphrey Bogart, wearing a hat and coat in the style of the 1930s and early '40s. In another photo, he poses with brothers and sisters in a sepia-toned world. In another, he's with his mother and father, stern-looking people who died before I was born. There's a picture of their two-story family home near Lebanon Junction, Kentucky. I stare at these images, trying to glean some clues about people I'm related to by blood, who are complete strangers. For my art projects years ago, I created a photo-etching collage of my father's life from birth to death. As I looked at his image in all the pictures and the story they created, I began to feel that I knew him better. I imagined my "good" father into being. I imagined him, but I didn't know who he really was, and I never will. Doing autobiographical art helped me to resolve some of the confusion and pain about him.

Nearly forty years after his death, I decide it's time to put my father's ghost away and find out more about him as a real person. With my newly discovered first cousin, I visit Lebanon Junction, a village near Louisville, where my father went to school as a young boy. The name reminds me of *Petticoat Junction*, a 1960s TV show. The village is situated on railroad tracks, and huge deserted fields hold the ghosts of the old buildings where my father began his career in the L&N Railroad so long ago.

My cousin and I walk to the site of the roundhouse in the freight yard where my father first worked. I stand by silent, rusty tracks and imagine the hustle and bustle that would have made this sleepy town an exciting place. As a boy, he crisscrossed the very land where I was standing. He would have followed the seasons here, celebrated Christmases and birthdays. He went to high school in this town and graduated. He woke up and went to sleep here before and during World War I. My heart hurts for all I don't know about him, the mystery of the boy who became my father.

In the local library, we discover a book about the town and find photos of my father as a little boy, sitting on his chair at school, his scuffed lace-up shoes pigeon-toed and crossed over each other. The boy has big ears that stick out, and thick, dark hair. His grin tells me it's him, Emerson—Em, as he was known then.

young Em

My cousin and I find out where the Myers farm was and locate some of the land deeds. We learn the location of the cemetery where our ancestors are buried and make our way through greenly pastures where cows graze by moss-covered stones, tilting and barely readable. On a map, we discover a Myers Lane and a Ricketts Road. We stand at the intersection where both sides of my father's family made an impression strong enough to have roads named for them.

I laugh out loud. Well, Gram, in the battle of who was better off, Em wins. He went to four years of high school, but you lied about graduating from high school. He had some college, but you never did. His family was middle-class; yours was not. Well. Finding the facts does help—they tell me all those fights were stupid. Of course, I already knew that.

On Ancestry.com, I begin my searches and locate generations of his family. His mother, Laurinda, is descended from Dutch ancestry going back to the 1600s. His grandfather on the Myers side was born in Frankfurt, Germany, and immigrated to New York in 1834, at age nineteen.

Full name: Emerson Clifford Myers
Called Cliff by my mother and grandmother, he is Em to his family as he grows up.
Born 1904, the youngest of six children.
His father owns land and runs a lumber mill.
Em completes four years of high school, then goes on to business school, before starting to work at the L&N Railroad in 1924.
1914: World War I. He's ten years old.
1918: After the war, he finds jobs on the local L&N Railroad at fourteen.
1923: His mother dies. He's nineteen.

1930 Census
Rate clerk, L&N Railroad.
He is twenty-five. He lives with Evelyn, age twenty-three; he married her when she was twenty and he was twenty-three.

Maude, his sister, lives with them. She is married at age nineteen.

1934
Age thirty.
Clerk, L&N Railroad.
Louisville, Kentucky.
Address: 4429 S. 3rd.

1940 Census
Lives with Evelyn M. Myers in a rooming house, Chicago.
Chief clerk, L&N Railroad.
Divorced.
Income: $24,000 per year. (He's making good money already.)

July 16, 1942
Enlists in army, Davidson, Tennessee. Private.
Branch: Warrant Officers, Camp Forrest.
Family rumor says that he was involved with a woman, Katherine, who killed herself shortly after he left.

May 29, 1944
Marries Josephine Hawkins, my mother. He's forty; she's twenty-nine.

March 1945
I am born.
Em is known as Captain Myers in a birth announcement.
Leaves the family later, in 1945.
Marries Hazel, 1948.
Continues to climb ladder of L&N.
Invests in Ramada stock; becomes a "millionaire."
Moves to Arizona in 1968.
Dies in 1971.

At the end of the excursion to Lebanon Junction, I visit my father's burial place, at a mausoleum in Louisville. Memories of the day he was buried return to me: my exhausted grieving for him only ten days after Gram died, the feeling that I never knew him. When we finally started to talk, even though we avoided the difficult stuff, we began to speak our minds, but he died before we were able to heal everything. My secrets weighed heavily on me—everyone in his family at the funeral had idealized him; he was the golden boy who made good. He gave money to family members when they needed it and was seen as generous, charming, and rich. My experience was that he and Gram fought continuously about money until the end of their lives. My father did not put me in his will, but he told his wife to give me money.

But this summer day, visiting the stone carved with his name, I feel nothing. The marble is warm, a flecked pink color. I touch it and wish him well, wherever he is. The story is over.

CHAPTER 21

Aunt Helen on Ancestry.com

Aunt Helen seemed ageless, but she must have been in her sixties when I came to live with Gram in Enid. Her mirthful laugh boomed out from her generous belly, and her goodwill, loyalty to our family, and willingness to help out in her Southern-hospitality way wove a comforting thread through my life.

All these years later, I looked for her on Ancestry.com and noticed sadly that no one had listed her in their family tree—she had no children of her own. Uncle Maj was in the listings, though. He was widowed and had two daughters; I found him entered on someone's family tree. The only "wife" listed was the daughters' mother. Aunt Helen was not listed at all. I know that Aunt Helen passionately loved his children and grandchildren—she'd told me she loved them as if they were her own. How sad it was to see that she was missing on the family posts. Did they not know her or remember her, or was the family tree a place where only "blood" family was welcome? How could she not exist in the records connected to the family?

What do you do with someone who was not "officially" your relative and not really your aunt, but who was one of the most important people in your life? Well, I added Aunt Helen to *my* tree. I brought her back to life on Ancestry.com by claiming her for myself. I had to wipe away a couple of tears as I heard the cadence of her voice in my mind when I uploaded her photograph; in it, she's laughing her belly laugh, saying, "God love ya, darlin'," in her Southern accent, making you feel loved all the way through.

On Ancestry.com, I also found her mother, Miss Daisy. Her career was listed as "music teacher." I'd forgotten that long ago, when I was six, her very old mother, Miss Daisy, lived with her and taught piano lessons at the house. Aunt Helen's birthplace was Knoxville, Tennessee. I discovered that she had lived in Austin as a little girl; she was listed in the 1910 census. After Uncle Maj died, in 1971, she went back to Austin.

She ended up living with her sister-in-law, Dot, the widow of her brother. Dot and Helen had been girlfriends for decades when they were young, and when they were old, they shared a lovely house in Austin. The last time I saw her, in 1975, was in Austin. I took five-month-old Amanda to meet her. Aunt Helen adored the baby, acting the way I always wished my mother and grandmother had. She cuddled her and talked baby talk, told me how much Amanda looked like me, and gave me what normal family members do: adoration of my child and validation of me as a mother. I ached for more of her kind of love.

As my life played out in chaos through the years, she wrote many letters that I still have, giving me kind instructions on how to live better and how to manage my difficult grandmother and mother. She had a perspective and knew the stories I didn't. Though she loved my grandmother, she did not agree with everything she did and wasn't afraid to say so. She was probably the only person alive, except her husband, who would dare to speak a truth to Gram that she didn't want to hear.

From a letter by Aunt Helen that I found in my archives, written the year I went to Illinois when I was twenty years old:

> *Of course, Gram will always hate your father, which is a pity. He may not always do as you think he should, no parent ever does, but he is a fine man and I know he loves you. . . . Gram won't let herself be happy, really happy. Something will be wrong. It is too bad to pick flaws in everything. Don't ever get that way. Always look for the good, and try to ignore the unpleasant, which I think you do. If she can find something for which to berate your father, she finds it delightful.*

Though I have my memories of how my grandmother acted, in the mists of time, I wonder about those memories: Were they real? Was it that bad? Seeing Aunt Helen's words years later reminds me that she was my witness for Gram's behavior. She knew and saw and tried to help me.

Aunt Helen also told me that Burt, the husband whom Gram left year after year to travel to England, had started to divorce her but died before he could. Interesting—the woman who criticized and put down men was supported for the rest of her life by a man.

When I talked with Helen on the phone in the early 1980s, I was heartbroken to discover she seemed to be losing her memory. At the time, I was a single parent with three children, had just been divorced, and was working and going to school, so I couldn't visit her. I also didn't think I could bear to see her and have her not know me. When I finally contacted her, the phone had been disconnected. For several years, guilty that I'd not been able to thank her or help her, I wanted to know about the end of Aunt Helen's life. I wrote the Texas Bureau of Records to ask about an "aunt"—you have to be a relative to get a death certificate—but didn't hear back.

A year later, I got a letter asking if I wanted to pursue my inquiry again. I paid $10, and the death certificate came in the mail. She had died in a nursing home near Tyler, Texas. How she got there, I will never know. Nothing could ease the ache in my heart about her having been alone at the end. We had no good-byes, and she faded away. But getting her death certificate made her real again, as did finding her on Ancestry.com. Because of her, I knew I was loved, hugged, fed, petted, and adored as a little girl and as a young woman. She was the only "mother" who wasn't afraid to beam her adoration toward me. She told me truths I would otherwise not know. And I always admired her loyalty to her friend, my grandmother.

I watched Aunt Helen waft her love into the darkness of our house, never failing to be my grandmother's ally. Now they're connected again, and on Ancestry she's mine once again, beloved.

CHAPTER 22

The Lady Who Traveled on Ships

Back row, far left, Frances on board ship

When I consider the eras that Lulu Who Became Frances lived through, I understand more about the historical context of her life and how that shaped her. She was born during the Edwardian era in England, a time featured in the early episodes of Downton Abbey, when a woman never showed her ankles and never went unchaperoned if she was unmarried.

You certainly didn't elope, either. But Lulu did, in 1911, three years before World War I, the war that changed everything. After burying one stillborn child in 1914 and having my mother in 1915, she had left her marriage by the time the Roaring Twenties arrived. It was mutually dissolved, or my grandfather left her— no one ever said what happened. Then she lived on her own, working first in Des Moines as a telephone operator. Most likely she lived in a rooming house, common for working women at the time.

Let's review the context of the times. In 1927, Lindbergh flies the Atlantic. In 1929, the stock market falls and a global depression begins. In 1930, Frances marries her second husband, Burt Hurlbut, and takes fifteen-year-old Josephine back to live with her. I can only imagine the strife that must have ensued. I discovered those details of their history when little green leaves sprouted up on their Ancestry.com profiles to let me know there was new information to investigate.

I found the date of her second marriage and ordered a copy of the marriage certificate through Ancestry.com. Sure enough, Frances lied about her age! He was forty-five, and she was listed as thirty-three, when she was really thirty-six. I knew she was vain and wanted to appear younger—not an abnormal desire, especially in a woman in middle age—but she was only in her thirties. I imagine she wanted to be seen as young and attractive, and perhaps she was beginning to see her beauty fade. Her desire to seem younger was a trait that later would be borne out in not wanting to be a grandmother, which to her meant she was old, though when I was born, she was only fifty-one.

I began to discover the amazing ways in which Ancestry.com offers up clues to old mysteries. I'd linger there, sometimes for hours at a time. One night, several little green leaves popped up and waved at me. Little did I know that even after having done searches for her for several years, I would still discover surprising new facts about Lulu Frances Hurlbut.

I clicked and was led to the international listings, which required a fee to view them. I got out my credit card to upgrade my membership, my heart pounding. What could it be? I couldn't track the listing fast enough. My kitties, who often are my companions when I use my laptop on the couch, must have been startled by the yelp I gave as I discovered documents I had never seen before or known about. There were ship manifests for not just one but several trips starting in 1933 to England and Scotland. Frances made all these trips to Great Britain? I had no idea she had traveled that much—and on her own.

Where did she go, and what did she do? Dozens of questions ran through my mind, and it was tough to realize they could never be answered, though I was somewhat comforted that the facts on the ship manifests affirmed the reminiscences I'd heard so long ago when she talked about England and castles.

The first listing was in 1933, her passport issued on June 13 of that year. There's conflicting evidence of the passport number: 137042 or 32871. Perhaps she was given a new number in 1935, when she renewed it. Her name was listed in several different ways on the manifests, from Lulu Hurlbut to Frances to L. F. Hurlbut to another, even stranger name: L. F. S. Hurlbut. I wondered if these were trips for some kind of work, but her occupation was always listed as "housewife." I believe that if she'd had any other title, she would have used it, having always wanted to elevate herself above her working-class origins.

Her husband, Burt, to whom she'd been married three years by the time of her first voyage, must have funded her travels. So, for a while at least, she was privileged to live a different kind of life, thanks to her marriage. Even as a kid, I got the impression that Burt was well off. After he died, she never had to worry about money and managed her investments with Uncle Maj's help. She took care of me all those years on her own, bought a new car every year, and made sure to purchase our clothes at the most expensive shops.

The dates told me that Frances began traveling the year my mother turned eighteen—perhaps because Frances was free of responsibility for her then. Perhaps she'd always wanted to travel and this was her first chance. The story I made up in my mind was that after my mother's annulled marriage when she was seventeen, things were not calm in the household, so my mother moved out, leaving her mother free to have her adventures.

These are some of the facts my research uncovered, beginning with her first journey:

1933
Departs Quebec
Arrives London, July 1, 1933
Ports of arrival: Plymouth, Havre, and Loden
Ship: *Ausonia*, a Cunard ship from Quebec; eleven passengers in first class
Name: Lulu F. Hurlbut, c/o T. Cook & Sons
Age: thirty-seven
Occupation: housewife
Address: Berkley, St. WC1

August 4, 1933
Departs Glasgow
Arrives Quebec, August 12, 1933
Ship: SS *Letitia*
Name: Lulu Hurlbut
Age: thirty-eight
Address: 56 Princes Street, Edinburgh

I kept following the clues, amazed to find several more voyages on various ships. Not all listings showed both her arrival and her departure, there were age and name discrepancies on various documents, and some records were missing, no matter how many obsessive searches I did, wanting the facts to line up perfectly.

The next listing is of only a return trip in 1934. Her first trip lasted for a month, so I imagine this one did, too.

August 11, 1934
Departs Southampton
Arrives Quebec, August 19, 1934
Ship: *Ausonia*
Name: Lulu Hurlbut
Age: thirty-nine
Address: 6152 N. Hermitage Avenue, Chicago, Illinois

I turned to Wikipedia to find the following information about the *Ausonia*:

> The Ausonia was built in 1921 by Armstrong Whitworth
> & Co. in Newcastle, as the third of Cunard's six post–
> World War I "A Liners." On August 31, 1922, she
> departed on her maiden voyage, Liverpool to Montreal.
> In 1927 she was refitted for the new cabin, tourist- and
> third-class configuration. In 1939 the Ausonia was
> requisitioned as an armed merchant cruiser, and in 1942
> she was purchased by the Navy and then converted into
> a repair ship.

I was pleased that to find the history of these ships online and to learn how they played a role in World War II. I also researched the news of 1930s Europe, focusing on the years Lulu visited. The time of her visits to England coincided with the uptick to World War II and various other major events in Britain and Germany.

In 1935, there is no listing; her next voyage was in 1936. That year, King Edward VIII of England abdicated the throne for his love of Wallis Simpson, creating a scandal of enormous proportions—nothing like that had ever happened in English history. Research reveals that both of them were pro-Nazi. In1933, Hitler became chancellor of Germany, and continued his anti-Semitic policies all the way to the Holocaust and the deaths of more than twenty million people. The 1936 Olympics were held in Berlin, where evidence of what Germany was up to regarding discrimination of Jews was temporarily removed to fool the world about Hitler's true intent. Jesse Owens, a black athlete from the United States, won the gold medal in track, which enraged Hitler.

In September of 1938, in Munich, British Prime Minister Chamberlain declared "peace for our time" in an agreement signed with Hitler—who had already annexed Austria, and soon moved on to take over the world. World War II started in September 1939, forever changing the world and Frances's beloved England, which would suffer bombing for six long years. Buckingham Palace, where she might have watched the Changing of the Guard, was bombed, narrowly missing the King and Queen. In fact, most of London was bombed, creating a firestorm that left St. Paul's Cathedral, one of the finest examples of Christopher Wren's architecture, standing amid smoldering rubble. The fires were put out by the firewatchers and priests at the cathedral, but many of Wren's churches were completely destroyed. I imagine that Frances would have enjoyed seeing those churches as she investigated the city.

I wonder what she did in London. Did she go to St. Paul's for a service and walk Fleet Street, the area destroyed by bombing in 1941? Loving art, she would have gone to the National Gallery at Trafalgar Square, and perhaps she had tea at the Ritz or the Savoy. I can see her there at an expensive high tea, sipping daintily, her little finger curled. Did she know the country was in a depression and many were out of work? I can only wonder how much the social milieu of the real England, not the imagined myths of Henry VIII and the other kings and queens, was visible to her.

1936
Departs Quebec
Arrives Southampton, May 31, 1936
Ship: *Montclare,* Canadian Pacific Line
Name: Lulu Hurlbut
Age: forty-one
Address: American Express, Haymarket, London

August 7, 1936
Departs Liverpool
Arrives Quebec, August 15, 1936
Ship: *Montclare*; five passengers in first class
Shipmaster: W. S. Brown
Occupation: housewife
Age: forty-one
Note: passport renewed 1935–37

Again I turned to Wikipedia, this time for information about the ship *Montclare*:

> The ship Montclare was launched in December 1921. Her maiden voyage, on 18 August 1922, was on Canadian Pacific's Liverpool–Québec-Montréal service. In 1929 Montclare later moved to the Antwerp and Hamburg services. She made her last regular Hamburg–Canada sailing in November 1933 [the year Hitler became chancellor]. She made her last Canadian Pacific voyage on 21 July 1939 and was taken over as an armed merchant cruiser in August 1939.

I know only that on this trip Frances stayed in London and eventually made her way to Liverpool, where she embarked for Montreal. This trip in 1937 appears to have been Frances's final one to England. The return voyage is listed two different ways.

August 11, 1937
Departs Belfast, Ireland
Arrives Quebec
Ship: *Duchess of Bedford*
Name: Mrs. L. F. S. Hurlbut
Six passengers

August 13, 1937
Departs Greenock, Scotland
Arrives Quebec, August 19, 1937
Ship: *Duchess of Bedford*; sixteen first-class passengers
Name: Lulu Frances Hurlbut
Age: forty-two
Home address: 6152 Hermitage Avenue, Chicago, Illinois
Passport #32811, issued June 13, 1933

Wikipedia links about the *Duchess of Bedford* revealed:

The Duchess of Bedford was launched on 24 January 1928 by Mrs. Stanley Baldwin, wife of the then prime minister. It was one of several Canadian Pacific liners known as Drunken Duchesses for their lively performance in heavy seas.

Troopship
At the outbreak of war in September 1939, the Duchess of Bedford *was commandeered by the Admiralty to bring civil and military officials from England to India.*

The Duchess *was among the ships that evacuated Singapore in 1941. The* Duchess *transported 1955 men of the 18th Infantry Division to Singapore before it fell. The* Duchess *was joined by an "empress" sister ship in this convoy duty. The convoy departed with evacuees on January 30. Her war service included support for the Allied*

invasion of Sicily in 1943. Her original accommodation
was for 580 in cabin class, 480 in tourist class, and a crew
of 510.

Echoing in my ears as I read about the ship named the
Duchess of Bedford is my memory of Aunt Helen and Uncle Maj
calling Gram "the Duchess" as we sat down around Aunt Helen's
perfect white tablecloth arrayed with pretty dishes and silverware, Uncle Maj's and roses in vases on the table in summer.
They would all fall out laughing as they used her nickname, and
Gram would wear a sly little grin. I never knew why it was a term
of endearment for her, but I wonder now if it's because of this
ship—the last ship she took to England.

I kept searching for more information on Ancestry.com,
sometimes for hours, still trying to learn more. One day, an odd
listing popped up:

1942
F. Hurlbut, age forty-eight
American SS *Domino*, crew of thirty-three
In port March 26, 1942, South Boston via new York
To sail March 30, 1942, to Cuba
From Tarafa, Cuba
Belongs to the American Sugar Refining Company
Eleven passengers.

I checked and rechecked the listing—the name and age
were right. My grandmother, the woman who loved misty castles
and English manors and high tea, went to Cuba? I gave another
yelp, startling the kitties once again. My grandmother—Cuba?
This did not fit with anything I knew or could imagine about
her. I knew that Cuba in the 1940s and '50s was a party place,
like Las Vegas, but I had her pegged as someone more restrained,
someone who preferred tea and scones to Cuban coffee, though

she loved her coffee: "I like my coffee to have body!" she'd say, after hearing complaints from friends that hers was too strong.

Online, I researched the SS *Domino*, named after the Sugar Company in Cuba. I discovered that three months after America entered the war, in December 1941, Gram was sailing up and down the East Coast on the *Domino*, where, we know now, German U-boats were patrolling. Two months after she had been onboard, the *Domino* had an encounter with a U-boat in which shots were fired, though the *Domino* was not damaged. What the heck was my grandmother doing in the middle of a war on a ship that might be endangered by U-boats? Why had I never heard of a trip to Cuba? And why did I know of only one of several trips to England?

My brain did some twists and turns as I tried to absorb this "new Frances." I sat on the couch with my laptop humming, wondering how well I had known her after all. Had I misunderstood her somehow? This grandmother, this Frances, was more of an adventurer than I'd ever imagined.

It's been over forty years since she died, and seventy years since she had her adventures on those ships. All these years since her death, I've held a certain view of her—defined primarily by those tough final years, when the darkness closed in. But I can close my eyes and see her smiling as she told me about dining at the captain's table on the ship—which one, I don't know. I think about how her face lit up when we traveled on the train to Iowa, when she enjoyed her coffee served in silver pots and cookies on china plates. Perhaps she was remembering other, finer trips with style and service. As the train chugged along, she closed her eyes and smiled. She loved exploring, figuring out which roads to take when we drove to Iowa, finding hotels and restaurants with class.

But how much can you know someone, really? Perhaps we're all full of secrets, even from ourselves. Or from our children and grandchildren, who can never know the fullness of our lives.

More questions arise: What was her husband doing while

she was gone? I don't even know his profession. I could find only one listing for him besides the marriage certificate, and that's his death record: he died in 1946, in New York, and was buried there. When did they split up? What did he die of? What was that relationship all about? Gram told me that one reason she married him was that he didn't drink. I imagine another was that he had money. When she spoke about him, it was with great respect, but I don't remember her talking about anything like love. They married during Prohibition, but, especially in Chicago, liquor was plentiful in speakeasies. I wonder if her firm stance on alcohol had to do with Blaine's drinking and whatever had happened between them. Still, despite all my research, so much of the story is lost.

Aunt Helen's earlier revelations to me that Frances had dealings "with men" when she was on her own implied involvements besides her husband, but I doubt she was overtly sexual with them. On the other hand, I didn't know how independent she was, either, or that she had traveled to Cuba. I suppose anything is possible. Have I misjudged her? Misread her? She was a dark and frightening figure to me for so long, it seems impossible to reimagine her, but I like this new Frances much better than the Gram I knew. We have something in common: she offered me her love of England and her passion for history and World War II, and I've followed in her footsteps

I have wondered if my interest in England and in World War II stems from Gram's love of Churchill. She often told me that he was one of the greatest statesmen in the world, and that his savvy about Hitler and the war helped to save England from invasion. Or was it the many times she fervently exclaimed, "England stood alone!" that hooked me into being fascinated by England and the war? It might be simply that I read a lot of English literature; perhaps watching war movies and documentaries about

World War II with her all those years ago was what ignited my own search to learn more about the history she'd witnessed.

I know that one factor in my obsession was seeing Hitler on the cover of *TIME* magazine as Man of the Year in 1938 while I worked at the University of Illinois library in the '70s. As I paged through the article, and drawing on the hindsight afforded me thirty years after the war ended, I saw how Hitler's lies and manipulations had fooled the German people. He had found a way to get people to follow him, and I was curious about how that could happen.

Gram's stories about the war, along with the information in the magazine, began my quest to read extensively about World War II, starting with William Shirer's *The Rise and Fall of the Third Reich*, and countless books after that about Germany, the Jews, the Blitz, and England during the war. I learned more about the internment camps—millions were dead because of the power of a man now known to have been insane and on drugs.

I believe I'm discovering that Frances must have mourned the loss of the England she'd known in the '30s, the England before the war. That she had lived through all the headlines about the war that have appeared in newspaper archives and in the historical documentaries I've watched over the years. Just like Blanche, Frances was inextricably woven into the history she'd lived. We all are.

I've inherited from Gram a love of England and have traveled there several times, not by ships at sea, but gliding through the sky in the sleek airplanes of the modern era. In twelve hours, you traverse time and space and arrive in another world. In 2007, I made my third trip to England to explore the history of World War II and to research material for a novel. I had a guidebook that mapped out bombed areas of London, showing what happened, and when and where. I knew from reading about life in London during the war that the destruction was extensive and tragic, starting with the Blitz in 1940. Later, deadly V-1 and V-2 rockets, early missiles, killed thousands without warning.

Night had fallen when I followed a route in the Bloomsbury area, where Virginia Woolf had lived with her husband, Leonard, which was bombed. Cars honked and sped down the main streets, but the side streets were quiet. The city had been rebuilt, but I found a strange satisfaction in tracking the buildings and landmarks that had been there before the bombing, imagining how they had crumpled into the street. Now the buildings were several stories high, and if you didn't know the history, you'd never know what had happened. I felt compelled to be a witness to these events nearly seventy years after they occurred, though I couldn't explain to myself exactly why.

I walked by a tennis court where the Coram children's orphanage had been in the nineteenth century, a place that inspired Dickens's *Oliver Twist*. I had a sense of purpose in following what took place there seventy years ago in a time-traveling mental state, only to be startled awake by honking horns and the hiss of modern busses. You can't see the wounds of the war anymore, but the ghosts are there. People and cities alike carry their silent injuries.

On the last day of that trip, I made my way to the bluffs of southeast England overlooking the English Channel where the River Ouse flows into the sea. There, in 1940, was where the "little ships," had made their way to Dunkirk to rescue three hundred thousand British and French soldiers.

My fingers traced the steel of the gun battlement pointed toward France. It was a clear day, and I could almost see to Dieppe across the Channel. I turned around, and laid out before me was a quintessential English countryside landscape: green hills swelling in the distance, lit by the afternoon sun under a perfect blue sky dotted with puffy white clouds that made the green shimmer in different tones, from chartreuse to grass green to dark shadows. As I watched the clouds drift across this dream of England, I heard intonations of Churchill's speech just after the Battle of France as if he were broadcasting from a radio in my head:

I expect that the Battle of Britain is about to begin. Upon this battle depends the survival of Christian civilization. . . . Hitler knows that he will have to break us in this island or lose the war. If we can stand up to him, all Europe may be free and the life of the world may move forward into broad, sunlit uplands.

Like the rest of the world, Gram would have heard that speech on the radio. I stood awestruck at the view from the bluff of the uplands before me while I thought about the weavings of history. I whispered a thank-you to her, wondering if she had come to this place where the chalk cliffs of Dover overlook the Channel, the England where she brought her heart and shared it with me. Whenever she went here, or why, her heart would have been broken when she heard about England and the bombings and the war.

I turned my attention to the English Channel as it flowed onward, peaceful and sparkling all these years later. All was quiet now; the guns were silent. The silence of peace and the long passage of time gathered around me as I turned toward the path down the hill.

CHAPTER 23

The Last Song

They are always singing under that big sky, the shush of corn as it waxes and wanes, the whisper of the wheat. Insects and the call of birds. The wheat fields that live in my heart's memory are tall, reaching nearly to my chin. The wheat stalks embrace me, soothe my body into calm, as the wind murmurs across the huge Great Plains.

As I finished the final drafts of my first memoir, *Don't Call Me Mother*, I found myself yearning for the wheat fields I cherished all those years ago when I was young. I decided to search for wheat at its full growth, just before it's harvested in June. I was curious to see how accurate my memories were: Were the fields truly golden? Did the wheat fill the landscape with beauty the way I remembered?

I landed in Kansas City and followed the westward wagon-train trails, pointing my car toward a pink glow on the horizon. I discovered that the glow was the dust from the combines cutting the wheat, dust illuminated by the long gloaming of a summer evening near the solstice. I was dismayed to see that great swaths of golden fields had been shorn into rows and rows of small stubs, as if they'd gotten a bad haircut. I drove faster, praying that I hadn't entirely missed the wheat at its apex, remembering that day in May so long ago when I stepped my full body into a wheat field. The moment had imprinted itself upon me—the magic of the wheat, the feeling of being embraced by it—and now I was overcome by the desire to return to it.

After an hour or so of seeing bad wheat haircuts as the sun set, I sighed in relief as I saw fields of uncut stalks appear in the dim light of early evening. I knew I had to wait until the next day to immerse myself in a field and take photographs of the golden wheat against blue sky, renewing my memories and giving me another moment like that, of timeless worship of a landscape I'd loved since I was young.

The next morning, I made my way to side roads surrounded on all sides by wheat fields, only to find that something was wrong. Though uncut, the wheat stalks were short, reaching a little over twelve inches, just above my ankles. I was heartsick—what happened to the beautiful wheat fields of my memory? Where was the tall wheat that feathered under the azure sky? Nearly in tears, I crouched down and put my face beside the wheat, camera at the ready. I ate a little dirt that day, but it was worth it. I found the trick I was looking for: angling the camera upward to frame the amber plants against the sky. Was it possible I'd never again walk into a wheat field and feel it engulf me with its nutty aroma and tickly stalks? I grieved for how it was so long ago, when, in all innocence, I never imagined losing it.

Later, I found out that the wheat had been genetically altered to create a short stalk. In a way, I suppose I never did lose the wheat fields. Memory has offered me a replay of those delicious moments. But no more will I feel the wheat caress my body again, or feel my whole body embraced by its beauty.

Life is full of these small grievings—the realization that there are moments we will never experience again, places we can never go that make up our internal landscape. Despite these vivid memories of the past, it's a shock to realize that you can never go back in real life.

I know now that I'll never go back to Aunt Edith's house and listen to the clocks ticking out their everlasting time. I'll never sit at her kitchen table and have coffee and pie. No more digging in the garden with Blanche or watching the flames leap in her wood cookstove. It's the loss of Edith's house, my other home, that causes the most pain. It symbolizes the loss of the place where she and Uncle Willard always welcomed me. And Blanche would always be there, embroidering, digging in the garden.

Then there was the Billy problem. In fact, Billy and his pedophile tendencies were the issue that brought everything to an end—and led to my decision to confront him. Shortly after Edith died, just a year after my mother, I watched him groom a younger girl cousin to be receptive to his advances, and realized with shock that he might still be dangerous to other children in the family. After thinking about it when I got home, I wrote him a confrontational letter and called him. He denied having done anything, ever, and I suppose it shouldn't have been a surprise that he was hostile. Deciding to break my silence completely, I outed him to the rest of the family. From one of my older cousins, I found out that their parents had never allowed them to be alone with Billy. What? I guess my grandmother missed the memo. The whole family had been silent about this. What other children besides me might have been afraid to speak out?

When my memoir was published in 2005, I wrestled with whether or not to overtly reveal his molestation in the story, but I wasn't ready to lose the Iowa family yet. For many years, I had visited Iowa and relived the moments when I was young there, enjoying the scent of dark earth, still hearing in my mind the cadences of Blanche and Gram's voices during those formative times. I'd stay with Billy's brother and his wife and visit with the few remaining relatives. During that time, I was researching the history of my mother and grandmother. But during what turned out to be my last trip to Iowa, Billy's brother K. let me know, with biting certainty, that he didn't believe my story about Billy's having touched me or that he'd behaved improperly all those years, though he admitted that his young daughters had asked that Billy not babysit them anymore. He said, "Hell, kids say anything. You can't read anything into that."

It was impossible to miss the disgust and even hate in K.'s slitted eyes that day while his wife fluttered about in distress. She had always been nice to me, but she was clearly afraid of him and his anger. With some amount of glee, K. let me know that he and one of my uncles had made fun of me for living in California, wearing hats and "thinking you were somebody." As I listened, I saw that, just like my grandmother and mother before me, I was truly an outsider in that family. I remembered how the family had made fun of Gram for her nice clothes and her trip to England, and here we were, fifty years later. It was odd to be in the same boat with her, but then I understood: I was different. I was a therapist, a seeker, an artist, and an outlier. This time, I knew it wasn't about bad blood. It was because we were from another line of the family. We were descended from Louis, the boy who'd marked us with his beauty. We were different, and a threat. I knew what I had to do: leave their house and accept that I was not welcome there.

The grieving started that afternoon. I put my things in the rental car and left K.'s house, trying to manage the tsunami of memories that flooded me, layers of sorrow for what I'd give up if I had no Iowa relatives to be "my family." In a crush of insight, I understood what my therapist had been saying for years: "You idealize them; you are not seeing them clearly. They are not really *your* family." It was true. The only connection was through Blanche and Edith, and they were gone. I'd created a sense of family out of the deep need to have one I could call my own. But I was truly an orphan, a wispy thing blown by the wind all those years, needing whatever shelter and comfort I could find. It seemed to work until I broke the silence and told the truth.

That day, the Great Plains put its arms around me and wept, too. Gray clouds hung over the cornfields; misty rain covered the marble gravestones in the cemetery where Gram and Blanche were buried. I said good-bye, whispering a prayer, my fingers touching the e. e. cummings poem I'd had engraved on Gram's stone: WHEN EVERYTHING'S DONE AND SAID/ AND IN THE GRASS LIES HER HEAD/ BY OAKS AND ROSES. Everything that happened was so long ago, in the dim mists of the past, where we all end up.

I drove to Wapello, where I talked to my mother, who rested beside her father, Blaine, in the cemetery there. I told her I would not return to her grave again and wished her well, wherever she was. I knew she'd suffered and had found peace perhaps only at her death. I did have the last word, though. On her gravestone, I'd had engraved MOTHER OF LINDA JOY. There would be no more denial of me as her daughter.

I said good-bye to the little house with its hollyhocks and sunny white curtains where I met Grandpa and Bernie when I was eight. I drove a few blocks to the house where my mother stayed with her grandfather as a little girl, and imagined her then, innocent, wearing a white dress, as she played in the yard. On Main Street, I bowed my head at the site of the newspaper office Blaine's father owned. Across the street was the apartment where the newlyweds Lulu and Blaine lived after they eloped. I imagined them young, dreams in their eyes, so long ago. The street was wet and empty now, the buildings shabby and careworn.

I drove by mist-filled cornfields to the sites of the old houses where Edith, Gram, and Blanche used to reminisce. I could still hear their low voices and see their faces suffused with memories as they relived times long gone. Now, I was nearly as old as they had been, on my own memory journey.

I stood by the banks of the Mississippi River, watching its endless flow toward the Gulf of Mexico. It was timeless, having flowed between its banks for centuries before our family came to this place. It was the Great River. I took some comfort in its timelessness as I said goodbye to this spot on the planet where I was part of something, a family that was now gone.

I needed one more thing from the river: its blessing, to feel its waters upon me like a baptism. I took off my shoes and bathed my feet in its coolness, my body bowed down with a grief so deep I could hardly bear it, but I knew it was time to let go. I'd spent the summers of my childhood here and returned for the last forty years, still looking for connection and meaning. For a place where I belonged. This place, where my family arrived in the nineteenth century, was the home of my heart. I knew the past was truly gone, but the love I felt for this site of birth and death and family would live in my heart always.

We shall not cease from exploration
And the end of all our exploring
Will be to arrive where we started
And know the place for the first time.
—T. S. Eliot, *Four Quartets*

Epilogue

It's 1:30 in the afternoon, the best time of day to meet my older son for lunch. Though by now, I'm used to how he looks, it still grabs my heart to see him lurch down the street as he approaches the café. In the early 2000s, he was diagnosed with early onset Parkinson's, and now lives in an assisted living center because of how the medications have affected his brain. His father, Dennis, and I are grateful that we could find him a place to live where he's safe, with a roof over his head, and that we're able to help him, but we could find no contacts in the medical system or Parkinson's resources that offer support for people like him. Without family assistance, our son would end up on the street.

Sprouting a greying beard, my son greets me with a kiss and hug as always. I'm grateful to see he's clean and well kempt, a quick assessment I make to determine the state of his mental health. I slide into my seat, glancing around at people nearby who, naturally, gaze at us. His arms and body fling themselves in different directions and his facial expressions are distorted at times, but he's aware of the world around him—of politics, news, and his son Seth's latest baseball game or scouting trip. We both laugh when we talk about how much Seth loves my kitties. His mother is allergic and can't have pets, so when Seth visits me every week or so, he sinks into their fur, immersing himself in their friendly purrs. Over the years, I've passed on to him Blanche's skill at pulling weeds and planting baby vegetables, and I shared with him my love of roses, thanks to Uncle Maj.

There are blessings along with heartache in this part of my story: Dennis and his wife arrive every year to visit. We meet to have a glass of wine and talk about how our son is doing, then slip into nostalgic discussions about the "good old days" when we were young. Dennis and I spent our early twenties together, and he's been with his current wife for over forty years. He's still friends with Steve, my second husband. We all came of age during a special era—the '60s and '70s—a time of upheaval and idealisms. But when we sit across from each other, each of us with gray hairs and wisdom wrinkles, talking about our children and grandchildren, it's as if no time has passed. We're family, and we're connected by love.

I feel blessed by the love of family I enjoy with my daughter and her children. Recently, I was surprised when my granddaughter Zoe Joy told me she wanted to visit England. It happens that a few months earlier, I'd made my fifth visit to the UK, following in Gram's footsteps for part of the journey, from London up to Edinburgh. As I made my way up to Scotland, the mist and rain creating the quintessential Scottish experience, I wondered if our family's wanderlust for England and Scotland was some kind of genetic memory, a yearning for a place that's deeply embedded in our DNA.

When I asked Zoe why she wanted to visit the UK, she told me she wanted to learn more about history, and see the places that the books she's read describe. Unlike Gram, she hasn't read great tomes of English history and literature, but thanks to the

Internet—its own kind of time travel—books, and her imagination, she understands that a place where something important
has happened has power. She knows that place holds history and
story. I told her that I'd take her where her great-great-grand-
mother went, and I'm planning our itinerary.

When I was in Scotland, like Gram did, I saw castles in
the rain and listened to the docents talk about the hundreds of
years of history that mark such a place. But unlike Gram, I don't
want to live in the past. As I made my way through the castles, I
thought of her comment, "I was born at the wrong time." On my
trip, I knew myself to be a writer, a grandmother, and a teacher
who is tethered, happily, to my own time. As the mist dampened
my face, I thought of her, perhaps walking on this same path,
in search of something—what, I don't know exactly. I do know
that my writing, healing, and teaching connect me to the stories
of the world that need to be told, and that each adventure is a
seed for a future story.

In 2016, I celebrated Keith's seventy-fourth birthday with
him over the phone. He seems to have had at least nine lives,
having had several surgeries and near-death experiences. We're
forever connected by our memories of Enid, the wheat fields,
and the music. There's always a catch in his voice when he tells
me about listening to Bach, or singing in a choir. "It fills my soul
like nothing else," he's fond of saying. Like me, he holds close
to his heart the years we played cello together, a sacred time of
beauty. My best friend Jodie has lived in Italy for forty years, a
professional cellist. We Skype and email now, remembering our
young selves. We talk about the orchestra, about Enid and our
memories of long ago.

As I see it now, my grandmother broke all the rules. She got
"'too big for her britches." She had a vision of going beyond her
origins, and saw that people who had more education went further in life than those who didn't. Being of a curious mind, and
through books and her travels, she educated herself and enjoyed

the world more as a result; and she was eager to share this flowering with me. It has taken me a long time to feel appreciative about how harsh she was with me, and how she made me be so vigilant for signs of lower-class behavior, whether it was licking your knife or using grammar improperly.

Now, I realize she had learned the hard way as made her way from working class to middle class. The way women bettered themselves was to "marry up." She'd observed that the women in her family were trapped by drudgery and limitations. Aunt Edith, for instance, didn't graduate from high school and never learned to drive. None of the women in that family were independent. By contrast, their half-sister was a woman who had "escaped," married up, and traveled alone to Europe several times on her own, bringing the stories of her adventures back with her. Even now, all these years later, I'm seen as "adventurous" because I'm not afraid to travel alone—nearly one hundred years after my grandmother made her way into a larger world.

For all the tragedy and pain I saw in my family, and lived through, doing the research for so many years and stepping into my grandmother's life has given me a depth of understanding that has not only helped to heal me, but has provided an ongoing practice in compassion and gratitude.

The beauty, the tragedy, all of this, weaves the fabric that we call life, its ebb and flow. And I am grateful.

T. S. Eliot says it best:

Dawn points, and another day
prepares for heat and silence. Out at sea the dawn wind
Wrinkles and slides. I am here
Or there, or elsewhere,
In my beginning.

Acknowledgments

*T*his memoir is not only a compilation of stories to be told but the collective energies of all the inspiration I've received over many years from many people, too many to name. This book lived for over thirty years in my imagination, pieces written that seemed to come to me without conscious choice. The source of my work has been generations of a fractured family that I was determined to bring whole through my stories. Many of us struggle with how to cope with and transform pain and family patterns, and while there's no easy answer, creativity, especially writing, offers us a path to peace. And so, in the end, I'm grateful to the family that has given me so much to write about.

My fellow passengers on the writing journey give me hope and support. For the last fifteen years my writing group, The Bellas—Amy Peele, Betsy Fasbinder, and Christy Nelson—have been my constant companions. Month after month and year after year we have met to laugh, read, cry, and most of all share how to find the words to create the worlds that are alive in our imagination. Thank you, dearest Bellas, for all you have given me.

Brooke Warner, my colleague, friend, co-teacher, editor, and publisher, has helped me to discover new ways to write and think about writing. For all she does and gives to me and to women writers through her teaching and as the publisher of She Writes Press, I'm deeply grateful.

Through the years many people have joined me in the desire to plumb the depths of emotions, heart, and healing—Ron Kane, Kathleen Adams, Jerry Waxler, and Sharon Lippincott in particular. I'm also grateful to Melissa Cistaro, Dr. James Pennebaker, Sue William Silverman, Mark Matousek, Tina Games, and Denis LeDoux. Thanks to Nina Amir, Melissa Cistaro, Hollye Dexter, Amy Ferris, Judy Newton, Donna Stoneham, Judy Reeves, Susan Sparks, and the team at She Writes Press and BookSparks for being my champions, along with so many other people who love memoir writing and who talk with me and help spread the word about the magic of memoir writing. And I'm blessed to work with students of writing and life who put their trust in me to help them to heal the generations of their families, and to find a new way to live in the present.

I'm lucky to still know three friends from my childhood—Keith, Jodie, and Lloyd—who remember "the old days" and who enjoy reminiscing with me about times gone by when we were innocent and hopeful, when music lifted our hearts and allowed us to experience magic. I feel blessed that my daughter, Amanda, and her family have given me permission to write about them, trusting that I will present our story in a way that can help others.

About the Author

*L*inda Joy Myers is president and founder of the National Association of Memoir Writers, which offers free and membership programs to memoir writers. She is the author of two memoirs, the award-winning memoir *Don't Call Me Mother* and *Song of the Plains*, and two books on craft: *The Power of Memoir* and *Journey of Memoir*. A writing coach, she teaches memoir workshops and co-leads courses through the program she co-founded, Write Your Memoir in Six Months program. A therapist for thirty-eight years, Myers speaks about family, the importance of legacies, memoir writing, and the power of writing the truth. She lives in the San Francisco Bay Area with her two cats and dozens of rose bushes.

Author photo © Reenie Raschke

Selected Titles from She Writes Press

She Writes Press is an independent publishing company founded to serve women writers everywhere. Visit us at www.shewritespress.com.

Don't Call Me Mother: A Daughter's Journey from Abandonment to Forgiveness by Linda Joy Myers. $16.95, 978-1-938314-02 -5. Linda Joy Myers's story of how she transcended the prisons of her childhood by seeking—and offering—forgiveness for her family's sins.

The Beauty of What Remains: Family Lost, Family Found by Susan Johnson Hadler. $16.95, 978-1-63152-007-5. Susan Johnson Hadler goes on a quest to find out who the missing people in her family were—and what happened to them—and succeeds in reuniting a family shattered for four generations.

Scattering Ashes: A Memoir of Letting Go by Joan Rough. $16.95, 978-1-63152-095-2. A daughter's chronicle of what happens when she invites her alcoholic and emotionally abusive mother to move in with her in hopes of helping her through the final stages of life—and her dream of mending their tattered relationship fails miserably.

Rethinking Possible: A Memoir of Resilience by Rebecca Faye Smith Galli. $16.95, 978-1-63152-220-8. After her brother's devastatingly young death tears her world apart, Becky Galli embarks upon a quest to recreate the sense of family she's lost—and learns about about healing and the transformational power of love over loss along the way.

Don't Leave Yet: How My Mother's Alzheimer's Opened My Heart by Constance Hanstedt. $16.95, 978-1-63152-952-8. The chronicle of Hanstedt's journey toward independence, self-assurance, and connectedness as she cares for her mother, who is rapidly losing her own identity to the early stage of Alzheimer's.

Secrets in Big Sky Country: A Memoir by Mandy Smith. $16.95, 978-1-63152-814-9. A bold and unvarnished memoir about the shattering consequences of familial sexual abuse—and the strength it takes to overcome them.